Vocation
Our Response to God's Call

Our Sunday Visitor

Curriculum Division

www.osvcurriculum.com

Vocation: Our Response To God's Call Student Edition
ISBN 978-0-15-902053-1
Item NUMBER: CU1149

6 7 8 9 10 00287 16 15 14 13 12
RR Donnelley; Menasha, WI, USA: April 2012; Job #196790

Contents

A Look Into the Future

Can you remember the last time someone asked you, "What are you going to be when you grow up?" We sometimes laugh now about our younger ideas of being "grown up," particularly when we look back and remember trying on some adult's shoes and walking around clumsily, or watching someone perform, and thinking, "That's what I want to do, too!"

Now when people ask about your future, particularly about the next year or so of your life, they are more specific: "What school?" "What job?" "What major?" "Stationed where?"

- Perhaps you still answer with some excitement, pretty sure of the direction your life is taking.

- Perhaps you avoid the questions, with no desire to think about the future so quickly approaching.

- Perhaps you spend more time thinking about the questions than you'd like to admit.

One thing is for sure: You **are** thinking about the future.

- In health or guidance classes, or at extracurricular club meetings, you hear talk of "career goals."

- You might have taken aptitude tests along with the unavoidable SAT's or ACT's, or some version of standardized testing.

- You've been getting brochures and e-mails from colleges or trade schools.

Now, here you are taking a course on Christian vocations. This course and this book invite you to reflect on and explore your vocation—which is more than simply your job, your years at college, or your relationships. What is God calling you to be? Where does the spiritual dimension of your life fit in with all the other issues you have to pay attention to right now? This time offers you an exciting challenge—to get a clearer idea of the ways that you can serve God and your neighbor through the gifts that God has given you.

> One and all are called to work for the coming of the Kingdom of God according to the diversity of callings and situations, charisms and ministries. This variety is not only linked to age, but also to the difference of sex and to the diversity of natural gifts, as well as to careers and conditions affecting a person's life. It is a variety that makes the riches of the Church more vital and concrete.
>
> Blessed John Paul II, *The Vocation and the Mission of the Lay Faithful in the Church and in the World*, #45

Every moment in history has brought its own unique challenges to those who live as disciples of Jesus Christ. Today is no different. Our world longs for the loving, healing, compassionate touch of Jesus. It awaits the next generation of people—you and your peers—who will rise to the occasion, capture this moment, and place your gifts, talents, and all that God calls you to be, in the service of humanity.

God invites you to recognize the unique gifts he has given you, and to meet the needs of the Church and the world by identifying and using those gifts. During this course, you will discover that, by virtue of your Baptism, the Church invites you into a life worthy of your attention and your energy.

About This Course

Here are just a few of the core ideas that this course on vocation presents:

- Vocation is how each Christian, in his or her own unique way, regardless of state of life or career, lives out God's call. Vocation is founded on Jesus and on our baptismal call to discipleship.

- We each have a *vocation to beatitude*—that is, we are each invited to participate in God's life and in his kingdom.

- We participate in the Church's mission as we discern our calling to be a lay person (single or married), ordained minister, or consecrated religious.

- The Eucharist and other sacraments nourish and give us the grace we need to serve others, and to hear and respond to God's call for us. The sacraments guide our life of faith and the discernment of our vocation to know, love, and serve God completely.

Using this book and participating in class discussions and activities will help you to:

- Revisit as a young adult the universal call to holiness and the Christian's baptismal mission as it is revealed in Scripture and lived in the Church.

- Come to a greater appreciation of, and give serious thought to, whether you want to live out your Christian vocation in the lay single life, consecrated religious life, ordained life, or married life.

- Reflect on who you are now—your gifts, talents, likes, and dislikes—and consider what these personal insights say about your vocation.

- Think and pray about the person you will become, based on your present gifts and interests, and the things you find yourself called to do.

- Consider the influence of your own family and the place family life will hold for you in the future.

Features

A Closer Look Each chapter begins with "A Closer Look: Who Are You?" Using a short survey, self-rating scale, or series of choices, you will examine some aspect of your personality or your attitudes about specific life issues. You won't be tested on any of these, nor will you be required to share them with anyone. However, some sharing may take place for those who wish to do so. Completing these activities will help you look honestly at yourself before you read the material in the chapter.

Each chapter ends with "A Closer Look: Who Will You Become?" This section links with the "Who Are You?" feature, challenging you to think about your future in the light of your answers to the first section and the material you've studied in the chapter.

The "A Closer Look" segments focus on topics such as:

- Self-awareness
- Living Faith in Everyday Life
- Values
- Prayer
- Service
- Relationships
- Communication
- Measuring Success

The role of family and friends runs throughout each of these topics.

Spotlight Each chapter contains several "Spotlight" features that draw attention to some organization, community, program, or project in which Christians act as disciples in some specific way. They take the general idea of "vocation" and offer particular examples of how people have been called by God to serve others.

Some of these spotlights will feature groups already familiar to you; others will be new. They are only a small collection of the many people, places, and organizations that could have been chosen. Let them be a springboard for you to find your own local groups to spotlight. Many of these groups include teenagers in their activities and membership, and most have websites linked for you at **www.osvcurriculum.com**. Who knows? Maybe you'll find a group or a project to join.

Group Talk Saying your ideas out loud can help to clarify them, and listening to other people's ideas can enrich and sometimes challenge your thinking. Each chapter offers several "Group Talk" activities designed to help you and your classmates hold that part of the chapter up for closer scrutiny and discussion. The conversations are for small groups of three to six people. Don't worry! You don't have to reveal anything too serious about yourself. But **do** plan to take advantage of these activities to help you get to know yourself and other people better and also to help you understand the information in the textbook.

Each person has "multiple intelligences" and needs to use more than one or two of them to really know and understand class and textbook material. There are eight types of intelligences, ranging from the verbal/linguistic to inter- and intra-personal learning skills.

Faith Activity Each chapter offers several "Faith Activities" that will take you out of the textbook into other source material, and into your own creativity. You will be invited to do research, write personal reflections, produce visual learning aids, write poetry, even create dances or write music. These activities provide the opportunity to learn in ways you may not have considered in the past. The finished product that results from these activities isn't as important as the process you go through to produce it. But you will probably be pleasantly surprised at some of your finished products. Good use of the Faith Activities will be one of the keys to meeting the personal vocational goals of this course. It will also help to form your faith, to help you make connections between your daily life and your Catholic faith.

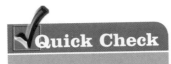

Quick Check

▶ **Quick Check** Each major section of the chapter concludes with a Quick Check, four questions intended to help you capture the major points you've considered in that section. These questions will also appear in a different format in the Study Guide, which concludes the Chapter Wrap-up. If you can't answer one or more of them, go back and find the answer.

▶ **Here I Am Lord** Several people agreed to be interviewed for this segment of the book, telling something about their vocations—what they do and how God called them. Something these people say might intrigue you or challenge you to explore other vocations in ways you hadn't considered.

Are they role models? Perhaps. But they weren't chosen because of heroic or unusual qualities. *They are ordinary people like you, your friends, and your families.* They made the same decisions about their vocations that you are starting to make about yours.

You will meet:

- a college student searching to know what God is calling her to do

- a permanent deacon and his wife who serve in a suburban parish

- two single lay people who are active in their parishes and in giving service in the wider community

- a religious brother who works with youth

- a missionary priest from Sri Lanka

- an engaged couple from a rural community

- a married couple with twenty children—sixteen of them adopted

- a religious sister who works to end racism in many ways.

Prayer Prayer is an important component of this course. Some of the Faith Activities invite you to reflect or to write a prayer. You might like to start a notebook for these prayers and reflections and any others you come up with on your own.

Each chapter ends with a prayer celebration. Some are short, not designed to take more than a few minutes. Others are a bit longer. But they are all designed to immerse you in a reflective mood of discernment. Throughout this course, you will engage in several different types of prayer—psalms, prayers from saints, quiet reflection, and shared prayer.

These prayer celebrations can be used in many ways. Perhaps your teacher will want to begin the chapter with one, instead of praying it at the end—or perhaps you'll use it both times. The prayers can be expanded by adding songs, more time for reflection and shared prayer, or time for intercessions for various needs.

You can also pray the chapter prayers alone, if you wish. Whether you use the prayers here, from other prayer sources, or simply prayers in your own words, try to pray often. It is an activity that can help you in your discernment process.

Pray for yourself and for your classmates and other young people who, like you, are discerning what God is calling them to do in life.

Study Guide The Study Guide consists of sixteen questions that correspond to the Quick Check questions and four Develop and Apply questions. These questions challenge you to apply what you've learned in the chapter, developing conclusions and making connections about faith and life.

Study Guide
▶Check Understanding
▶Apply and Develop
▶Key Words

CALLED BY GOD

CHAPTER 1

CHAPTER GOALS

In this chapter you will:

★ explore the idea of vocation.

★ discover the foundations of Christian vocation in the lives of the men and women of the Old Testament.

★ see how Jesus' mission led him to call disciples to follow him to his Father.

★ consider how—from the earliest days of the Church until now—a Catholic's understanding of vocation is founded on Jesus and his or her baptismal call to discipleship.

★ be introduced to a college student who is discerning whether she is called to the religious life.

who are you?

Take a few minutes to fill
out the boxes below.

Your best school subjects

Subjects that are hardest for you

Sports and/or extracurricular activities you've been involved in.
Place a star next to those you've particularly enjoyed and done well in.

Volunteer work you've done and paying jobs you've had or have
Place a star next to those you've particularly enjoyed and done well in

Now spend
some time
thinking
about these
questions.

★ Do you see any patterns or connections among all the
things you enjoy or at which you excel?

★ What are some of the skills, interests, and talents
that you use in these school courses, extracurricular
activities, and volunteer/work situations?

★ In what other ways might you use those skills,
interests, and talents now and in the future?

The Idea of Vocation

It sometimes might seem you have no control over your destiny. Yet if you look back on decisions you have made in days, weeks, and years past, you can see their effects today. Certainly some things you do today will have an effect on your life ten years from now.

Similarly, if you feel certain about the future and have everything planned out to the minute, at some point something will happen that is out of your hands. You can expect some detours and surprises on the way to your life goals.

What has been your experience so far? Do you have dreams for your future? Have you set any goals? Do you have any ideas about what might be your calling in life? All of these questions pertain to the term **vocation**. Vocation comes from the Latin verb, *vocare*, which means "to call." Another Latin word, *vocatio* means "a summons." These root meanings give insight into the English word *vocation*. Both Latin words imply a second form of influence involved in your choice of a profession. If you have a vocation (a calling), from whom does the call come? Certainly you are not calling yourself. Who is calling you? And for what?

From one perspective, it's reasonable to say that a calling comes to a person from the needs or invitation of another person, a group, the world, or society. You might see that society needs more carpenters, doctors, or newspaper reporters. Based on your gifts, abilities, and interests, you therefore might choose to answer a call to one of those professions. In common use, the words *profession* and *career* are often considered interchangeable with *vocation*. In reality, however, *vocation* is more than a profession, career, or job. It connects with the deepest needs of humans, like the need for comfort, food, shelter, and clothing. It taps into what makes you truly happy and what you are most passionate about.

GROUP TALK

Think about jobs you and your friends have or had recently.

1. Can any of the jobs you or your friends have, or have had, be considered vocations?

2. Could any of these jobs become vocations for you? What would you have to do to make the job a vocation?

3. Do you know of any adults who have a vocation connected to the kind of work you do at your job?

4. In a real sense, how can any job or occupation we have become a vocation?

A Call *from* God and *to* God

In a Judeo-Christian use of "vocation," the call might come from the community or society, but ultimately it comes from God. The first and ultimate call of each person is the call from God to know him, to love him, and to serve him. He created humans for this exact reason: for us to be in relationship with him, to share in his life and love, to find true happiness that comes from him, and to serve others. In order to do all of this, he created us in his image and likeness. We are free to think, love, and serve, reflecting our God who does these things. And God gives us the grace to help us live our lives as a response to this vocation to become his adopted children, to choose good, to love him and serve others. This grace draws us into the community of our triune God—Father, Son, and Holy Spirit. So, humans are religious by nature; it's part of our make-up. It differentiates us from the rest of creation. It's human nature.

> The desire for God is written in the human heart, because man is created by God and for God; and God never ceases to draw man to himself.
>
> *Catechism of the Catholic Church,* 27

We're Not Alone If humans are religious beings—capable of knowing God, being directed toward him, and serving him and our neighbor—we are also social beings by nature. God did not create us to be alone. He established a chosen people in the Old Testament, and Jesus established a Church to carry on his **mission**. The Church's mission—or vocation—includes

FAITH ACTIVITY

The *Catechism* and Vocation The *Catechism of the Catholic Church* uses the word vocation in many different contexts. Work with classmates to look up the following *Catechism* paragraphs: 44, 1533, 1699, 1719, 1877, 1878, 1998, 2232, 2253. Compare your findings in response to the following question: How would you sum up the *Catechism's* view of the Christian's ultimate vocation?

every individual person's vocation. In this sense, the individual's personal vocation is viewed as part of the Church's vocation. The Church is called to participate in and to help build God's Kingdom on earth, to spread the Good News of Christ's transforming life, to show God to others, and to be an example of the love among the three Persons of the Trinity: Father, Son, and Holy Spirit. That vocation of the whole Body of Christ can only be carried out if the Church and her members listen to and follow the guidance of the Holy Spirit.

The Church grows when each member of the Body discovers and lives out his or her personal vocation. As we look at the gifts and talents God has given us, and grow to understand the needs of the world around us, we ask ourselves what we need to do to be faithful to God, to worship him, and to participate in the building of his kingdom.

When do Christians receive this individual call to be part of the vocation of the whole Church? While the idea of vocation seems to culminate in adult life, each and every person is called to believe in and follow Christ. This universal call to holiness is to become Christlike, to follow the Son's example and to love and serve the Father as he does. Certainly it takes our whole lives to live out our particular vocations, but we were first called at Baptism, even though most of us were baptized as infants. And how we live out our lives individually is a response to this first call.

As a teenager, you can live your Christian vocation now by using your God-given gifts. God does not wait until you are an adult to give you graces and blessings. You are already a member of the Church, already part of the worshiping community, and already contributing to the building of God's Kingdom. You already experience the Holy Spirit's work in your life, drawing you to what gives you joy and pride.

GROUP TALK

The *Catechism of the Catholic Church* states that, "the first vocation of the Christian is to follow Jesus" (*CCC*, 2232). Think about this statement and consider how it is reflected in your life. Discuss it in a small group. Then, discuss the following questions:

1 In what ways are you living this vocation today?

2 How does following Jesus affect your life choices?

3 How often is prayer part of your response to a difficult or complex situation?

4 Can a person's moral life and decision-making skills be separated from his or her first vocation?

The Choice of a Way of Life

The Church uses the word *vocation* in general terms, to refer to a person's response to one's baptismal calling to love and serve God and others. This vocation can be lived out through the various states of life: as a lay person (single or married), an ordained minister (bishop, priest, or deacon), or as someone in consecrated life (most often as a religious sister or brother, or life priest). Members of the consecrated life and ordained ministers take vows or promises for life. Married lay persons promise to be faithful to each other as long as both people live. People in each of these states of life may have different jobs or careers, but in some fundamental way they are doing what brings them a sense of accomplishment, happiness, and fulfillment.

Many people say that it was more than their acting on what made them uniquely who they are and choosing a state of life. God and the community chose them as well, calling them to be a priest, a religious brother or sister, a husband or wife, or a dedicated lay single person.

At this time in your life, you have a lot of decisions to make—about college, your future career, or jobs leading up to that career. And making these decisions can be very rewarding. You are in a time of **discernment** about your vocation—you are gathering information, seeking advice, praying for guidance, and noticing how your personal gifts seem to be steering you toward particular careers and lifestyles. Beyond educational and job choices you have some much deeper discernment ahead. Is religious life as a sister or brother in your future? Are you called to the single life? Is married life your vocation? Is God calling you to ordained ministry?

This book has been written to help with that discernment. This chapter will explore the history and uniqueness of the Christian vocation in general. The chapters that follow will investigate each of the particular states of life and offer ideas for discerning what life God is calling you to live.

Believe in yourself. Know and trust that you are important to God and others. Your ancestors, family, friends, parish priests, teachers, and everyone else in your life are praying for you, asking God to guide you in this time of discernment. Your vocation is important for all of God's creation. When you were baptized you were "claimed for Jesus Christ" and became a member of the Christian family. The Church will guide you, with your cultural background, gifts, and unique qualities, to answer God's call and to be part of the building of his kingdom here on earth. God invites you to share his Good News at work, at school, and in the home, by making choices that are consistent with Jesus' message and by participating in the Sunday Mass and other sacraments. Your life choices are important—they are going to have an impact on your future, as well as the future of the Church.

The Discernment Process

Explore | Explore opportunities by finding information about possibilities available to you. With the right motives, seek what is good and true.

Seek | Seek direction by looking to Scripture, Church Tradition and teachings, and to your convictions about what you want your life to mean. Look to the stories of prominent figures of our faith—prophets and leaders in the Old Testament, Gospel evangelists, or saints—for guidance. Also seek direction from a qualified spiritual director (priest, deacon, lay woman or man, religious brother or sister).

Ask | Ask advice from the wise and knowledgeable persons of integrity in your life. Seek a few people you can talk the matter over with, confide in, and rely on for sound, honest insights.

Assess | Assess your needs, abilities, experiences, and relationships in terms of what God might be calling you to be or do. Explore how your ancestors responded to God's call on their lives. What would this particular state of life require and what possibilities and opportunities does it offer?

Pray | Take time to pray privately to participate in the Mass devotion to Mary and the adoration of the Blessed Sacrament, and take part in the Sacrament of Penance. Prayer is essential for the life of faith, and it is necessary for listening to God's call. Scripture, the Church's liturgy, and the virtues of faith, hope, and charity are a foundation and starting point for prayer. Reflect on how the gifts and skills you've received from God can help you live as a Catholic in today's world.

✓ Quick Check

1. What is the deeper meaning of vocation that the Church presents to us?

2. When do Christians first receive their vocation and when and how can they start living it?

3. What is the mission, or vocation, of the Church and how does it connect to an individual's vocation?

4. Describe how the Christian vocation can be lived out through various states of life.

Beginnings of Vocation in the Old Testament

From the beginning, God has called all of humanity to salvation. God has revealed the mystery of himself gradually to humans. He has communicated through deeds and words that are collected in Sacred Scripture. The Bible recounts key elements in our salvation history. On our own, humans would know something of God, but God has actually revealed himself to us directly and given himself to us. No one could imagine so much love from a divine being!

God's first revelations were through the things he created, but soon he spoke to men and women directly when he created them. Our first parents walked and talked with God and knew what he expected of them. In spite of that, they disobeyed him; in turn, God banished them from the garden. God did not abandon them, but promised them eventual salvation. He ratified his promise through a **covenant** with humankind. God made that covenant official and everlasting with Noah and all who were alive after the Great Flood. (See *Genesis 9:9–17*.)

▲ *The Sacrifice of Isaac* (1931) by Marc Chagall

The story of our salvation continues with an extraordinary man, Abraham. It might seem to be the story of only one man's vocation. On the contrary, Abraham's vocation to follow where God led is the story of the vocation of the people of Israel, and it is also the beginning of the call of the Church. It is a prime example of how God does not call an individual for that person's sake alone.

The Call to Become God's People

They were named Abram, and Sarai, and were from a nation that worshiped many gods. God chose to reveal himself as the one, true God to Abram. We can only surmise the depth of Abram and Sarai's faith in the one true God that enabled them to make the leap from polytheism to monotheism. God's grace moved their hearts and souls to realize the revelation that there is only one God. Abram believed this revelation and realized that God had singled him out.

Though his wife, Sarai, joined with him in his journey, perhaps others in his family or tribe thought he was crazy. At times he may have doubted his own sanity. It didn't take long for this personal, single God to begin to ask things of Abram:

Now the Lord said to Abram, 'Go from your country and your kindred and your father's house to the land that I will show you. I will make of you a great nation, and I will bless you, and make your name great, so that you will be a blessing. I will bless those who bless you, and the one who curses you I will curse; and in you all the families of the earth shall be blessed.' So Abram went, as the Lord had told him and Lot with him.

✝ Genesis 12:1–4

GROUP TALK

Imagine for a moment that you are in Abram's sandals. Based on all you had learned of the gods of your tribe, would you trust this newly revealed God? Would you have gone where he led you? Would you leave your familiar home, family, and tribe to go to some unknown land? Abram's great faith enabled him to follow God's directive. Abram took his wife Sarai, Lot, his nephew, and others with him. (See *Genesis 12*.)

Read Genesis 12:1–5 and reenact some possible scenarios of Abram preparing to leave Haran with Sarai, Lot, and others.

Abram's story in the Book of Genesis spans chapters 12 through 25. It reads as a **prototype** for all other stories of vocation. You watch Abram travel into danger, take great risks, make mistakes, meet opposition, and continuously receive God's calling to an increasingly closer relationship. Eventually God made a covenant with Abram promising that Abram would be the father of a multitude of people and that God would be their God. To seal this covenant, God gave Abram (a name that means "revered ancestor") the new name "Abraham" (meaning "ancestor of multitudes"). He also renamed Abraham's wife Sarai, "Sarah."

FAITH ACTIVITY

Answering the Call Read Hebrews 11:8–16. The author of this letter states that Abraham's faith was the reason he was able to answer God's call and to fulfill his calling for him. Compare your own faith to the description of Abraham's faith in this passage from Hebrews. Write a reflection or a prayer about your discoveries and how God is calling you today.

FAITH ACTIVITY

Vocation in the Old Testament
Look up some of the passages in the chart below, then discuss the following.

★ What was God asking? How did each person respond at first? What did God do or say?

★ Why do you think the Old Testament includes so many examples like this? What lessons can we apply to our own vocational discernment?

Reluctant Responses God has continued to call the descendants of Abraham and Sarah through the ages. Vocation is a common theme that weaves through the entire Old Testament. God calls scores of people in some significant way. In many cases, the person called doesn't want to be called, or doesn't understand why God is calling him or her. There is usually some argument with God about this—a "Why me?" conversation. The person called is afraid he isn't good enough for the call or isn't up to the job God is asking of him.

In every case, God gives the same answer, simply put: "It isn't up to you; it's up to me. I will be with you." In the Old Testament vocation stories of people such as Moses, Samuel, Gideon, Isaiah, Jeremiah, and more, God is clearly in command. He reveals his power and his love for humanity through the deeds of those he calls to act for him and through the words of the prophets he calls to speak for him. He chooses some unlikely and reluctant people to fulfill his will. There can be no doubt, when reading these stories, that the power to speak for God, to fight for him, or to rule and judge on his

Other Old Testament Vocation Stories

Besides Abraham and Sarah, Moses, Aaron, Samuel, and David, the Old Testament gives us insight into the call of many other important figures.

Isaiah Isaiah 6:1-8	"Then I heard the voice of the Lord saying, 'Whom shall I send, and who will go for us?' " (*Isaiah 6:8*).
Jeremiah Jeremiah 1:4-10	Now the word of the LORD came to me saying ' . . . before you were born I consecrated you . . . ' " (*Jeremiah 1:4-5*).
Ezekiel Ezekiel 1–3	"He said to me, Mortal, I am sending you to the people of Israel . . . " (*Ezekiel 2:3*).
Judith Judith 13:18	Then Uzziah said to her, "O daughter, you are blessed by the Most High God above all other women on earth."
Miriam Micah 6:4	I brought you up from the land of Egypt . . . and I sent before you Moses, Aaron, and Miriam.
Jonah Jonah 1–2	The Lord said to him, "Go at once to Nineveh, that great city, and cry out against it . . . " (*Jonah 1:2*).

behalf, comes from God. The Old Testament vocation stories can be considered prototypes of our own vocation stories. They model the trust we can place in God, the ability to overcome our own fears or perceived limitations, and the sense of meaning and purpose that can come from doing what we believe, even when it challenges us or is difficult.

Consider for a moment the role of Moses, who we learn about in the Book of Exodus. (See Exodus 3:1–10.) This book is the pivotal book of the story of the Hebrew people. Moses was the hero who led God's people out of Egypt, on a forty-year trek through the desert and into the Promised Land. It was through Moses that God revealed his Law to his Chosen People. When God called to Moses from a burning bush and revealed his vocation, Moses could only stammer that he wasn't up to the job. Feeling he didn't have the influence and power needed to confront the Pharaoh and lead the Hebrew people to freedom, Moses said, "O my Lord, I have never been eloquent. . . I am slow of speech and slow of tongue" (*Exodus 4:10*).

God provided an answer for each argument Moses made. Each answer came down to the same core truth: "It isn't up to you; it's up to God."

GROUP TALK

When you are asked to do something new, or feel challenged to move in a new direction, what arguments do you make to yourself and others? In what ways do you feel you are not up to the challenge? What could you say to a trusted advisor? What could you say to God?

FAITH ACTIVITY

One on One with God Reflect on and record your thoughts to the following questions.

★ When are your best times for quiet prayer? How does God speak to you then?

★ Who can you go to for advice and spiritual direction about what you hear?

★ At what other times or in what other ways might God be speaking to you?

Who Calls and Who Is Called?

The Old Testament also includes examples of people who did not recognize God's call at first. In the First Book of Samuel we read that Samuel was someone special from the very beginning. His mother, Hannah, was barren until she prayed at the Temple where the priest Eli saw her. Eli sent her home with the promise that God would answer her prayer for a child.

Hannah conceived and gave birth to her son, Samuel. When he was old enough, she took him to the Temple and put him under the supervision of Eli, the same priest who had told her God would send her a son. However, even with this special beginning, Samuel at first did not recognize when God called him. Samuel awakened Eli in the middle of the night several times before Eli realized it was God calling the boy. Eli directed Samuel to answer, "Speak, LORD, for your servant is listening" (*1 Samuel 3:9*). When he did this, Samuel learned it was, in fact, God speaking; and he began the life of a **prophet**, receiving messages from God to give to the Israelite people.

Do You Mean Me? Sometimes other peoples' reactions to your ideas about your vocation can be confusing or disappointing. Family members and friends can often be good resources for advice or feedback because they know you well and can recognize your gifts and talents. Sometimes they know you *too* well and they tend to focus on your limitations. Or they've known you so long, they haven't noticed how you've changed. We see some of these reactions in the story of Jesse.

David was almost overlooked when God sent Samuel to anoint a successor to King Saul. Samuel only knew the future king would be a son of Jesse. When Samuel arrived in Bethlehem and explained his visit, Jesse was happy to bring all his sons in to meet him. As he met the strong, handsome young men, Samuel was ready to anoint each one. But God rejected them. God explained to Samuel, "The LORD does not see as mortals see; they look on the outward appearance, but the LORD looks on the heart" (*1 Samuel 16:7*).

Samuel met all seven sons of Jesse, but learned from God that none of them had been chosen to be the next King of Israel. He believed there must have been another son.

There was, in fact, one more son, but he was very young; Jesse hadn't called him home from his work of watching the family sheep. It hadn't occurred to Jesse that God might be calling his youngest son, David. Yet when he came in, God said to Samuel, "Rise and anoint him; for this is the one" (*1 Samuel 16:12*). Ultimately, David became one of the greatest kings of Israel and ancestors of Jesus.

GROUP TALK

1 What do you think some of David's brothers said to him that day? How do you think David might have responded?

2 How do you usually react when a nay-sayer puts you down or doubts your abilities?

3 Do you think your family and friends recognize your potential? What do you do about people who don't? How can they be an obstacle for you? How can they actually be of help?

4 What can you learn from the call of David about your own calling?

Quick Check

1. What was so extraordinary about Abraham given the time in which he was alive?

2. What were some of the common responses of those who were reluctant to answer God's call, and what was God's basic answer to all of them?

3. What were Moses' arguments when God called him to lead his people out of Egypt?

4. What was surprising about the successor of King Saul?

Connected to the Past Evidence from the Old Testament helps us sum up the religious sense of "vocation" this way: When God calls, answer "yes." Keep saying "yes" to God today, tomorrow, and every day thereafter. Response to a call from God will set you on a new course—you'll turn in some new direction, or start a new kind of living. You'll receive a mission, and you'll spend the rest of your life fulfilling it. You'll meet others who share your mission, and they'll become your community.

God's calls to Abraham, Sarah, Moses, Deborah, Ruth, Samuel, David, and the multitude of others before the time of Christ kept leading God's People toward Jesus. Those people, responded to God's calling and prepared for Christ's mission of salvation. They were our **ancestors in faith** and vocation. Because they believed in God and answered his call then, we can do so today.

The Catholic Parish: Where Disciples Are Formed and Fed

" The parish initiates the Christian people into the ordinary expression of the liturgical life: it gathers them together in this celebration; it teaches Christ's saving doctrine; it practices the charity of the Lord in good works and brotherly love . . .

(*CCC*, 2179).

There are nearly 220,000 Roman Catholic parishes in the world. Nearly 19,000 of them are in the United States. Parishes can be as small as a few dozen families and as large as thousands of families. They are located in every type of city, town, or rural area in every country of the world, using buildings that range from small wooden huts to massive marble cathedrals.

Some parishes have a resident priest and some do not; some may even have more than one priest in residence. Each parish has some type of priestly presence–only in this way can parishioners have the Eucharist. And all parishes celebrate the Eucharist on a regular basis. All parishes make the other sacraments available, too. People are baptized, reconciled, confirmed, married, and anointed in their parish churches. At the end of life, people have their funerals there.

Some parishes have a full-time parochial school; all offer religious education for at least some, and often all, members. A visit to any parish in the world can offer many clues about the "style" of the parish. Mass–the Eucharistic Liturgy–is celebrated in every Parish, usually in the language of the local people. However, some parishes celebrate Mass in Latin, and some offer a multi-language menu of Masses to serve the many ethnic groups who live nearby.

You will find large choirs with pipe organs and instrumental ensembles at some parishes. Others might have a piano or a guitar or no musical instruments at all. You will always find music in the parish–sometimes it is of professional quality, sometimes it is not.

Some parishes have large staffs of ordained, consecrated, and lay people. Others have just one or two paid staff. No matter what the size, all parishes depend on every member, every Christian disciple, to carry out the parish's mission. They sing, teach, clean, launder, counsel, type, file, answer the phone, visit the sick, cook meals, stuff envelopes, babysit, drive, build, or count money. Each person can be depended on in a crisis. Above all, they gather at the parish to pray. A parish couldn't be a parish without all of them.

FAITH ACTIVITY

Comparing Your Parish to Others
Go in small groups to your own and other parishes with predominant cultures that are not your own, asking for permission to do a profile of the parish by interviewing staff members and parishioners. Take cameras, notebooks, tape recorders, and video recorders and visit groups and individuals; attend Mass and other services, religion classes, meetings, and other activities. Identify the mission statement of the parish and illustrate in your profile how it is being carried out. Notice how young people are being challenged to think about their vocations.

Vocation in the New Testament

FAITH ACTIVITY

Skepticism Read Luke 4:14–37 to see the context of Jesus' mission statement. Why do you think people reacted to him the way they did that day? Has anything like this ever happened to you or any of your friends? Have you ever been skeptical about the abilities of someone you know? What do you think causes people to be so negative about the talents of some local young people your age?

The New Testament is filled with stories of Jesus calling people—to repentance, to believe, to hope, to trust in the Father, to follow him. Jesus himself models how we are to listen to and respond to the Father. Jesus was sent by his Father to live among us and to die for our salvation, lasting the fullness of time. God the Father "revealed himself fully by sending his own Son" (CCC, 73). The covenant that God the Father first established with Noah and Abraham was established forever in his Son, Jesus. His mission was to bring salvation to all humankind. Once he set out on that mission, he never turned away from it. God the Holy Spirit was with Jesus in this mission. Jesus described his work this way.

The Spirit of the Lord is upon me,
because he has anointed me
to bring good news to the poor.

He has sent me to proclaim release to the captives
and recovery of sight to the blind,
to let the oppressed go free,
to proclaim the year of the Lord's favor.

Luke 4:18-19

Each of his followers, from the first Apostle to you today, shares in that mission with him in varying ways. Jesus' entire life taught us how to live our own lives as his disciples. Everything he did—his miracles, prayers, his love for the poor—made his words a reality. Everything he said and did was the fulfillment of God's Revelation. The entirety of what he did on earth culminated in his sacrifice on the Cross for the salvation of the world and in his Resurrection from the dead. (See *Catechism of the Catholic Church, 561.*)

Setting the Stage

We see in the Gospels, that, as Jesus' birth approached, some people of the Old Covenant set the stage for his coming. The Holy Spirit inspired these people to hear and answer God's call.

Zechariah and Elizabeth In the beginning of the Gospel according to Luke, we read the story of the priest Zechariah and his wife Elizabeth. Elderly and childless, they were part of the **faithful remnant** of Israelites who still awaited the coming of the Messiah. They were thrust into the center of the story, to be the parents of the prophet John the Baptist.

Zechariah was a priest who was taking his turn offering incense in the Temple. The angel Gabriel came to him there and told him he and Elizabeth would have a son, whom they would call John. Gabriel assured Zechariah that John would be a very special man who would lead many people to God. Zechariah had some trouble believing that the elderly Elizabeth would have a son. Because of his unbelief, he spent her entire pregnancy unable to speak. It wasn't until he wrote the message that the new baby's name would be John that his voice was returned to him. When Zechariah could finally speak after the birth of his son, he proclaimed, "Blessed be the Lord God of Israel, for he has looked favorably on his people and redeemed them" (*Luke 1:68*).

Before John's birth, when Elizabeth was in her sixth month of pregnancy, her cousin Mary, who was newly pregnant with her Son, Jesus, came to visit. Elizabeth felt her baby leap within her. She "exclaimed with a loud cry, 'Blessed are you among women, and blessed is the fruit of your womb'" (*Luke 1:42*).

Elizabeth and Zechariah shared a vocation. Inspired by the Holy Spirit, they both spoke prophetically. Their mission was to raise the man who would announce the arrival of the Messiah in a faithful Jewish home. For them, responding to God's call meant remaining where they were, and starting to live as parents at a very old age. We can only imagine all the challenges they faced, but we can be sure that John's love for God, his passion for the truth, and his courage were deeply influenced by their faith and love.

Mary and Joseph At last, the time had come for God's age-old promise of sending a Messiah to be fulfilled. By the power of the Holy Spirit, Mary conceived a Son—the Messiah. The Father gave the world his Son, Emmanuel, "God-with-us." (See *CCC*, 744.)

Mary answered the angel Gabriel when she learned that God wanted her to be the Mother of his Son, "Here am I, the servant of the Lord; let it be with me according to your word" (*Luke 1:38*). With this consent to God's

FAITH ACTIVITY

Starting with Prayer The Church's daily prayer, the Liturgy of the Hours, includes two prayers from the beginning of Gospel according to Luke. The Canticle of Zechariah (see *Luke 1:68-79*) is prayed every morning, and Mary's Magnificat (see *Luke 1:46-55*) is prayed every evening. Pray one or both of them as prayers to discern what your own vocation might be.

▼ *The Vision of Saint Joseph* (ca. 1636) by Philippe de Champaigne

plan, Mary became a collaborator with the work of salvation her Son would accomplish. Before she accepted her vocation in this way, however, she was like those called in the Old Testament—surprised and not sure why God had chosen her.

She didn't ask for proof, but the angel offered it to her: her elderly cousin Elizabeth was pregnant and would give birth to a child, "For nothing will be impossible with God" (*Luke 1:37*). Surely this news stirred both joy and amazement in Mary's heart. With God's grace, she found the courage and faith within herself to answer, "Yes!" to his amazing call.

Joseph must have been as surprised as Mary, and he, too, freely said "yes" to what God was calling him to. He learned that his espoused wife was already pregnant, and he knew he wasn't the baby's father. He decided to end his betrothal to Mary privately. But God sent an angel to help Joseph. Joseph saw the angel in a dream, telling him not to be afraid to take Mary as his wife because it was through the power of the Holy Spirit that Mary had conceived the child. Implicit in Joseph's exchange with the angel was that Joseph also believed that nothing is impossible with God.

He did believe, and Mary and Joseph began to fulfill their vocation to care for and help raise the Messiah to adulthood. They didn't have an easy vocation. From the beginning they faced great dangers, long hours of travel, and years away from their home in Nazareth.

The mystery of the Incarnation teaches us that God who is true God, became true man in Jesus. Mary and Joseph faced the reality of the Incarnation in ways no one else ever could. The second Person of the Blessed Trinity, the Son of God, assumed human nature and became man while remaining God; Jesus Christ is both true God and true man. That's what the Incarnation means. And because of this mystery of faith, Jesus is "the one and only mediator between God and man" (*CCC*, 480). This baby was born while Mary and Joseph were far from home and family, with only a stable for shelter. The birth of Jesus meant diapers, nursing, and dealing with tears, teething, and childhood illnesses. It also meant escaping death by traveling to Egypt, and finding ways to feed, clothe, and shelter themselves and their child.

Jesus learned much of what made him a man—his learning, his values, his work ethic, and his passion for truth—from his Mother and his foster father. In their home he learned the prayers and practices of the Jewish faith. Mary and Joseph had the joy and challenge of raising a very bright Son. The Gospel according to Luke gives us a brief glimpse into their daily life with Jesus, describing one of the family's annual trips to Jerusalem for Passover. (See *Luke 2:41–52*.) It isn't hard to imagine the frantic feelings Mary and Joseph must have felt as they searched for their missing Son. It isn't hard to imagine their hurt and confusion when Jesus told them he needed to be in his Father's house. After this incident, Jesus "went down with them and came to Nazareth, and was obedient to them" (*Luke 2:51*).

✓ **Quick Check**

1. What was Jesus' mission and how did he accomplish it?

2. Why were Elizabeth and Zachariah important figures in the history of salvation?

3. How did Mary and Joseph respond to God's call?

4. Not every Apostle in the Gospels immediately got a direct call from Jesus to follow him. How did others come to follow him?

The Disciples of Jesus

"Come follow me," Jesus said to a band of fishermen and other workers. In the Gospels we see Jesus directly calling people to be his **disciples**, and we see the variety of answers he received.

The call to be a disciple of Jesus was reminiscent of Abraham's call. Disciples had to change their direction in life, leave home, and go into the unknown. We read in the Gospel according to Mark that, when Jesus called the fishermen, Simon Peter, Andrew, James, and John, "immediately they left their nets and followed him" (*Mark 1:18*). Jesus got the same immediate response when he called the tax collector Levi, or Matthew. (See *Mark 2:13–14*.)

Some of the Apostles got their call to follow Jesus because of the influence of another Apostle. Philip told Nathanael about Jesus, but Nathanael's first reaction wasn't so positive. "Can anything good come out of Nazareth?" he scoffed. (See *John 1:46*.) But after speaking with Jesus, Nathanael could tell he was a prophet, so he also became an Apostle.

Some who were called decided not to follow Jesus. A rich young man who was keeping all the commandments still wanted to do more. But when Jesus told him what he needed to do next, he wouldn't follow that call. Jesus said,

"If you wish to be perfect, go, sell your possessions, and give the money to the poor, and you will have treasure in heaven; then come, follow me." When the young man heard this word, he went away grieving, for he had many possessions.

Then Jesus said to his disciples, "Truly I tell you, it will be hard for a rich person to enter the kingdom of heaven. Again I tell you, it is easier for a camel to go through the eye of a needle than for someone who is rich to enter the kingdom of God."

✝ Matthew 19:21-24

Peter asked what would become of the Apostles, who had given up everything to follow him. Jesus told the Apostles that all who left their homes and families for his sake would inherit eternal life. (See *Matthew 19:27–30*.)

Youth Ministry and World Youth Day

The Church at all levels—the parish, the diocese, the U.S. Bishops, and the Holy Father in Rome—cares deeply for youth and reaches out with many forms of youth ministry. Pope John Paul II made ministry for and with young people a priority of his papacy. In 1986, he proclaimed Palm Sunday to be World Youth Day (WYD) each year. This started a tradition of world and diocesan gatherings of youth every two to three years. On these occasions, youths gather from culturally diverse churches worldwide to point out the local and universal dimensions of discipleship.

Each diocese plans its own events to celebrate and reach out to young people who are already part of youth ministry programs at local parishes. These diocesan events help youth see that they are part of a Church that goes beyond the boundaries of a single parish. At diocesan youth gatherings young people gather to pray, celebrate, and share their faith and mission with one another.

World Youth Day takes on a global dimension. Pope John Paul wrote of these international events that "young people are called periodically to make a pilgrimage along the roads of the world. In young people the Church sees herself and her mission to mankind: with them she faces the challenges of the future, aware that all humanity needs to be rejuvenated in spirit. This pilgrimage of the young members of the people builds bridges of brotherhood and hope between continents, peoples and cultures. It is a journey which is always in action, like life, like youth" (from the Letter of Pope John Paul II to Cardinal Eduardo Francisco Pironio).

FAITH ACTIVITY

Researching WYD Contact your diocesan youth ministry office to find out what events are being planned for the next World Youth Day. Research what events have taken place in the past. Where have the youth of your diocese gathered in the past few years? What were the goals of these gatherings? Speak to people who attended any of these events when they were in high school. Find out what impact World Youth Day had on them.

To what different countries have young people gone on pilgrimages as part of World Youth Day in the years it has been celebrated globally? Interview someone who has attended an International World Youth Day gathering. What were their experiences and what effect did these experiences have on their faith?

You can find links about World Youth Day at www.osvcurriculum.com. Check to see when and where the next one is scheduled.

GO online

Pope John Paul II arrived for World Youth Day vigil in Toronto on July 27, 2002 ▶

The Christian Vocation: A Call to Discipleship

With ancestors in the faith like we have, it's no wonder Catholics take vocation so seriously. By studying the vocational models from both the Old and New Testaments, the Church has come to have a very well-developed understanding of vocation. We don't wonder whether or not we have a vocation; we know we do. A vocation is a holy calling from our God to love and serve him and others, it is part of who God created us to be. In Baptism we are called to be Jesus' disciples. The Christian vocation is a call to all people regardless of circumstances: young and old, rich and poor, married and single. All Christians are called to discipleship.

The *Catechism* describes the vocation of all Christ's disciples as "a vocation to holiness and to the mission of evangelizing the world" (*CCC*, 1533). The Apostles after Jesus' Resurrection heard this call and were **commissioned** to go forth and share the "Good News." Jesus said, "Go therefore and make disciples of all nations, baptizing them in the name of the Father and of the Son and of the Holy Spirit, and teaching them to obey everything that I have commanded you." (*Matthew 28:19–20*). This call to share Jesus' "Good News" is a call to **evangelize**. It remains the Church's mandate today.

"Why Are You Standing There?"

There's a sense of urgency about the commissioning of the Apostles. They were sent by Christ; it was time for them to begin their mission. Yet, there was a short delay. Jesus explained it himself before he ascended into heaven: They still needed to receive the Holy Spirit, and Jesus promised it would happen in a few days. Only then could they become his Church—built, given life and energy, and made holy by the Holy Spirit. In the meantime, the Apostles were confused and undoubtedly afraid. Jesus told them he'd always be with them, and then he ascended into heaven. They stood staring up after him, unwilling or unable to move. Then two white-robed men confronted them and asked, "Men of Galilee, why do you stand looking up toward heaven?" (*Acts 1:10–11*).

GROUP TALK

1 Have you ever hesitated before starting a new task? Why?

2 Take some time to reflect on how you start a new task. How do you come up with the strength and courage you need to begin?

Filled with the Holy Spirit

After the Ascension, the Apostles returned to Jerusalem, but spent ten days praying together with Mary and other disciples, speaking of all that had happened, and choosing a replacement for Judas Iscariot. On the day of Pentecost a violent rush of wind and divided tongues of fire signaled they were filled with the Holy Spirit. They received the Spirit that Jesus had promised, and the strength, courage, and ability to begin their mission.

The story of the descent of the Holy Spirit on Pentecost is full of energy. (See *Acts 2*.) We read about what sounded like a rushing wind, and what looked like tongues of fire burning over each head. Suddenly, men who had been hiding behind a locked door went forth boldly and spoke in languages they had never spoken before. From that moment on, the story of the Church has vibrated with energy. The Holy Spirit has never stopped moving through the Church and the world, calling more and more people to know Jesus Christ and to bring his Gospel to others. The tongues of flame over the Apostles' heads never went out, but multiplied into infinity, so that they rest over our heads now. We might not see them burning, but we see the power of the Holy Spirit everywhere.

It's likely your Baptism did not include violent wind and tongues of flame, but it did fill you with the Holy Spirit and empowers you to live your Christian vocation. Called at Baptism, that call is now confirmed at your Confirmation. Through the power of the Holy Spirit you received the gifts of wisdom, understanding, knowledge, counsel, reverence, courage, and awe and wonder. You need these gifts of the Holy Spirit to help you to carry out your mission. The Gifts of the Holy Spirit can be found in the book of the prophet Isaiah. (See *Isaiah 11:1–3*.)

FAITH ACTIVITY

Gifts of the Holy Spirit Consider the seven Gifts of the Holy Spirit. In small groups, discuss what each one means. How do they play out in your lives now? Which can be strengthened within you? Do you have any of them in abundance?

Gifts of the Holy Spirit

Wisdom	This gift gives us the power to see things from God's perspective. We develop this gift as we meditate and contemplate on his presence, action, and guidance in our lives. This kind of reflection helps us clarify what we believe and guides us to make right judgments and good decisions. Through wisdom we have the power to love what is of God and to value all of his creation.
Understanding	This gift gives us a way to understand Jesus' teachings and the Tradition of the Church. It helps us get to the heart of revealed truth even when we do not fully understand its entire meaning. It gives us a real confidence in the revealed word of God and leads us to draw orthodox conclusions from Scripture and doctrine. It is the power to know how to live our lives as followers of Jesus and to apply the teachings of the Church to our lives.
Counsel (Right Judgment)	This gift, also called counsel, helps us know what we should do in difficult situations. It helps us judge our own actions correctly. It is the power to know how to make right choices and good decisions that are consistent with Jesus' teachings. This gift often involves asking others for help, and offering good, moral advice to others.
Fortitude (Courage)	This gift, also called fortitude, ensures a confident spirit of resolution, firmness of mind, and strong will to persevere knowing that God's providence (by which he guides his creation toward its perfection yet to be attained) will enable us to overcome all obstacles. It helps us persist in the practice of virtue even when we do fail or are persecuted for trying. It is the power to stand up for our beliefs and the values of Jesus' message especially when it is difficult.
Knowledge	This gift enables us to judge what is happening in relationships, the environment, and social situations. We are able to see God's providence in what happens in our lives. This gift is sometimes called the science or knowledge of the saints (see *Proverbs 30:3*) because those who have knowledge can distinguish between impulses and the inspiration of grace.
Piety (Reverence)	This gift places us in a right relationship with God. It enables us to see God as our loving Father. Pope John Paul II described it as a gift that opens our hearts to "tenderness towards God and our brothers and sisters . . . expressed in prayer." Through it we develop a loving obedience toward God. It is the power to see God's presence in all people and life experiences.
Fear of the Lord (Wonder and Awe)	This gift inspires us with awareness of God's majesty and the fact that he has created us in his image. Wonder and awe helps us appreciate the mystery of the Trinity and respond with love and goodness to God's initiative of love by which he sent his Son to atone for our sins, and the love by which his Son, Jesus, freely offered himself for our salvation. Through this gift we know we have a spiritual dimension and are able to be in relationship with God. It is the power to recognize how awesome he truly is.

Called to Eucharist

Their mission did not become clear to the apostles and other disciples immediately—even after they received the Holy Spirit. They experienced stops, starts, and wrong turns as they began their lives as Christians. However, from the very beginning, they knew they were to return to what they had been taught and given at the Lord's Supper—Jesus' Last Supper with them before he died. They broke the Bread together and drank from the cup. They knew that they were eating the Body of Christ. They knew the wine they drank together was actually his Blood that would be poured out for them.

They remembered the story of something that had happened right after Jesus died and rose from the dead. Jesus appeared to two disciples who were leaving Jerusalem on their way to Emmaus. Still in shock over the violent crucifixion of the man they thought was the Messiah, and confused about the reports of some disciples that he had risen from the dead, they were talking about it in sorrow. Suddenly, Jesus came up to them and asked what they were discussing. They didn't recognize him, and they told him about the tragedy that had befallen their small group.

▼ Detail of *The Last Supper* (1520-1525) by Andrea del Sarto

Then Jesus spoke to them about how the Messiah needed to die to save God's people. He used passages from Scripture to make his point. Later, the disciples reported that as he spoke they felt as if their hearts were on fire from his words. When they got to Emmaus they invited him to stay with them for the night. As they sat at supper with him, he broke bread and blessed it. With that, the two disciples recognized him, and he disappeared from their sight. Those two weary men then found the energy to run back to Jerusalem to tell everyone what had happened and that, indeed, Jesus had risen from the dead. They drew strength for their mission to tell everyone about the Resurrection of Jesus. (See *Luke 24:13–33*.)

The early Church cherished this story, and we still do today. "How will we know he is with us?" they would ask, knowing the answer: They would know him in the breaking of the bread.

This command from Jesus to "take and eat," and to "do this in remembrance of me," continues for us to this day. We affirm our discipleship and membership in the Church by receiving the Body and Blood of Christ. From this Eucharist we are united more closely to Christ and his Body on earth. We draw our strength for the journey and the mission as disciples have done since the very beginning.

Called to Service

Jesus did something else at his Last Supper that he commanded us to do also. The Gospel according to John reports that Jesus washed his Apostles' feet. When he was finished, he told them, "If I, your Lord and Teacher, have washed your feet, you also ought to wash one another's feet. For I have set you an example, that you also should do as I have done to you" (*John 13:14–15*). Jesus was a servant, as well as king, and we ae called to follow his example.

The Church has taken this mandate very seriously throughout her entire history. You may have seen the foot washing take place on Holy Thursday at the Evening Mass of the Lord's Supper as symbolic obedience to this command. The real obedience can be seen in every institution of charity established and maintained by the Church. Catholic hospitals, orphanages, homes for the poor, soup kitchens, missions, clinics, schools, and other types of outreach to give service are directly connected to the Last Supper foot-washing.

FAITH ACTIVITY

How Would You Respond?
Prayerfully read John 13:1-17. Try putting yourself into the place of one of the disciples in the story. Write, draw, sculpt, or compose a response to Jesus as you imagine him washing your feet and telling you to do likewise.

Foot-washing, or service of all kinds, can also be seen in the actions of each individual disciple. A parent consoling a child, a teacher working with a student, a nurse changing a bandage, a chef serving a meal—each person is washing feet as Jesus commanded them to do. They do so when their motives spring from their faith and take them beyond a mere sense of duty.

GROUP TALK

Read the story of Jesus washing his disciples' feet. (See John 13:1–20.) Consider Peter's embarrassment and refusal when Jesus comes to wash his feet. Then consider how Peter recants his refusal, and instead asks Jesus to wash not only his feet, but his hands and head as well.

1 What do you think was the source of Peter's refusal?

2 If you have ever had your feet washed during the liturgy of Holy Thursday Mass, how did you feel before, during, and after?

3 If you haven't had your feet washed, imagine that you have just been selected for the foot washing. How do you feel?

4 How would you describe our call to service that is modeled in the foot washing?

▶ A Sister of Saint Joseph of Brentwood, New York, and principal of The Mary Louis Academy in New York addresses the junior class at their Commissioning Ceremony for Christian service that they will perform in and for the local community.

The Knights and Ladies of Peter Claver

The Knights and Ladies of Peter Claver is the largest African American lay Catholic fraternal order in the United States. It was founded in Mobile, Alabama, in 1909, for the express purpose of giving service to the local Catholic Church community. Today its national office is located in New Orleans, Louisiana. The order has over 40,000 members in 86 dioceses across the United States. There are four divisions of membership: Knights, Ladies, Junior Knights, and Junior Daughters.

This fraternal order of African Americans honors Saint Peter Claver, a Jesuit Missionary from Spain who served in Cartagena, Colombia, in the early 1600s. At that time, Cartagena was a port used for the passage of enslaved Africans to the New World. Father Peter Claver was sent to minister to the Catholic citizens of Cartagena, and was appalled by the conditions in which the enslaved Africans were living. He ignored the social ostracism and disapproval of his Spanish community and went to minister to the Africans. He sought out enslaved Africans who were injured or ill, then fed them, bound their wounds, and advocated for better conditions for them.

Father Claver served the Church this way for forty years. His gentle ministry led to the Baptisms of nearly 300,000 Africans. Besides ministering to the enslaved himself, he chose a small group of enslaved people to help him serve. Today's Knights and Ladies of Peter Claver point back to that chosen group of enslaved Africans who served others who were enslaved as the "first real Knights and Ladies of St. Peter Claver." Father Peter Claver died in 1654, and was named a saint in 1888.

Knights and Ladies of Peter Claver help their own members and people in their wider communities. When people of color were unable to get burial insurance, or were refused admittance to many hospitals, the Knights and Ladies of Peter Claver provided help and care for families who needed assistance. Today, the Knights assist the bishops and clergy of the Roman Catholic Church in Apostolic work by "planning, promoting, sponsoring and executing commendable works of Catholic Action wherever and whenever possible."

In parishes that have a chapter of the Knights and Ladies of Peter Claver, members work with their pastors to help parishioners in need, to evangelize and welcome new Catholics, to contribute to the upkeep of parish buildings and grounds, and to promote vocations to the priesthood, religious life, and lay ministry among young people. Nationally, through contributions from all local chapters, the Knights and Ladies of Peter Claver award two college scholarships each year, maintain a charity fund which awards grants to worthy applicants, provide money for treatment of, and research on, sickle cell anemia, offer tutoring, and provide grant money for groups working on humanitarian projects that promote social justice.

FAITH ACTIVITY

Researching Fraternal Orders Do some research about the Knights of Peter Claver and the Knights of Columbus. These two orders now often work in tandem. Find out how each contributed to the support of immigrant Catholics in the early part of the twentieth century. How have these orders adapted to changing times and needs in the Church and in their communities? Contact people from their national offices or from local chapters and ask for literature about these orders. Would you consider being a member of one of these orders (or of their ladies' auxiliary orders)?

Meet Elyse Heinrich, She's a junior at Illinois State University, where she is seeking a degree in elementary education, in preparation to teach middle school. She's also discerning whether she has a vocation to a consecrated life as a sister in a religious order.

INTERVIEWER: When did you first get the idea you might be called to a consecrated religious life?

ELYSE: The summer after my junior year in high school, my older brother and I went with our parish youth ministry group to help clean up an inner-city neighborhood. Some Benedictine Sisters were in charge of the project. That was the first time I'd met any sisters, and I was interested in their mission and calling as soon as I met them. I've been going back to work with them every summer since.

I: What was it about them that drew you in? Were they really the first religious sisters you'd ever met?

E: My Catholic grade school had no sisters, and I was in public high school. I guess part of their attraction was that they ran a Catholic girls' high school in the city. The sisters were so much fun and so genuinely happy in just helping any way they could. Oh, I don't mean they went around smiling all the time. It was hard work in hot weather, but when things got tough, the sisters knew how to bring all of us back to a good space. They seemed to always be able to look on the bright side of everything. And some of the stories they told were hilarious!

I: Some people might find it hard to believe religious sisters have a sense of humor, do you remember any of their stories?

E: I can't remember anything specifically . . . no wait, I remember this one. They told me about a time when they walked into a store and everyone went from cutting up and having a good time to near silence after they walked in. But then one of the sisters said to everyone, it's OK to smile, God loves you, and everyone became happier and more at ease again. The way they told it was really cute. I'd love to be able to tell stories like they do.

I: What led you to consider actually joining them?

E: I didn't consider it at first. I just liked their style—down to earth, simple, honest. It took a couple of summers working with them to get me thinking. This summer project has meant a LOT to me. It's one time I know I'm really making a difference. It's a way I really connect to Jesus in the Gospel. I feel called to be of service like that.

I: Do you ever think about getting married?

E: Sometimes. I've dated a few guys, but I haven't met anyone yet who I'd be interested in spending my life with. Maybe I will. But maybe I'm going to be a religious sister. I don't have to decide right now.

I: But what are you doing about it right now?

E: I'm writing to a sister who gives me spiritual direction and answers my questions. I pray every day and attend Mass as often as I can—every Sunday, of course—but I like to go to daily Mass sometimes, too. Oh, and I'm going on a vocation awareness retreat next month. I went on one last year and it was great to talk and pray with other people who are trying to discover what God wants them to do in life.

who will you become?

Take a few minutes to fill out boxes below.

Where do you imagine yourself four or five years from now? What kind of work do you see yourself doing? What kind of life will you be living?

Look back at the interests, skills, and talents you identified at the beginning of this chapter. How might they be gifts from God and ways to make a difference in the community?

How could you use these talents and skills in a future profession or career?

How might you use them as a way to respond to your baptismal call to grow more like Jesus?

How might they help you figure out what vocation God is calling you to?

Praying to God with Mary

Leader: Everyone has a vocation to be a disciple of Jesus. Mary has often been called the first and best disciple of Jesus. Today we will pray her Magnificat in union with all in the Church who pray this prayer each day. Let's pray for each other, that we will each come to know what God is calling us to do in life. We begin:

All: In the name of the Father, and of the Son, and of the Holy Spirit.

Left Side: My soul proclaims the greatness of the Lord,
my spirit rejoices in God my Savior
for he has looked with favor
on his lowly servant.

Right Side: From this day
all generations will call me blessed:
the Almighty has done great things for me,
and holy is his Name.

L: He has mercy on those who fear him
in every generation.
He has shown the strength of his arm,
he has scattered the proud in their conceit.

R: He has cast down the mighty from their thrones,
and has lifted up the lowly.
He has filled the hungry with good things,
and sent the rich away empty.

L: He has come to the help of his servant Israel
for he has remembered his promise of mercy,
the promise he made to our fathers,
to Abraham and his children forever.

All: Glory to the Father,
and to the Son,
and to the Holy Spirit:
as it was in the beginning,
is now
and will be forever. Amen.

Study Guide

►Check Understanding

1. Describe the deeper understanding of vocation the Church presents to us.

2. Explain when Christians first receive their vocation and when and how can they start living it.

3. Summarize the mission, or vocation, of the Church and how does it connect to an individual's vocation.

4. Identify how the Christian vocation can be lived out through various states of life.

5. Give examples of what was so extraordinary about Abraham given the time in which he was alive.

6. Outline some of the common responses of those who were reluctant to answer God's call and recall God's basic answer to all of them.

7. Restate Moses' arguments when God called him to lead his people out of Egypt.

8. Describe what was surprising about the successor of King Saul.

9. Explain Jesus' mission and how he accomplished it.

10. Why were Elizabeth and Zechariah important figures in the history of salvation?

11. Account for what might have made Joseph's vocation so difficult at first.

12. List the different ways disciples came to follow Jesus.

13. Detail how the events of Pentecost affected the Apostles and influenced their mission.

14. Explain what it means to evangelize and how the first Apostles accomplished this task.

15. Give examples of what Catholics believe about the Eucharist and why is it so important in our lives.

16. Describe what we learn from Jesus' washing of his Apostles' feet at his Last Supper.

►Apply & Develop

17. Support, in writing, the importance of discernment in the lives of Catholics. Include explanations of the various aspects of discernment and concrete examples of what someone can do in each.

18. Illustrate how the call of David to be anointed as future king is a prototype for the experience some young people have as they try to discover their gifts and talents today.

19. Compare and contrast the vocational calls of Mary and Joseph. How are both models of faith for us today?

20. Choose three Gifts of the Holy Spirit you feel are most needed in the lives of people your age, supporting your explanation with specific information about the Gifts.

►Key Words

See pages noted for contextual explanations of these important faith terms.

ancestors in faith (p. 20)

commissioned (p. 27)

covenant (p. 16)

discernment (p. 14)

disciples (p. 25)

evangelize (p. 27)

faithful remnant (p. 23)

mission (p. 12)

prophet (p. 19)

prototype (p. 17)

vocation (p. 11)

CALLED TO COMMUNITY

CHAPTER 2

CHAPTER GOALS

In this chapter you will:

★ consider what faith is, how it impacts the way you live out your baptismal call as a member of the Body of Christ, and how it influences your vocation awareness.

★ learn how the Church's moral teachings are a clear guide for Catholics in all walks of life, how these teachings can help you live out the common call to holiness now, and discern your future vocation.

★ discover how the sacramental life of the Church is an essential part of responding to God's call to know, love, and serve him.

★ see the importance of family and a Catholic home environment in introducing us to the faith and encouraging our vocations.

★ meet a permanent deacon who serves a parish community.

who are you?

Take a few minutes to consider the examples below.

Have you ever wondered what being a Catholic has to do with who you are as a person, what life choices you will make, what career or occupation you will have? Would you be surprised to find out that many mature Catholic adults include their Catholicism as a deciding factor in how they live their lives? Consider these examples:

- a Catholic store owner who sets her and all her workers' hours so that everyone can get to Mass or to their own church service each weekend

- Catholic parents who choose to sacrifice some material needs so they have enough money to pay for Catholic educations for their children

- Catholic travelers who search for a Catholic Mass to attend on Sunday no matter where they are traveling

- a Catholic banker who spends one night a week helping at a homeless shelter

- a Catholic mother of four young children who drives an elderly neighbor to kidney dialysis twice a week

- Catholics who make decisions about how they spend their money, use their time, speak to others, or vote based on their faith

Now spend some time thinking about these questions.

1. Can you think of any other examples of faithful Catholic living you have observed in your family, friends, or other people you know?

2. Do you think being a Catholic has influenced who you are? If so, how? If not, why not?

3. Do you know any other examples of Catholic adults who live their faith in their everyday activities—home, work, school, and so on?

4. How do you live your Catholic faith as a high school student today?

You'll revisit these at the conclusion of this chapter to see how God might be acting in this area of your life.

The Path to Vocation Awareness: Living a Faithful Life

How can you come to know what God is calling you to do with your life? What can you do to become aware of your vocation? You won't find quick answers and you probably won't reach out and grab the first idea that comes along. Every state of life—dedicated lay single, married, consecrated religious, ordained minister—is a calling, an invitation from God that asks for a response.

> The Christian, whether laborer or judge, doctor or farmer, business person or professor, is recognized by the way he or she practices the commandment of love for God and neighbor....Whatever place you take in society, whatever profession you carry out, you are called to do as a service.
>
> —Papal Message to College Students at Villa Nazareth in Rome June 8, 1996
> *Sons and Daughters of the Light*, p. 12

But how do you recognize what you're being called to do with your life? You can look at your abilities, skills, activities, and relationships. It is there that God motivates us and calls us. Self-discovery is a life-long process, and a very important part of the discernment process. You have to know yourself to know how God is calling you to know, love, and serve him.

Know Yourself Well Enough to Make a Life Choice
Recognize your abilities, what you can give.
Understand your needs.
Know what makes you happy.
Know how you best relate to others.

Don't overlook the importance and role of your family, neighborhood, and parish and school community.

Since God is calling you right here where you are, one important aspect of discerning your vocation is to live each day faithfully. One key to this is realizing how important you are to those around you, and how necessary it is to take part in the community and to use your gifts and talents for the benefit of the Body of Christ near and far.

So, notice who is around you. How do they love you, and how do you love them? What do they need that you could give them? What do you need that they can give to you? Where do you fit? What do you do well? What do the people around you—your community—need you to do? How might that translate into the future?

"But," you might argue, "how is that being a disciple? Doesn't everybody have to live like that? It isn't only Church people who have to get along with others!" While that is true, it is also true that faith-filled people are called to add a faith dimension to everything they do.

GROUP TALK

1. What do you think is most difficult about figuring out your vocation in life? How often do you pray for guidance?

2. What do you need to know and want to learn about yourself before deciding permanently on a way of life?

3. When do you usually seek someone else's guidance or advice? How have close friends and family members been helpful or unhelpful when you seek advice?

Faith: a Divine Gift and a Human Response

Faith might be a word you haven't thought a lot about. You've been raised in a particular community of faith and you might just take your own faith for granted. That's true for many young people. You, or people you know, might struggle with questions and ideas about the faith of their families and communities and wonder if they actually have that faith or any faith at all.

Faith begins with God, not with us. It is a supernatural gift freely given by God that requires our cooperation. And we are free to respond, and when we do, that faith is a real, concrete human act. In an act of faith we hold firm to God, who has made himself known to us. When we profess faith, we accept the entire truth of what our triune God has revealed. Our most important profession of faith is in the Blessed Trinity: the three Persons in one God: God the Father, the Son, and the Holy Spirit. God the Holy Spirit makes it possible for us to believe, stirring our hearts, heads, and souls to turn to God, helping us see things as he intends.

It is up to each individual person to decide what to do about this offered gift and this action of the Holy Spirit. In fact, his grace connects to the deepest desires of human freedom, calling us to accept and cooperate with his grace, which can lead us to the perfect use of our freedom. We each have an **intellect** with which we consciously come to know about ourselves, the world, and God. We each have a free will with which we make decisions and choose how we will behave. These two gifts of intellect and **free will** set us apart and give us a special dignity among God's creatures. Our choice of faith is part of what makes us members of the People of God, the Church. Baptism is also necessary for entering God's people, to which all are called. God never works with us outside of our human nature.

So, faith next requires something from us—the act of believing. Here's how the *Catechism* expresses this:

> " Faith is a personal adherence of the whole man to God who reveals himself. It involves an assent of the intellect and will to the self-revelation God has made through his deeds and words. "
>
> *Catechism of the Catholic Church*, 176

Our choice of faith is part of what makes us members of the People of God, the Church. Baptism is also necessary for entering God's people, to which all are called.

Faith-filled Catholics striving to live out their Baptism and the universal call to holiness will look at the everyday occurrences in their lives through eyes of faith—the decisions made, the actions taken on behalf of someone else, the way they respond to their parents and loved ones, the way they accept or critique the values of society, their priorities, the DVDs they watch, the music they listen to, the way they choose to spend their free time, the way they use their gifts and talents, their participation in parish events. Often subconsciously, people of faith are influenced by what they know about God the Father's love and mercy, by Jesus' example of just and true living, and by the Spirit's motivation to act in ways that bring us closer to him, the Son, and the Father.

GROUP TALK

In small groups, discuss the following questions:

- Why do you think faith has to begin with God's action?
- Would it be faith if a person didn't freely choose it?
- How do intellect and free will give us a special human dignity among God's creatures?

The Nicene Creed and You Refer to page 249 of your text for the Nicene Creed. Carefully read over each belief statement, or doctrine. Honestly evaluate yourself by asking for each doctrine:

- What do I really know about this doctrine of the Catholic faith?

- How have I ever taken any action based on my belief in this doctrine?

- Where or when have I seen or experienced the Catholic Church acting on this belief?

- What parts of these doctrines are easy for me to understand?

- How does this doctrine challenge me to understand and live my faith differently?

- When the wording of the Nicene Creed changed slightly in 2011, did I understand or experience these doctrines differently? If so, in what way?

The Faith of the Church, the Body of Christ What Catholics believe is no secret. We proclaim our faith out loud every Sunday during Mass when we recite the Nicene Creed. Each statement describes something each individual Catholic believes, but it also reflects our shared Catholic faith that is professed by the whole Church as a community of believers.

We do not believe in a vacuum. The Holy Spirit moves us to believe, and a significant way he does so is through the Church. Our faith flows from the faith of the Church, the visible sign of God's love and salvation.

- The faith of the Church, of all those who have come before us and articulated what it means to be Catholic, is the faith we share and grow in.

- The faith of the all those who make up the Body of Christ, the Church, encourages us so that our faith grows and develops.

- The faith as revealed and passed down from the Apostles through the teachings of the their successors, the popes and bishops, forms our own faith.

- The faith of the Church provides for our belief, holding us up and supporting us as we try to understand and accept all that God has made known to us.

- The faith of the Church gives substance to what we believe and teaches us in our faith.

We cannot separate our own belief from the Church's belief, for we are part of the Church, the Body of Christ. In Saint Paul's First Letter to the Corinthians we read:

"For just as the body is one and has many members, and all the members of the body, though many, are one body, so it is with Christ. For in the one Spirit we were all baptized into one body—Jews or Greeks, slaves or free—and we were all made to drink of one Spirit. . . . Now you are the body of Christ and individually members of it."

1 Corinthians 12:12–13, 27

Another term used to speak of the Church as the Body of Christ is **Mystical Body** of Christ. This metaphor indicates the intimate connection of Jesus and his disciples. He is the head; the faithful are his body. The Church cannot be separated from Christ; our life comes from him, and we live for him and his message of hope. And, Christ is with his Church always, making it possible for us to continue his mission and to use our diverse abilities and interests to show others what it means to believe in the Good News. In this way the Church is visible and spiritual, human and divine, an earthly, institution, and the Mystical Body of Christ.

The Church is the Temple of the Holy Spirit who is the soul of this Body. The Holy Spirit gives Christ's Body—the Church—her life and her gifts. Because of the Holy Spirit, we are united as one Body while still being a diverse gathering of people from all times in history and all places in the world.

Living as Christ's Body Day to Day We return to the theme of everyday living. Here you will get glimpses into what God is calling you to do. As you live a faithful life within the Church, you are encouraged to become more involved as a member of your parish community. Often, other members will invite you and recognize gifts in you that the community needs. You may notice people serving in ways you'd like to serve, too. You may notice people in need, and you may want to help them.

Active Catholics participate in their parishes. As an active Catholic you will participate in Mass each Sunday or Saturday evening. As you do that, you may be called to engage in a particular ministry, depending on your time, gifts, and abilities. You may have already been asked to serve in a particular ministry (such as server, lector, or volunteer at a soup kitchen) at your parish, or you may be as people get to know you. Just as Paul described the many gifts he saw in the Church of his time, we see them now. You may be called to help teach young children, perhaps; or to be part of the music ministry, or a lector, or part of a group who reaches out to those in need. There are many ways to "try out" aspects of your future vocation as you live the life of an active Catholic.

FAITH ACTIVITY

What Is the Body of Christ?
Look up Paul's First Letter to the Corinthians, Chapter 12, where Paul discusses the Body of Christ. Then look up his Letter to the Ephesians, 4:1-16. How do his words speak to you about your place in the Body of Christ? Work alone or with one or two others to create a visual expression—a poster, painting, collage, or any other form of art—of some aspect of these passages.

Quick Check

1. What is faith?

2. How is faith unique to humans?

3. What is the Church's role in our faith?

4. How are we the Body of Christ?

The Moral Life and Following God's Call

Life can get complicated with so many things to do, people to see, and places to go. Trying to sort out all of the things we need to do and want to do can cause a lot of stress. The pressures of school, family, friends, and jobs may be compounded by the big questions that face people your age: What am I doing after I graduate? What do I plan to do with my life? What are my goals? What is going to make me happy? How does being Catholic make a difference when I'm thinking about all of these things?

All of these issues are real, and they can occupy so much of our time that we start to lose perspective. We can get so wrapped up in the changes and tensions between the present and the future that we overlook what has the most meaning for us today. No matter where we end up, no matter how God calls us to live, we all share that basic call to know, love, and serve God. We can do just that now, however uncertain or clear our future may be; we can do that as we journey through jobs, college, relationships, and self-discovery; we can do that as we discern how we will respond to God's call and what vocation we will live. In many ways, knowing, loving, and serving God can be considered the foundation of simply living life faithfully, day by day.

God's people during the time of the prophet Micah struggled to know how to approach God, how to offer him the worship that was his due. Micah challenges the people to see that their offerings and sacrifices are not all that is required of them.

With what shall I come before the LORD,
and bow myself before God on high?
Shall I come before him with
burnt offerings,
with calves a year old?
Will the LORD be pleased with thousands
of rams,
with ten thousands of rivers of oil?
Shall I give my firstborn for my
transgression,
the fruit of my body for the sin of
my soul?"
He has told you, O mortal, what is good;
and what does the LORD require of you
but to do justice, and to love kindness,
and to walk humbly with your God?

✠ Micah 6:6-8

Micah tells his listeners to "walk humbly with your God." This is sage advice to us today. It reminds us that our lives are a journey to and with God. The attitude we bring to that journey makes a big difference for the paths we take. Do we take the paths that are good, that lead to love, justice, and the example of Jesus? Or do we take the paths that lead us away from the goodness in ourselves, and in others, and ultimately the happiness that God wants us to find in him? Are we led by our conscience, the voice inside of us telling us what is right or wrong, or are we swayed by what is popular and acceptable by society's standards? And what do we do when we take the wrong path, but realize it and want to change? We can find comfort in Jesus' words and actions, for he spent a lot of his time and energy accepting people for who they were and calling them back to the path to the Father.

GROUP TALK

Look again at the threefold advice of Micah. How does this advice relate to our common vocation to know, love, and serve God? How do Micah's words speak to people in the twenty-first century? Think of some ways you could share the wisdom of this passage with other people—in art, music, drama, dance, or writing.

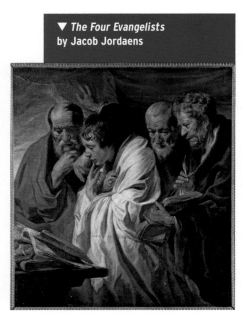

▼ *The Four Evangelists* by Jacob Jordaens

The Path to Take

How do we know the right path? Even the Apostles asked Jesus that question. In the Gospel according to John we read that, at the Last Supper, Thomas said to Jesus, "Lord, we do not know where you are going. How can we know the way?" Jesus said to him, "I am the way, and the truth, and the life. No one comes to the Father except through me" (*John 14:5–6*).

Guides on the Path Explorers in uncharted territories can tell you: It takes a lot of extra energy to go first. The first explorers of an area often have to draw their own maps, or make major corrections on the ones they were given. They often make their way slowly because they have to open a path first by cutting away underbrush, moving huge obstacles, and finding detours around hazards. Anyone coming that way later will reap the benefits of the first explorations by following well-drawn maps, walking well-cleared paths, and meeting few, if any, hazards.

If you want to know how to follow Jesus and how to live a good life, you don't have to go into uncharted territory and figure everything out for yourself. Wise guides have come before you, leaving clear directions, cleared paths, and careful warnings about possible hazards. Among these wise guides are the Apostles, the evangelists who wrote the four Gospels, Paul who wrote many of the New Testament letters, early Church fathers, and men and women saints who recorded their journeys and left advice and direction from their own experiences. Following these guides, we have a focus and a path for our own journeys. We learn from the ways they discerned God's call in their lives, and we gain insight into how we can interpret God's action in our own lives. We have a clearer sense of what it means to be a disciple.

We get specific guidance from the ways our popes and bishops have interpreted, applied, and presented the moral teachings of the Church. Through the Tradition of the Church, we gain a sense of how God calls us to live based on the Ten Commandments given to Moses and on the Beatitudes taught by Jesus. From all this Catholics have a body of moral teachings to guide us to live faithful lives and respond to God's desire for us to know the freedom and true happiness that only comes from being in relationship with him.

But some people might object, "Those are all lists of rules! They don't give us freedom; they just tell us what we can't do!" The gift of these rules and moral laws is that, in some ways, they work like guidebooks for a traveler. Far from tying you down, they direct you in how to live out your relationship with God, those you love, and even those you may not know. These moral teachings protect you and free you by directing you to put trust in God, to look for the things in life that will give you real happiness. In this way, you can handle the problems, distractions, and obstacles that might arise on your journey of faith. Most importantly, these moral teachings are intended to help you avoid sin, which is completely contrary to true freedom. Sin in many ways enslaves people, creating a cycle of actions that lead them away from God and true freedom. They then find that they actually have very little choice about how they live their lives.

GROUP TALK

Choose one activity you engage in–driving, dating, or getting a job, for example. Work with one or two other people to discuss the following.

1 List all the rules you can think of that apply to this activity–Church teaching, civil laws, family rules, etc.

2 How do these rules restrict your freedom to engage in this activity?

3 How do these rules give you freedom as you engage in this activity?

4 Where do these rules come from?

The Precepts of the Church It is in and through the liturgy that we express and celebrate our moral living and we get the spiritual nourishment we need. The *Catechism* indicates five precepts that the Church has given us that concern the connection of our moral life and our liturgical life.

The Precepts of the Church	
1. You shall attend Mass on Sundays and holy days of obligation and abstain from servile labor.	We are required to participate in the Eucharistic Liturgy on all Sundays and holy days of obligation.
2. You shall confess your sins at least once a year.	This is the minimum required of a Catholic. It is only required of a Catholic if one has committed an unconfessed mortal sin since one's last worthy confession. The reception of the Sacrament of Reconciliation continues the Holy Spirit's work of conversion and forgiveness and ensures that we are prepared to receive the Eucharist.
3. You shall receive Holy Communion at least once during the Easter season.	This, too, is a minimum requirement. It is hoped that most Catholics receive both Reconciliation and the Eucharist more than once a year. This precept, however, highlights the importance of the Easter season, for the feasts of Holy Week and Easter are the origin and center of the Catholic liturgy.
4. You shall observe the prescribed days of fasting and abstinence.	The Church prescribes certain days when we are to fast (eat only one full meal) or to abstain from eating meat. These days prepare us for liturgical feasts and help us practice control of our instincts and appetites.
5. You shall provide for the material needs of the Church according to your abilities.	There could be no liturgical life to support our moral life if there were no church buildings, liturgical vestments and objects, and parish personnel. Each Catholic is expected to contribute to the material needs of the Church as well as the needs of the larger community and the world.

You might wonder what the precepts of the Church have to do with vocation. There are several connections worth considering. First, we all have a responsibility to offer our lives to God.

- We do this by sincerely talking to God, and being open to his Spirit, in personal prayer. We offer our hopes, concerns, joys, and needs as we participate in the Church's liturgy, most particularly the Eucharist.

- We are called to look at our personal challenges and struggles as a way to connect to Jesus' suffering and his ultimate offering and sacrifice on the cross as the one, true priest.

- Our participation in the Eucharist commits us to those who are poor and in need, and to offering our time, talent, and treasure for their benefit and the benefit of the whole Church.

The precepts guide us by emphasizing our obligation to participate in the Mass and to work on behalf of those in need. We are strengthened by the grace of the Eucharist, united more closely to Christ and with his Body. The Church does not want us to deprive ourselves of this amazing share in divine life. This grace makes it possible for us to have faith, and to respond in faith in our daily lives.

Second, an important part of discerning our vocation and responding to God's call is assessing our current lives and praying for guidance. The Church teaches us to pray always, for no matter what is happening, we can pray. In fact, to live the Christian life one must pray. You cannot separate prayer from living as members of the Church.

If we are honest with ourselves, when we evaluate who and what are important in our lives, how we communicate, the values we honor, and what talents and abilities we have to offer God and the world, we might see the need for change in some areas of our lives. Taking a serious look at our lives opens us to conversion and the Holy Spirit's transforming power. If we are open to that conversion, we will be led to the grace of the Sacrament of Penance and Reconciliation. We need that grace if we have committed such a grievous sin that our relationship with God is broken; we need his healing and forgiveness in order to be able to hear and respond to his will for our lives. We also benefit from the regular celebration of the sacrament as a way to strengthen our will to make the right choices in our lives.

Quick Check

1. What does the prophet Micah teach us about what is "good" and how does this relate to our moral life?

2. Who and what are the guides we have on our path to the Father through the Son?

3. What are the precepts of the Church?

4. What is the common priesthood of the faithful and how do the precepts connect to it?

Peer Ministries: Operation Snowball and S.A.D.D.

It is never easy to make a good moral decision all alone, especially when surrounded by people who are making bad moral decisions. While this is true for everyone all through life, the burden of peer pressure is often common and especially difficult to deal with when we're in high school and college. Sometimes we get more freedom than we can handle, or we're faced with situations we haven't had enough experience to know how to deal with yet. Often, we might insist on taking care of pressures and problems head on, and without consulting friends, parents, or other adults in authority positions. This is part of adolescence, the long process of becoming an adult.

Many young people are more willing to seek help or advice from someone their own age rather than from an adult family member, teacher, coach, counselor, or youth minister. Recognizing this, several groups concerned for the health and safety of young people have developed programs that involve teen peer ministry—the service and support of young people by young people. These programs include training in leadership and in communication skills. Young people are empowered to help each other. A teen's natural tendency to reach out to other teens, is the basis for any kind of peer ministry.

Both Operation Snowball, which was founded in 1977, and S.A.D.D., founded in 1981, were formed due to concern over the use of alcohol, tobacco, and drugs by teenagers. In fact, S.A.D.D. began as an acronym for "Students Against Driving Drunk," but by 1997, young members of S.A.D.D. had petitioned for a broader scope for their organization, and it became the acronym for "Students Against Destructive Decisions." Operation Snowball got its name from the idea that one person's good effect on another person can "snowball" so that a school, Church, or neighborhood can become a "Community of Caring."

S.A.D.D. has chapters in 10,000 middle schools, high schools, and colleges in the U.S. Operation Snowball has chapters in Illinois, Indiana, Wisconsin, North Carolina, New York, China, Colombia, Lithuania, and Poland. Both of these peer ministry organizations stress education for the prevention of alcohol, tobacco, and drug use. They provide leadership training for teens who will reach out to help their peers, and they teach effective communication skills. Both organizations include interaction and training with adults who serve to support and guide the teen groups. Both hold extended training sessions, publish a monthly magazine or newsletter, and hold an annual convention.

The success of these peer ministry programs can be seen in the decline of the number of students involved in drunk driving accidents in the past thirty years.

▼ Teens at a S.A.D.D. event in Florida.

The Sacramental Life and Hearing God's Call

The *Catechism* tells us that the moral life is "a spiritual worship." (See *CCC*, 2047.) Faithful living gives praise to God and is closely connected to how we worship within our faith community. It is essential to our faith growth that we take part in the liturgy—the Church's official public prayer. The liturgy includes the seven sacraments and the **Liturgy of Hours**, by which the whole people of God mark the day with prayer at set times.

Our participation in the **sacraments** is fundamental to who we are and who we will become in the future. The sacraments—as effective signs of God's grace instituted by Christ and given to the Church so that we might share in divine life through the Holy Spirit's action—make it possible for us to experience God's welcoming, nourishing, healing, forgiving, and consecrating presence in our lives. The specific ritual words and actions that celebrate each sacrament signify and make present each sacraments' distinctive graces. These graces will produce their desired effects in those who receive them with the right disposition.

The sacraments open us up to the action of Christ in our lives so that we might know him as his first disciples did, and therefore be lead to a deeper relationship with Father, Son, and Holy Spirit. The sacraments "strengthen faith and express it" (*CCC*, 1133).

> "The seven sacraments touch all the stages and all the important moments of Christian life:[1] they give birth and increase, healing and mission to the Christian's life of faith. There is thus a certain resemblance between the stages of natural life and the stages of the spiritual life.
>
> *Catechism of the Catholic Church*, 1210

As we've discussed in this chapter, living a life guided by faith is the key to any vocation. We've looked at the significance of the Sacrament of Baptism in our journey of faith, and we will continue to consider it and Confirmation (two of the Sacraments of Initiation) in this and following chapters. We will focus on the Sacraments at the Service of Communion (Holy Orders and Matrimony) in later chapters that address the ordained life and the married life. The Sacraments of Healing (Penance and Anointing of the Sick) provide strength and grace along the journey of all Catholics no matter what their state of life. These sacraments encourage the ongoing conversion and healing that is so important to our growth in every stage of life and as we seek to know and live our vocations, all of our Catholic life finds its "source and summit" in the Eucharist. (See *CCC*, 1324.)

The Eucharist: At the Heart of the Church's Life

The Eucharist unites all of us in the Church to Christ in his ultimate sacrifice, offered to his Father once for all of us on the cross. We know that the event of Jesus' Resurrection turned his suffering and death into a sacrifice of praise and thanksgiving by which he poured out the graces of salvation on his Body, the Church, for all eternity.

We need to balance the power, mystery, and central importance of the Eucharist to the entire Church community with the personal, intimate aspects of the Eucharist. It is important to remember that what Christ does for his whole Body, the Church, he does for each individual member. Therefore, it would not be possible to discern or to live out our vocations separate from the Eucharist.

It would also not be spiritually healthy to do so. Each time you receive the Body and Blood of Christ:

- You become more closely united with Jesus, and the bonds of love between him and you are strengthened.

- Your union with him contributes to the unity of the whole Church with Christ.

- All your venial sins are forgiven if you are sorry for them.

- Your life of virtue is strengthened.

- You are given more protection from the evil of mortal sin.

Communal Worship Sometimes you will hear people say, "I don't go to church on Sunday because I can pray better alone, or when I'm out in nature." That would be fine, if going to church on Sunday was about private prayer, but it's not. Sunday Mass isn't about private prayer—it's for worship and liturgy, which is the public prayer of the whole community. The Eucharistic Liturgy—Mass—is a prayer of the community. The liturgy is our participation in God's work.
There are other times and other places for private prayer. At every Mass, together as a community:

- We hear the word of God from Scripture proclaimed.

- We offer praise and give thanks to God the Father for all his gifts, especially the gift of his Son.

- Bread and wine are consecrated and become the Body and Blood of Christ.

- We are always invited to receive his Body and Blood in communion with all those who have gathered for the celebration.

All the prayers and actions of a single Eucharistic Liturgy are not a collection of personal prayers; they constitute one single act of worship. Liturgical prayer is public prayer.

Public prayer may also be personal to you because you bring your own personality to it. Likewise, when you or anyone else chooses to be absent from the Church's liturgical prayer, you are missed as a person. You are missed because you belong to a community, a Church, a Mystical Body. If you take your personal spiritual life seriously, it will include private prayer every day. It will also include liturgical prayer—the worship of the community—at least once a week. This participation in the liturgical life of your parish will also guide you in your vocation discernment.

GROUP TALK

1 Discuss the statement; "Liturgical prayer is not private prayer." Why is it important to realize this?

2 What difference can it make in a person's decision about weekly Mass participation?

3 Do you think it really matters to your parish community whether you are at Mass each week or not?

The Liturgical Year: Getting the Whole Story

Why is it always harder to get a seat at Mass on Christmas Day and Easter Sunday? Perhaps you are among those who come to Mass every week and feel a sense of sadness when you see the crowds on those two holy days return to normalcy the following weekend.

One of the Precepts of the Church reminds us of God's command to keep holy the Lord's Day by participating in the Eucharist every Sunday and holy day of obligation. Why is that? It's not designed to burden us or to make us prove our faithfulness. So, how do you interpret and explain the precept? For some it is enough to say, "It's one of the rules; so we have to do it." For others, it makes no sense, and as a result they stay home for most Sundays of the year. However, the Church invites us to regular prayer because we meet Christ and receive the grace to be his Body.

Far from looking at Sunday Masses as a set of isolated weekly events, the Church unfolds the whole story of our salvation in the course of the liturgical year. We remember and celebrate the whole of Christ's **Paschal Mystery**— Christ's work of redemption through his Passion, death, Resurrection, and Ascension. From Advent and Christmas, when we prepare for and celebrate the Mystery of the Incarnation; through Lent, Triduum, and the Easter season, when we ponder Jesus' earthly life and teachings, his suffering and death, his Resurrection from the dead, and his Ascension into heaven; to the coming of the Holy Spirit on Pentecost; the story is told each week in the Liturgy of the Word. Our thanksgiving and words of praise are raised to God for these saving actions each week in the Liturgy of the Eucharist.

Through the year's feasts and seasons, we come to know Jesus in a different way. We come to a better understanding of what it means to be his disciples. People who only come two or three times a year never hear the whole story of our salvation in a logical progression. They miss the wonder the Church expresses; they arrive to celebrate events they haven't prepared for with the community and to hear the end of the story without being able to insert themselves and their own stories of discovery, conversion, and renewal into the community's story.

Taking an active role in the celebration of the weekly Mass can have a tremendous impact on you as you seek to know what your vocation in life might be. It is there you can see Christ's mission and ministry revealed gradually, as your vocation will be revealed to you. As you reflect on the readings each week, you'll also consider what they mean for you right now and what they might tell you about your future. As you worship God the Father and receive the Body and Blood of Christ, you'll be strengthened for your personal spiritual journey.

FAITH ACTIVITY

A Journey of Discovery Consider some of the major themes of the Church seasons, for example: preparation, anticipation, penance, conversion, forgiveness, acceptance, initiation, renewal, and hope. How can reflection on and celebration of these faith themes help you as you live out your baptismal call and consider what your vocation might be? How could these faith themes impact your family life now and in the future?

CROUP TALK

Discuss how the "whole story" of our salvation is laid out for us each liturgical year. Reflect on places in the life of Christ that most connect with your life. Which liturgical season is your favorite? Why? What liturgical season do you need to enter into more fully? Why?

Celebrating Mary and the Saints Have you noticed that we often call upon Mary and the saints when we are at Mass? They have gone before us to heaven to worship God there and because of this they can intercede on our behalf through prayer. This is the greatest example of the Church as the **communion of saints**, all the faithful Church members on earth, those being purified in purgatory, and the blessed already in heaven. The Church unites with their heavenly liturgy by commemorating them during Mass here on earth. The **Sanctoral Cycle** is the schedule of fixed dates on which we celebrate most especially different events in Mary's life, or commemorate the lives of the Apostles, martyrs, and other saints.

We've already considered how Mary responded to God's call and lived out her vocation as the Mother of the Son of God. The lives of Mary and the saints can lead us to a deeper understanding of living out the married, dedicated lay single, consecrated, and ordained life. We might be surprised at how some of them hesitated to answer God's call, or did not know how to act on it once they accepted it. If we learned more about their lives, we might be comforted by some of these ordinary people who trusted in God's plan and accomplished extraordinary things.

Quick Check

1. Why are the sacraments important to our individual vocations?

2. How does the Eucharist help a Catholic to live faithfully.

3. What is the liturgical year and how does it impact our journey of faith?

4. What is the Sanctoral Cycle and how does it help us respond to God's call in our own lives?

Parish Liturgical Ministries

Each week, without fail, Mass is celebrated in parish churches all over the world. Catholics gather in their parish and form an assembly to offer God thanks and give him praise. Candles are lit; bread and wine are ready to be consecrated; vestments of the correct liturgical color are clean and ready to wear. Usually a musician or a group of musicians and even a choir are in place with the correct music at hand. A reader is ready to proclaim the assigned readings from the Lectionary. How did all this happen? An amazing collaboration among people of different states of life living out their vocations.

A priest takes on many roles in a parish. In liturgies, he is the **celebrant**, or **presider**, who leads the celebration, prays the opening and closing prayers, usually preaches the homily, gives the blessing, and in the case of a Eucharistic celebration, consecrates the bread and wine, transforming them into the Body and Blood of Christ. The priest is indispensable in the celebration of the Eucharist.

Deacons, too, have many roles in a parish. Their liturgical roles allow them to preside at Baptisms, weddings, and Communion services. At Mass, deacons often proclaim the Gospel, at times preach the homily, lead the Prayer of the Faithful, and assist during the Liturgy of the Eucharist.

Other liturgical roles at parish Masses are carried out by the **laity**.

Sacristans take care of all material aspects of the liturgy, keeping all sacred vessels, vestments, and liturgical supplies in good order.

Ushers and **greeters**–also referred to as ministers of hospitality–see to needed hospitality, welcoming everyone, especially visitors and newcomers. They also make sure everyone can be seated and see to any special needs.

The **altar servers** might be children, teens, or adults. They carry the cross and candles in the processionals, and assist the celebrant as he needs them–sometimes holding a liturgical book, or bringing needed vessels to and from the altar.

The reader, sometimes known as the **lector**, proclaims the first reading at every Mass and the second reading on Sundays and special feast days. Lectors follow in the tradition of ancient storytellers. It is their task to proclaim the first two readings in a way that is easy to understand and reverent.

FAITH ACTIVITY

Parish Organizations As you participate in various activities in your parish church, be on the lookout for an adult who is involved in a parish organization in which you are interested. If possible, find someone you don't already know well. If necessary, introduce yourself to that person and ask him or her to tell you about the organization you've seen them involved in at your parish. Ask the person why and how he or she got involved in this organization. Find out what you'd need to do to join.

Parish Liturgical Ministries

The **cantor** leads the assembly in singing the responsorial psalm.

Liturgical musicians have roles all through the Mass. Choirs, choir directors, and instrumentalists provide music for the hymns and also for the ordinary parts of the Mass such as the Holy, Holy, Holy and the Great Amen after the Concluding Doxology.

Extraordinary ministers of Holy Communion help distribute the Body and Blood of Christ when the assembly is too large for the presider to do it alone or when there are no priests or deacons present to assist the celebrant. They also may take the Eucharist to parishioners in hospitals and to anyone homebound due to age or illness.

All of these service roles, together with the worshipping assembly, make it possible for the Church to participate in the sacramental work of God, the liturgy. As the People of God gathered for prayer, the assembly has an active role in he public worship of the Church. Those gathered need to respond with meaning, sing with heart, listen with attention, and offer themselves as all of those in liturgical ministry roles have offered their time and talent for the whole community.

GROUP TALK

Discuss with a group of classmates any liturgical ministries you have already participated in. How has participation in any of these ministries enhanced your experience of the Mass? What ministries would tap into your personality and natural abilities? What questions would you like to ask of both laity and ordained who are involved in your parish's liturgical ministries?

GO online For more information about **parish liturgical ministries,** visit the link to the U.S. Conference of Catholic Bishop's Committee on Liturgy on **www.osvcurriculum.com.**

The Family and Vocation

God is a Trinity of Persons who are in relationship with each other—the Father, the Son, and the Holy Spirit. This is the central mystery of the Catholic faith, only known to us because God has revealed it to us. Since the three Persons of the Trinity are in relationship with one another, is it any wonder that we who were created in God's image are called to live in relationship with other people?

We know that the whole Church is a communion of saints united in faith as the Body of Christ. But our deepest experience of close personal relationships is family. Our first experiences as people of faith and members of the Church happen in a family.

FAITH ACTIVITY

Catholic Family Experiences
Compare your experiences with other classmates—How old were you when you were baptized? Do you know where you were baptized and who your godparents are? How many generations of your family were/are Roman Catholic?

Introducing Children to the Faith

Shortly after bringing a new life into their family, Catholic parents bring that child to be born into new life in Christ through the Sacrament of Baptism. The parish community and the entire Body of Christ welcome this new child into the larger family of faith. He or she is united to Christ and becomes a member of the Church. Baptism forgives the Original Sin transmitted by our first parents—Adam and Eve. The new child is born again as a child of God the Father, a member of Christ's Body, a temple of the Holy Spirit, and a sharer in the priesthood of Christ.

Just as there are genetic imprints that indelibly mark a baby as a member of a particular family, there is permanent and indelible spiritual imprint, called the baptismal character, which marks a child's soul as Christian. This is why Baptism need not and cannot be repeated.

Catholic families pass on their faith to their children and typically bring them for Baptism as infants or young children. It is likely that you and most of your classmates were baptized at a very young age. However, the Church welcomes people of any age to celebrate the Sacrament of Baptism.

Your Baptism was the beginning of a lifelong journey. You began a relationship with God—Father, Son, and Holy Spirit—that would be fostered by family, friends, your parish and school community, and the way you choose to live your life. Baptism is the doorway to all the other sacraments, and so, by your Baptism, you entered into the sacramental life of the Church and participation in the mission of Christ.

Confirmation If you could compare notes with teens from various parts of the country, or even of your own diocese, you would find that the Sacrament of Confirmation is celebrated at widely different ages and stages of life. In fact, because it is one of the three Sacraments of Initiation—along with Baptism and Eucharist—adults who join the Church without previously being baptized, receive all three Sacraments of Initiation during one celebration at the Easter Vigil on Holy Saturday night.

Many Eastern rite Catholic Churches have maintained the ancient practice of giving Eucharist to infants at Baptism. When this is done, there is no separate "First Communion" for young children as is done in the Roman Catholic Church. In the Roman Catholic Church, the three sacraments usually are separated in time, often beginning with Baptism in infancy. Many Roman Catholic children receive First Eucharist between the ages of six and eight, and are then encouraged to receive it often. Eastern rite infants are usually chrismated (confirmed) and given Eucharist immediately after Baptism.

Like Baptism, Confirmation imprints a permanent spiritual character on the soul, so it can only be received once. Confirmation seals us with the Holy Spirit in order to:

- perfect the grace of our Baptism.

- root us more deeply as children of God.

- place us more firmly in the Body of Christ.

- strengthen our bond with the Church.

- associate us more closely with the Church's mission.

- bear witness to our Catholic faith both in word and deed.

GROUP TALK

Given the reasons for Confirmation you have just read, discuss with two or three classmates what you think the ideal age for Confirmation is and why. Do you think Catholic parents have a duty to see to it that their children are confirmed, or should they leave it entirely up to their children? What connection does Confirmation have with one's Christian vocation?

Catholic Parents: A Child's First Teachers

We can tell that the vocation of each Catholic child is very important to the Church, because the child's future is mentioned several times in the Rite of Baptism. It is clear that every baptized Catholic's vocation is connected to the priesthood of Christ. Of course, everyone doesn't have a vocation to be an ordained priest, but everyone *does* have a vocation to bring to others the Good News of salvation through Jesus.

Part of the vocation of all Catholic parents is the task of teaching their children about the faith. In the Rite of Baptism, the Church tells parents that they are the "first teachers" of their children, and then prays that they will also be the "best teachers." From the minute they bring a new child into the family, parents and other family members teach the child about the faith. They teach primarily through their love, dedication, and good example. They teach their children through prayer, worship, celebration, core beliefs, and morality, even before their child can begin to talk about these things. You began to learn to be a Catholic from what you saw your family do and say, and also from what they did not do and say. In later chapters of this book we will consider the role of parents and adult family members in creating a **domestic Church**, a holy community where children first learn about God through the love, teaching, and good example of parents and other family members.

FAITH ACTIVITY

Ideas About Vocations Reflect on the following questions: What ideas have you gotten about marriage, dedicated lay single life, priesthood, or religious life from your parents and other family members? Do you believe that their attitudes have had a big influence on you? Why or why not? Discuss in small groups.

Quick Check

1. What role do parents and adult family members have in a child's sacramental life?

2. Why is the Sacrament of Baptism so important to our faith life?

3. What happens in the Sacrament of Confirmation?

4. How are parents called to be teachers of the faith?

Nurturing Vocations No matter what your vocation in life will be, you have been and will continue to be greatly influenced by your parents and other family members as you try to discover what God is calling you to do. Catholic families need to understand clearly the responsibility God has given them to help children grow in their knowledge and practice of the Catholic faith and in discernment of their vocations.

Family members are role models for children, and as such they can have a positive or a negative impact. Attitudes toward their own vocations and those of others are noticed, absorbed, and adopted by the children of a family. Parents' marriages—not formal teaching of doctrine—are the first teaching that children receive about the Sacrament of Matrimony. Through such intense, up-close teaching about some of the challenges and blessings of married life, children learn lasting lessons about it. Families' attitudes toward unmarried family members influence children's understanding of a vocation to the single life. Children need to be encouraged to learn about the lives of priests, deacons, and religious brothers and sisters and to explore the possibility of a priestly or religious vocation.

Vocations do not spring out of nowhere; they are born, nurtured, and encouraged in homes where the Catholic faith is lived and celebrated.

The Little Sisters of the Poor

In an ideal world, every person would live within a family until death. Every elderly person would be cherished and cared for by family members. In our real world, sadly, that is not always the case. Some elderly people outlive their other family members, some are neglected by family members, and others have families who cannot properly care for the elderly or sick.

Among the many agencies, for-profit businesses, and charities that offer assistance to the elderly, there is one group that offers hospitality and different levels of care for elderly people who are poor. The group is called the Little Sisters of the Poor, and they were founded by Blessed Jeanne Jugan. Jeanne knew God desired her to give her life in his service, but at first she wasn't sure how this was to be accomplished. In 1839, she found an elderly, blind, destitute woman who had been abandoned by her family. Jeanne carried the woman home and put the woman in her own bed. Before long two other young women joined Jeanne and together they helped give other elderly people who were poor a home.

From those humble beginnings, the Little Sisters of the Poor has become an international order of religious sisters with homes for elderly people who are poor in thirty-two countries on five continents. When Jeanne began her ministry, she and her companions went out to work or to ask for alms each day to get the money and food needed to provide for their residents. To this day, the Little Sisters of the Poor still operates this way—since the Social Security or pensions their residents receive in no way cover the cost of their care, they rely on gifts of charity for which they beg or which they receive from admiring benefactors.

The headquarters—or Motherhouse—of the Little Sisters is in France, and each sister, no matter where she is from, spends at least a year in training there. While the Little Sisters want their elderly residents to call their houses "home," the sisters themselves vow to go to any house in any country where they are needed. They give up their homes in their native lands and cities in order to provide homes for these elderly guests. Each house is called a "Little Family," and everyone in that family calls the Sister Superior, "Mother."

Because the Little Sisters of the Poor do not run schools or orphanages, some thought that they might not attract new members and would not be able to survive. But from the time of their founding until today, women have learned of the mission of the Little Sisters of the Poor and of the gifts of their foundress, and have come in great numbers to care for elderly poor people who have been abandoned or need their assistance.

▼ One of the Little Sisters of the Poor in Kansas City, Missouri, pauses to laugh with a local resident before continuing with her job for the order, which is to round up enough food to feed the many in her care.

FAITH ACTIVITY

Caring for the Elderly Visit a house of the Little Sisters of the Poor or go to an assisted living facility near you. Consider volunteering to visit there on a regular basis. Talk to two or three of the residents about their memories of family life when they were young. Notice how the home you are visiting tries to make the guests feel at home and part of a family. How well do they succeed in doing this? How could you help?

GO online You can find a link to their website at www.osvcurriculum.com. Check it to see if there is a house of the Little Sisters of the Poor near you. If there is, pay them a visit. You'll find a joyful welcome there.

Meet Ed and Theresa Morrison. Ed is a permanent deacon; Theresa is his wife of thirty-five years. They are the parents of three grown children and have six grandchildren. Ed was ordained a permanent deacon in 1999 and was assigned to a large suburban parish. At that time he was still working as a college professor, teaching history. When he retired from teaching in 2003, he was able to give more time to his ministry at the parish.

INTERVIEWER: Have you always felt an inclination to give of yourself to others?

ED: Yes. I knew I that I wanted to have a wife and children, but I also felt called to serve the Church. Meeting Theresa was the best thing that ever happened to me, and we've had a happy marriage. We both are devout Catholics and raised our two daughters and our son in the Catholic faith.

I: When did you first know you were called to be a permanent deacon?

E: Back in my youth there was no such thing as a permanent deacon. After Vatican Council II, that began to change. The Church has always had deacons, but in modern times before the Council, there were no permanent deacons. At first I just thought it was interesting that this form of ordained ministry was being reestablished. I didn't think about becoming a deacon myself until a few years later.

THERESA: We both got the idea one night—at dinner with a priest-friend of ours. He was asking us about our life in the parish and noticing how active we both were.

E: Right! He asked me if I'd ever thought of becoming a permanent deacon, and as soon as he asked the question, I knew he'd hit on something that I ought to pay attention to.

I: Theresa seems to have played a big part in the decision.

E: She did! And that was very important. Married men cannot be ordained deacons unless their wives are part of the discernment and the training. I've known men who were unable to continue their training because their wives did not support their ordination for some reason. Theresa has always been real supportive of me, though.

T: (laughs) And I like it that he won't be able to get married again, if I die before he does.

I: Is that true?

E: Yes, those of us who are married may not remarry if we are widowed.

I: What do you do in your parish as a deacon?

E: In the Acts of the Apostles, we read that the Apostles decided they needed deacons to help with the distribution of food. (See *Acts 6:1-6*.) So, our first mandate is to be of service to the parish in any way the pastor needs. Besides my liturgical ministry, at my parish I'm in charge of the social outreach ministries. I organize people to assist the poor, to visit the elderly, and to do anything like that. There are two permanent deacons at the parish, so we each have some outreach responsibilities. We are also given certain roles in the liturgy. An important part of our work is assisting at Mass. We each have a turn to preach the homily at a Sunday Mass once a month. We also take turns celebrating infant Baptisms after Mass one Sunday a month. I've officiated at a few weddings and the pastor almost always has me run the wedding rehearsals. I also lead wake services for the dead and Communion services when no priest is available to say Mass.

I: I would think that ordination as a deacon has had a big effect on your spiritual life.

E: It has. Like those in the consecrated life and other devout Catholics, we deacons pray the Liturgy of the Hours every day. I spend time praying before the Blessed Sacrament, and I celebrate the Sacrament of Reconciliation twice a month. I also do spiritual reading and have a spiritual director. One of my prayers every day is a prayer of thanks that God has called me to be both a married man and a deacon. I take both sacraments very seriously and know that I'm in a unique group of men who are privileged to have received both these sacraments.

who will you Become?

Think about how you live your Catholic faith today. Now look ten years into the future.
How do you see yourself?

What tasks are you doing for, with, or in the Church?

What tasks are you doing for or with other people in need?

How do you envision these tasks and/or activities impacting your daily life? Are the tasks and/or activities themselves your daily life?

What one or two traits of your Catholic faith and identity would you want the people around you to see in you?

If your faith today could be a little bit stronger, what can you do to improve it so that ten years from now you'll be living more faithfully?

At the present time, which state of life do you feel inclined to pursue? The lay person (married or dedicated lay single), ordained, or consecrated life? Why are you so inclined?

At the present time, what career or profession do you feel inclined to pursue? Why are you so inclined?

Prayer

Leader: Let us unite ourselves with the Holy Trinity as we pray the Sign of the Cross, the Sign of our Faith.

All: In the name of the Father, and of the Son, and of the Holy Spirit.

Leader: The prayer of Saint Richard is a treasure of the Church which gives us words to express our simplest needs from God. Let us pray it together:

All: O most merciful Redeemer, Friend, and Brother,
May I know Thee more clearly,
Love Thee more dearly,
Follow Thee more nearly,
Day by day.

Reader 1: Read Micah 6:6–8.

All: O most merciful Redeemer, Friend, and Brother,
May I know Thee more clearly,
Love Thee more dearly,
Follow Thee more nearly,
Day by day.

Reader 2: Guide us today, Lord. Show us the way we should follow as we deal with school, friends, family, and job. Guide our steps, guide our words, and guide the decisions we make.

All: O most merciful Redeemer, Friend, and Brother,
May I know Thee more clearly,
Love Thee more dearly,
Follow Thee more nearly,
Day by day.

Reader 3: Guide us into the future, Lord. Show us how you want us to use our talents. Send your Spirit to guide our decisions about relationships, careers, and vocations. Help us to stay connected to you as we grow older and become more independent of our childhood homes and families.

All: O most merciful Redeemer, Friend, and Brother,
May I know Thee more clearly,
Love Thee more dearly,
Follow Thee more nearly,
Day by day.

Leader: Let us pause to pray our personal prayers in silence.
(After a minute of silence continue.)
We unite all our prayers in the one prayer that Jesus taught us to pray:

All: Our Father, who art in heaven. . . . Amen.

Study Guide

▶Check Understanding

1. Identify the different aspects of faith.

2. Explain what makes faith a unique human response to God.

3. Detail how individual faith flows from the faith of the Church.

4. Describe the images of Body of Christ and Mystical Body.

5. Expand upon how the prophet Micah's message related to our moral life.

6. Identify some of the guides on the path of discipleship, and identify their role.

7. Name the five precepts of the Church and tell what their purpose is.

8. Summarize how the precepts help us to live out the common priesthood of the faithful.

9. Give an explanation of the sacraments and what they mean for us as we live out our vocations.

10. Tell how the Eucharist helps a Catholic live faithfully.

11. Express in your own words the purpose of the liturgical year and its place in our journey of faith.

12. Explain the significance of the Sanctoral Cycle for our worship and for response to God's call in our own lives.

13. Describe the role of parents and adult family members in their children's sacramental life.

14. Identify the effects of the Sacrament of Baptism and why it is so important.

15. List the effects of the Sacrament of Confirmation.

16. Explain why parents are called the first teachers of their children.

▶Apply and Develop

17. Support with examples how having faith and being a member of the Body of Christ makes a difference in the daily lives of faith-filled Catholics. How can faith and membership in the Church make a difference as you discern your vocation?

18. Conclude from the chapter content how the Church's moral teachings guide us on our path and lead to freedom and happiness. Consider what specific guidance people your age would benefit from.

19. Compare and contrast the expression and role of private prayer and public prayer (liturgy) in our spiritual lives. Consider the implications of the liturgy as the spiritual work of the community on your participation in the Sunday Mass.

20. Compose a poem, prayer, or illustration that depicts the difference a Catholic family and home can make in discerning and living out one's vocation.

▶Key Words

See pages noted for contextual explanations of these important faith terms.

cantor (p. 57)
celebrant (p. 57)
communion of saints (p. 56)
deacon (p. 57)
domestic Church (p. 61)
faith (p. 42)

free will (p. 43)
intellect (p. 42)
lector (p. 57)
Liturgy of Hours (p. 52)
Mystical Body of Christ (p. 44)
Paschal Mystery (p. 55)

precepts of the Church (p. 49)
sacraments (p. 52)
sacristan (p. 57)
Sanctoral Cycle (p. 56)

CALLED TO THE SINGLE LIFE

CHAPTER 3

CHAPTER GOALS

In this chapter you will:

★ discover how the lay single life is a fulfilling vocation that leads people to respond to the desire to bring value and meaning to their lives.

★ see how the lay single life is deeply rooted in Baptism and nurtured by the Eucharist and Reconciliation.

★ consider possible life circumstances that indicate a call to the lay single life both transitionally and permanently.

★ learn about the significant role friends and family play in the lives of dedicated lay single persons as well as the various affiliations of dedicated lay single people in the Church.

★ meet a man and a woman who both found the single life to be their vocations.

who Are You?

When we value someone or something, a trait or characteristic, a way of acting or being, we show that he, she, or it is important to us. Valuing something assigns it importance and prominence in our lives.

Complete each statement below with your honest opinion.

You may choose to share your responses if you wish. You'll revisit these at the conclusion of this chapter to see how your values can help you respond to God calling you now and in the future.

Three things I value about myself are _____,

_____, and _____.

Three things that I value in my close friends are

_____, _____, and _____.

Three things that I value about my family are

_____, _____, and _____.

Now spend some time thinking about these questions.

What similarities do you see among the things you value in yourself, friends, family, and faith?
How do these values impact the choices you make in your everyday life?
How could these values help or challenge you to be a disciple of Jesus?

The Lay Single Life: A Life of Value and Meaning

Our values and priorities say a lot about us. They give other people insight into who we are and what matters to us. They impact the choices we make, the people we surround ourselves with, the work we undertake, the attitudes we bring to our study and work, the way we communicate with others. Values and priorities give structures to our lives and how we live out our vocation to love God and others.

It's logical that our values and priorities can help us discern how God is calling us to live our lives. If we consider what really matters to us, what's most important in our lives, we can then prioritize the practical aspects of our lives around those priorities. With so many influences pulling us in different directions, it won't always be easy to keep our priorities straight, but staying focused on your core values can help.

If we ask ourselves what we really need to be happy, and how can we satisfy those needs, we can get a better insight into where to place our priorities and values.

GROUP TALK

1. What values and priorities do you think characterize a Catholic family? a Catholic school?

2. What priorities or values do you think contemporary culture stresses? Of these values, which ones are not aligned with Gospel values?

3. What helps you periodically reset your priorities? How do your religious beliefs and practices help you do that?

What Do We Need to Be Happy?

Needs	What's Required to Satisfy Them
Physical Needs *with the hope of physical comfort and security*	• Sufficient food and adequate clothing • Clean, comfortable, healthy shelter • Good health and proper health care; enough sleep and physical activity • Reasonable physical comfort • Reasonable access to necessary transportation
Self-identity and Self-esteem *with the hope of psychological health and balance*	• Self acceptance, and belief that you're worthwhile and valuable • A sense of integrity, that you're a morally good person • Recognition and confirmation by others of your value • Understanding that identity flows from being a child of God.
Companionship and Intimacy *with the hope of emotional and spiritual well-being*	• A close relationship with God and a desire to grow in holiness • A close relationship with another person • Good friends, closeness to family members or relatives, to other members of your Church community • Active participation in the life of the Church, especially the sacraments • Amiable relationships with peers, colleagues, and co-workers • Appropriate affectionate physical contact with others
Self-actualization *with the hope of realizing your God-given potential*	• Service, giving of yourself, contributing to and helping others • Developments of your abilities, talents, skills, accomplishment or achievement • Enough opportunity to express your imagination and creativity • Enough relaxation and recreation • A well-rounded life

GROUP TALK

1. What's the minimum you think you'd need in order to satisfy each of your basic needs? In your family and community, who helps you meet your basic needs?

2. How do your real needs sometimes differ from what you think you need (or want)?

3. What do you think the greatest needs are of the world and the community you live in? How might your own deepest longings intersect with the greatest needs of your community and wider society?

Living for the Kingdom

How do what we need to be happy, and the ways we can satisfy them, relate to our faith? We can look to Jesus' Beatitudes for a clear presentation of what will bring us true happiness, a happiness that focuses on the values of God's Kingdom. We will examine the Beatitudes later in this book. It's important to consider them as the attitudes of Christians living in God's Kingdom today that lead us to the eternal happiness to which God calls each of us.

All people want to be happy, but how you use your gifts, talents, personality, and uniqueness to address those needs can give you some sense of how you can live out your call from God. Whether single, married, consecrated, or ordained, you will make decisions about what work you will do and what value you place on that work. It is important to keep the right emphasis on the spiritual aspects of your life. This becomes increasingly important as you experience more of what the world has to offer and as you meet and interact with people who have a diversity of values.

Many young adults want the opportunity to be independent but at the same time connected to others. They strive to develop their God-given potential and to explore the exciting possibilities in careers, travels, and meaningful relationships. Since many people are extending their education and personal development further into their years of adulthood, we have more and more single people living and ministering in the world around us. Yet being single describes many different situations. Some prefer to remain single. Others are single due to unfortunate circumstance—divorce or a spouse's death. Some remain single to devote themselves to caring for someone in need. For many, being single is temporary, a transitional vocation until they find a partner suitable for marriage, enter a religious community, or respond to a call to the priesthood.

FAITH ACTIVITY

Christian Attitudes Read the Beatitudes in Matthew 5:3-12. Discuss how the values presented in the Beatitudes can help you keep the right priorities and balance as you seek to meet the basic human needs described earlier.

Others are called to the dedicated lay single life, choosing to be single as a permanent way of life. They are not drawn to marriage. They find fulfillment in their careers and/or in their service of others and wouldn't have the time to meet the demands of marriage and family life. Living happily in this way might be an indication that one is called to the dedicated lay single life, to use his or her God-given talents to love God and others, as all of us are called to do in whatever state of life.

A Fulfilling Vocation How single lay people live out their vocation differs greatly depending upon their interests, commitments, age, and so on. As we consider the vocation to the dedicated lay single life, we need to take a couple of things into consideration. First, we need to acknowledge that ordained ministers and consecrated religious live a celibate single life with certain vows and commitments to the Church and/or a specific religious community. These states of life have some similarities to, but are distinct from, the lay single life, which is the focus of this chapter. Second, we need to realize that many are transitionally single as they discern a vocation to marriage, the consecrated religious life, or the priesthood; others permanently live as dedicated single lay persons.

Each Christian is to follow Christ and to help build his kingdom here on earth.

Some lay people are called to serve God in the dedicated single life, to spread the Gospel message within the world. These men and women work for God's Kingdom without a spouse and without a defined religious community. While perhaps the most overlooked state of life, this calling is a fulfilling, life-giving one.

- The dedicated lay single life is a valuable vocation that reflects God's love in its own unique way. Being single is a worthwhile, desirable way of life. It has its own blessings, relationships, advantages, opportunities, and challenges.

- The dedicated lay single life is the most flexible vocation. Single persons may have more personal freedom to befriend or help people. They may change their personal priorities and commitments as their needs and situations change. They have greater liberty to relocate or adjust personal and work schedules.

- Single women and men share their love and bring about life in ways unique to their calling, and they offer themselves to family, friends, and community in myriad ways.

A Radical Christian Calling Many elements of Christianity have their roots in the Old Testament. But the vocation to a dedicated single life is nowhere explicitly recommended in the Old Testament. But it is in the New Testament. We read in several of Saint Paul's letters advice for those who are married and single—whether never married or widowed. Saint Paul himself was single, but he wrote about living the life that each is called by God to live. (See *1 Corinthians 7*).

While marriage was not specifically prescribed for everyone in the Old Testament, it certainly was assumed to be the norm. It was each person's duty and calling to bring forth children to be part of the believing community. There was even some thought among some Jewish groups that one's son might end up being the Messiah.

So, among the many things he did that differed from ordinary Jewish practices of his time, Jesus did not marry—a circumstance that flowed from his unique identity. It seems that at least some of the Apostles chose celibacy for the sake of following Jesus and spreading his message of the kingdom. The only one who was definitely married was Peter, for we know Jesus healed Peter's mother-in-law. Being married and having a family would have been difficult with Jesus' lifestyle of preaching, traveling from town to town with little emphasis placed on how or when he would eat, and being available at almost all times to people in need. Most importantly, Jesus remained focused on building his Father's kingdom. When his disciples asked him if he thought it was better not to marry, he said that for most people marriage is the norm. Those given a vocation to the single life do so "for the sake of the kingdom of heaven." (See *Matthew 19:10–12*.)

Our values influence our actions. Our choices and lives tell others what we value. Because of advertising, mass communications, and consumerism, we are exposed to a wider variety of values today than before.

This wide variety in values, however, doesn't ensure depth in values. How do we value relationships, marriage, ethics, or faith? How do we value faithfulness, trust, and honesty? What value do we place on making sure other people have their basic needs met? What value do we give to spending time with family, being compassionate, and sacrificing so that others might have a better life? How do we value different ways people participate in the Church and their vocation?

GROUP TALK

1 What new insights do you have about being single as a vocation in its own right? How will this impact the time you spend as a single person?

2 Do you usually think of Jesus as a single person? How is he a model for single persons today?

Quick Check

1. What role do values and priorities play in our lives?

2. What description would you give to the dedicated lay single vocation?

3. In what ways is the call to the lay single life transitional for some people?

4. How is the lay dedicated single life a radical Christian calling?

Rooted in Baptism

We know through our Baptism, we all share in the universal vocation to holiness. We have discussed our baptismal calling and what it means to respond to live as a follower of Christ. As we consider the unique aspects of living the lay single life, it might be helpful to keep in mind that each state of life is a way of living out that common vocation we all share. So what does it mean to be holy?

> To be holy is to live according to the Gospel—to be grounded in Christ Jesus. It is the ever-present challenge to be a people of heartfelt compassion, kindness, humilty, gentleness, patience, and forgiveness (cf. Col 3:12). It is a call to embrace the beatitudes—to be poor in spirit, to comfort, to be meek, to be merciful, to be peacemakers (see Mat 5:3-11). It entails listening and meditating on the word of God and actively participating in the eucharist and the sacramental ife of the Church. It is to pray individually and as a community and to pray often.[1] It is an invitation to bring a heightened sense of the presence of Jesus Christ into the regular rhythms of life...
>
> United States Catholic Conference. *Sons and Daughters of the Light*, p.18

FAITH ACTIVITY

Holiness Synonyms In small groups create a holiness word web. Write the word *holy* in the middle of a large piece of paper. Then brainstorm any words that would describe someone living a holy life as described in this quote. Write the word or phrases around the word holiness. Choose one thing you can do differently this week to live a more holy life.

How is it possible to live a holy life? Through God's grace most especially received in the sacraments. People called to the lay married life and to ordained ministry celebrate sacraments in which they receive graces to live out their state of life. The dedicated single lay life is not marked by a Sacrament at the Service of Communion; however, the graces of this blessed calling flow from the person's call to live the Christian life, given to them at Baptism. This calling is strengthened by reception of Confirmation and the participation in the Eucharist and the Sacrament of Reconciliation.

Marked for Life Baptism is birth into new life in Christ. The grace given at Baptism—**baptismal grace**—is a powerful reality meant to last a lifetime and to continuously enrich our souls. From the moment of Baptism and through one's whole life, baptismal grace is present to:

- make us adoptive sons and daughters of God the Father
- make us members of Christ
- make us temples of the Holy Spirit
- incorporate us into the Church
- make us sharers in Christ's priesthood

You'll recall that both Baptism and Confirmation imprint a permanent spiritual sign or **character** on the soul. This mark, which remains forever, consecrates a person as a worshipping Christian. If a person decides to follow a vocation to the lay single life, no additional sacrament is needed. The indelible marks of Baptism and Confirmation and the graces that come with them and the other sacraments, especially the Eucharist, give single persons the divine assistance needed to fulfill this calling.

GROUP TALK

- Since there is not a separate sacrament for those who commit to the permanent lay single life, in what ways can parishes acknowledge the commitment of single lay persons?

- How can the Renewal of Baptismal Promises that often takes place during the Sunday Masses of the Easter Season be used to ritualize the commitment of lay singles?

A Share in Christ's Mission A faithful Catholic single person gives time, talent, and treasure to the building of the kingdom in very concrete and practical ways. Today's single people often can devote more time and energy to the Church and to people in need than they could if they were married with the responsibilities and commitments of raising a family. Furthermore, as lay people working in the world, they have opportunities to spread Christian values and build God's Kingdom that priests and religious sisters and brothers don't. The *Catechism* makes it quite clear that lay people have unique ways to share life in Christ's priesthood, prophecy, and kingship. Single lay people, as well as married lay people, serve in various ministries and in leadership positions at the parish and diocesan level. Sometimes this ministry is their paid profession, and other times it's volunteer service. Single lay persons bring their talents and dedication to their jobs or profession, to the Church, the community organizations, and to the wider society.

(See CCC, 897–913)

Christ's office of or mission	Lay participation in this office within the world	Lay participation in this office within the Church
PRIEST	All of their daily life–work, relaxation, prayers, apostolic undertakings–become spiritual sacrifices offered to God through Jesus. They build bridges between others.	With proper training, they may serve in liturgical ministries such as lectors, acolytes, and extra-ordinary ministers of Holy Communion when needed.
PROPHET	Their evangelization–by word and by the testimony of their lives–proclaims Christ within the ordinary circumstances of the world. They make moral and ethical decisions based upon Gospel values.	They may collaborate in ministries such as catechetical formation, in teaching theology, and in using communications media. They promote social justice and are concerned with the pastoral care of others.
KING	They are to first rule their own passions and then join forces to help remedy sinful institutions and conditions of the world and to bring moral value to culture and human works.	They can cooperate in the governance of the Church by serving on diocesan synods, pastoral councils, finance committees, and ecclesiastical tribunals.

Nurturing a Vocation

While the single life is rooted in Baptism, it is nurtured by the Eucharist. We also call this sacrament, in which we receive the Body and Blood of Christ, "Holy Communion." Christ offers himself to us in this sacrament, and we are joined more closely to him and the rest of his Body. When we step back and look at what we are given in this sacrament, how can we not take comfort in knowing that Christ is present in us? We are not alone when we participate in the Eucharist. Married or single, ordained, lay, or consecrated, male or female, we can all share in this communion with Christ.

For a single lay Catholic, such a communion with Christ can be a source of great joy and strength. This sacrament of love gives single Catholics a focus for their vocations, a center of meaning for their lives. Communion with Christ and with other believers helps keep solid Catholic values in perspective as commitments are lived out. The responsibilities and commitments of single people might not be as outwardly visible as married lay people, but you can rest assured that they do have them! Single persons have important relationships that involve responsibilities and obligations, and it takes extra time and effort to develop and maintain such relationships with people you don't live with and see every day.

Forgiveness and Healing We are all in need of forgiveness and healing in our lives. We have made the wrong choices, failed to do the morally right thing in our relationships, lost sight of God's presence and guidance in our lives. This is part of our human experience because we are free to love or not to love.

Remember, one of God's greatest gifts to us is our free will. Some might wonder how much easier things might be if God could just force us to do the right thing, or even if we were just made so that we'd never do anything wrong. Can you see the problem in that? What would it do to our relationship with God? How would our love be for God, or for anyone else, if we just loved because we didn't have any choice? Do *you* want friends who only love you because they have to? Why, then, would God want it to be this way? God wants us to want him in our lives. He offers his love and friendship, and he gives us the direction to follow his will. While asking us to be faithful, to keep all the commandments, and to seek to be as close to Christ's perfection as we can, God the Father never stops letting us start over when we fail or fall. Hopefully we learn from our experiences and grow to be more forgiving and reconciling in our own lives.

All of us, no matter what state of life, need the graces of the Sacrament of Penance and Reconciliation. It isn't always easy to admit we need forgiveness, or to ask for it, but it is offered freely to us if we are sorry and resolve to make a very strong effort to change. God forgives everyone who turns to him in repentance. So, in addition to being rooted in Baptism and nurtured by the Eucharist, single Catholics—and all Catholics for that matter— are forgiven and healed in the Sacrament of Reconciliation every time they return to God.

FAITH ACTIVITY

Mission in Action Create a visual presentation of people being priestly, prophetic, and serving in the world today. You can do this electronically or on poster paper. Use pictures from magazines, newspapers, or advertisements to illustrate scenes.

GROUP TALK

Why do you think it is sometimes difficult to ask for someone's forgiveness? What advice would you give to someone who needs healing in a relationship but is unwilling to grant forgiveness? How can forgiveness and reconciliation give a fresh start to relationships with God and others?

Intentional Living Every Catholic needs to live *mindfully*, asking important questions such as:

- What is God asking of me in this situation?

- What consequences will my decision have for others and for me?

- Is this material possession, pleasurable activity, or accomplishment really as important as everyone else says it is?

- How should I be treating this person?

- How should I be treating myself?

- Am I faithful to my prayer life, participation in Mass, and receiving the other sacraments?

- Am I a responsible member of my family of origin, the one in which I have grown up?

All too often we let someone else answer these questions for us, or we find ourselves in compromising situations because we aren't being mindful of what is going on. To be mindful we have to take the time to reflect on what is happening in our lives and why we think it's happening. This type of intentional living helps us make life choices and decisions that are true to Catholic values. It helps us keep our priorities straight as we discern what way of life God is calling us to live, and helps us live out that way of life to the best of our abilities.

Being intentional and mindful requires that we be truly honest and correctly name what is going on in our lives. God doesn't leave us alone in this task. God the Holy Spirit moves us to look at our lives through his eyes, and in doing so we become more open to his work and to believing. He calls us to continual **conversion** and repentance. These attributes involve genuine sorrow for the sins we have committed, sincere abhorrence of them, and a resolution to change. With true conversion, we know well what we have done wrong and also we really want to stop doing it. We see how our habits, thoughts, or actions draw us away from love of God and neighbor, and we admit that we need God's forgiveness and healing in order to re-direct our lives on the path of goodness, life, and love. In the Sacrament of Reconciliation, we are strengthened to live as disciples of Christ again and to respond to God's presence in our lives. God is with us as we search for meaning and purpose in our lives. He is with us as we seek fulfillment and joy by doing the best we can with the interests and talents we've been given.

FAITH ACTIVITY

Priorities and Purpose List your main priorities in life at present. Describe how you structure your life to put these things first. Then read again the questions on this page about mindful, intentional living. Which of your priorities lead you to reach your God-given potential? Would you need to reorder some priorities? Add some? Take some away?

✔ Quick Check

1. How are Baptism and Confirmation significant to the vocation of the lay single life?

2. What role does the Eucharist play in the life of the dedicated lay single person?

3. Why is the Sacrament of Penance important in living out one's vocation?

4. How can intentional living and conversion help us on our path to God?

The Catholic Network of Volunteer Service

There is a long tradition of volunteerism both in the Catholic Church and in the United States. Some people volunteer their time to a local cause on a weekly or monthly basis, before or after their work day or on weekends. Others give a full year or two of their time and leave home to volunteer at a foreign or domestic mission. Lay volunteers can be married or single. Some married couples do volunteer together, but most volunteers are single, and therefore more easily able to pause their regular lives and careers in order to volunteer full time.

Catholic adults of all ages are volunteers. Often, young adults will volunteer at a mission for a year right after they finish college and before they begin their careers. Other adults will take a sabbatical year from their established careers to volunteer at a mission. One growing group of single lay volunteers is the widowed. Men and women who have lost a spouse and do not have children at home to care for may give a year or two of service now that they no longer have responsibilities as a spouse and parent.

How do people find a place to volunteer, and how do organizations that need volunteers find them? Father George Mader, a priest of the Archdiocese of Newark, NJ, and his sister, Patricia, realized there was a need for some kind of bridge between people who wanted to volunteer and organizations that needed volunteers. In 1963, they established the non-profit organization Catholic Network of Volunteer Service (CNVS) to provide that bridge. From its headquarters in Takoma Park, Maryland, CNVS links thousands of volunteers each year to one of 200 missions and service programs that are members of its network.

CNVS publishes an annual directory, *RESPONSE-Directory of Volunteer Opportunities*, which lists thousands of volunteer opportunities. If on first thought you don't think you have a skill that would be needed in a volunteer program, you'll realize by reading the list of opportunities that you probably have a lot more to offer than you realize. Some of the skills that are sought include work in teaching, nursing, construction, art, music, accounting, farming, driving, library science, recreation, cooking, dentistry, and computer programming, among many others.

The programs that recruit volunteers through CNVS include such organizations as the Maryknoll Lay Missioners, the Volunteer Missionary Movement, the Society of African Missions, Passionist Volunteers International, Quest–Volunteers for Haiti, Jesuit Volunteer Corps, Mission Doctors Association, and the Catholic Relief Services Volunteers Program.

FAITH ACTIVITY

Do some online research about CNVS and some of their member volunteer programs.

- Why do you think there are so many people who see their involvement in groups like this as part of their discipleship?

- In what ways can you imagine you might participate in groups like this in the future?

- How are you living as a disciple who gives of him/herself to others?

GO online You can find a link to the CNVS website at www.osvcurriculum.com.

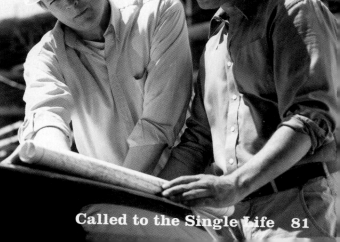

A Diversity of Paths

Ask a group of lay single adults why they are single, and you will probably get as many different answers as there are people in the group. It is unlikely that any would say that they always planned to remain single, or that they never thought of any other state in life. Most people at least consider Marriage as a possible life choice, and many will say they always planned to be married or even were married for a time. Some will report living in a religious community for a time or studying for ordination in the seminary. So, what are the circumstances that have led these people to see that they are called to the permanent vocation of dedicated lay single life?

A committed Christian vocation to the single state in life is an expression of a person's faith, just as the vocations to be married, ordained, or in the consecrated life are. The common denominator for all decisions and discussion about Christian vocations is faith.

We have already seen that believing is a free and conscious human action. The choice to believe must be followed by actions that express our belief. Adult Catholics keep their faith alive by making it central in their lives. Their faith informs how they live, and how they live expresses what they believe.

We have also seen that believing is a community action, an act of the Church, the Body of Christ. Being a member of the Church gives birth to an individual's faith and then supports and nourishes that faith. We express our faith as part of a family, a parish, a community. We express our faith by the choices we make about how we will live our lives within community—day by day.

"The Life for Me"

Often in today's society, a presumption exists that a person someday will be—or should be—married. A single person attending a wedding might be asked several times, "What about you? When will *you* be getting married?" Rarely does anyone ask, "Do you want to be married or not?" Married life has been engrained as a societal norm so strongly that some people find the notion of the dedicated lay single life unbelievable or impossible. They typically don't have a true understanding of what it means to have warm, affectionate relationships that are chaste—something we will discuss in depth later in this chapter. Additionally, many people don't realize the blessing of the committed single life.

Instead, some people regard the single life as a temporary and regrettable condition in certain cases, or a sign of failure in others. Instead of asking the question, "Do I want to be married?" and answering, "No, not really," young people who are called to the single life too often are found thinking, "I don't want to get married. What's wrong with me?"

In fact, nothing is wrong except the fallacy that says marriage is a requirement for a happy life. Granted, marriage is the choice of a majority of people, but that does not make it a requirement for everyone. We can hope that more and more young people, as they think about marriage, will at some point ask the question, "Is God really calling me to married life? Is it the right life choice for me and my gifts, talents, and interests? Will it bring me happiness? How will my life be life-giving?"

In a similar way, there are societal expectations about life in a vowed religious community or as ordained clergy. When a young person shows a great interest in the learning about the faith, takes prayer seriously, participates actively in the sacraments, is involved in campus or parish youth ministry, takes a leadership role on retreats, and feels called to serve others, it is often assumed that he or she has a vocation to the priesthood or vowed religious life. Because of a call to prayer, worship, and enthusiastic practice of the faith, a young person may feel pressured to enter a formal religious lifestyle. Here, too, a question should be asked: "Is life in a community of vowed religious or in ordained ministry right for me? Will it bring me happiness?" Prayer and service to others are not exclusive to religious life. Many married and single people have rich and varied lives of prayer and ministry and as we will see in the next chapter, the dedicated lay single life can be excellent preparation for a vocation to the consecrated life distinct from a religious community.

Despite the expectations of society, the dedicated lay single life may well be the life for you. You can be happy and whole as a single person. In fact, unless you are, you wouldn't be ready to make any other type of commitment—whether to marriage, the consecrated life, or the priesthood. Each vocation requires its special gifts. Your happiness will depend in a great degree upon whether the life you choose suits your needs for growing and your talents for giving.

FAITH ACTIVITY

The Single Life in the Media In small groups brainstorm ways the single life is portrayed in television shows, films, and Internet sites. Give some specific examples of the lifestyle, attitudes, and behaviors of single people of different ages. Explain how realistic or unrealistic these portrayals are, and point out the misconceptions, biases, or stereotypes you note. Then discuss how these images affect the perception that people your age have of the single life.

"You did not choose me but I chose you. And I appointed you to go and bear fruit, fruit that will last....I am giving you these commands so that you may love one another."

Most single persons are truly happy. Whether temporarily or permanently single, they are finding fulfillment. While you are single, look positively on your single vocation. To be happy, whether you remain single or marry or become an ordained minister or enter a religious community, you'll first need to discover a meaning to life that encompasses all states of life. You will find that meaning in letting God into your life and in loving and giving to others in the ordinary opportunities of your every day life.

GROUP TALK

1 What blessings, advantages, and opportunities do you see in the single vocation? Which ones appeal to you the most? Why?

2 What characteristics do you think are needed to live the dedicated lay single life successfully?

3 Which of these characteristics do you think you have? Which ones do you most need to develop as you prepare to live the adult single life on your own?

"Under the Circumstances"

You have no doubt heard someone say he or she did something because "I had no choice." This is a popular phrase used to express that something is so obviously necessary that no other choice could be considered. However, it is a phrase that is never really true. To believe we have "no choice" is to say we are not fully human and free to choose.

Even in circumstances where we are unable to do what we really want to do, we can and do choose how we will deal with these circumstances. We choose our attitudes, our reactions, our words, and our positions within the circumstances.

- The woman who remains single so she can stay with her aging parents to care for them might say she had "no choice" but to do this. Actually, she had several other choices. She could have left home; other people have done so. That choice would have left her parents with different choices of their own about how to manage their lives as they age. If she found the right man, she could have married and raised a family of her own. That choice would have provided not only more people for this woman to care for, but more people to help her care for her parents. However, the woman has chosen to respond to her vocation to love God and others by providing loving care for her parents.

- The widowed man who remains single so he can care for his young children left with him when his wife died might think that he has "no choice." He certainly has difficult circumstances, and of course he wants to provide his children all of the love and care he possibly can. Remaining single is certainly one viable choice he can make to accomplish this, but he has other choices.

Circumstances can lead a person to choose to remain single; they can greatly influence the decision. Circumstances, however, can't really force a decision. When a person decides to be single either temporarily or permanently, he or she may be recognizing clear signs of a call from God to live the baptismal commitment as a single person. This could be for the good of one or more family members, for the good of the community, or for the good a specific group in need. When the single life is fully embraced, the single person will be a joyful, productive, faithful Catholic man or woman who is an active member of a faith community.

A Career Track

Sometimes career involvement can be an indicator of whether a person has a calling to the dedicated lay single life. Some professions consume hours of time and physical and mental energy. Certainly, there are married people, priests, and religious brothers and sisters who are successful in these professions. However, because of their vocations, they are called to attend to a spouse, children, or a religious community or parish. They are often torn between loyalties. They have less freedom and flexibility to find a healthy balanced approach to life.

Sometimes someone getting started in a career will postpone Marriage, thinking they will pursue that vocation after they get their career going. And sometimes the person comes to realize that a vocation to the dedicated lay single life is more compatible with his or her. Hopefully the work we do is a source good in our lives—providing for ourselves, growing personally and professionally, achieving a sense of accomplishment and self-satisfaction. Work is an important way we participate in God's

Quick Check

1. What is common in the discernment and living out of any vocation?

2. What seem to be the societal expectations of people who have not yet committed to a particular way of life?

3. What are circumstances that might lead people to choose to remain single?

4. How can a person's attitude toward work and money affect their vocational choices?

work of creation; when hardships and burdens in work are endured in union with Jesus, work can be a source of holiness and redemption. Making life choices about work and careers should be about fulfillment and bettering ourselves and others, not simply about how much money we can make. This is true on the societal level, too. Institutional and civic development is more than economic. It should help people better respond to their vocations and how God is calling them to live.

Everyone who owns *anything* is called to be a good steward of what they own. We are given what we need and we are called to use our possessions to help build God's Kingdom. Money is a necessary part of life, enabling us to provide for our own needs and to reach out to others. We need to plan wisely and provide for ourselves and our futures as well as possible.

We also need a sensible attitude toward money and possessions. Becoming obsessed with making money for its own sake or the ability to multiply our material possessions will introduce unnecessary challenges into living a life of Christian values. When we get the idea that we are somehow entitled to these things, we forget that God is the Creator of all and the source of all we have. Jesus offered vivid imagery to express the dangers of being preoccupied with wealth:

Then Jesus said to his disciples, "Truly I tell you, it will be hard for a rich person to enter the kingdom of heaven. Again I tell you, it is easier for a camel to go through the eye of a needle than for someone who is rich to enter the kingdom of God."

✝ Matthew 19:23-24

By comparing the difficulty of a rich person entering the kingdom of heaven to a camel passing through the eye of a needle, Jesus seemed to be saying this was impossible for rich people to do. But Jesus went on to indicate nothing is impossible "for God." (See *Matthew 19:26*.) This is a statement that surely grabbed the attention of all his followers who had any amount of wealth.

GROUP TALK

Discuss other images you can use to convey this message from Jesus. Why do you think Jesus used such a startling image to warn about the danger of not having a balanced life and priorities, and being consumed by a desire to be rich? Do you think too much wealth makes it impossible to reach heaven today? Why or why not?

Faith in the Workplace

Think about any jobs you might have in the future. How do you intend to practice your faith while you are at work? Does that question surprise you? Perhaps, stepping back, it is easier to answer in terms of today. How do you already practice your faith while you are at school, at home, at work, or with friends?

We really do need to *intentionally* practice our faith in the various settings of our lives. That may mean having outward signs of faith visible in what you wear, in how you spend your free time, in how you work, in the good example you give, and in how often you speak to coworkers about your faith. Intentionally practicing your faith at work may also refer to your work ethic; how you treat customers, coworkers, and managers; and what you do with the money you earn at work.

When we look to the Church's teachings on work, we find instruction on the place of work in human life, the dignity of work, and the rights of workers.

In 1981, Pope John Paul II wrote *Laborem exercens (On Human Work)*. It has taken a while for many Catholics and Non-Catholics to appreciate and take this encyclical to heart. In it the Pope stated, *"Work is one of the characteristics that distinguish man from the rest of creatures. . . ."* Besides being necessary to live, work is also a source of our dignity, self-worth, purpose, and participation in family and society. In your job, there's more to think about than a paycheck!

Questions of faith and work are centuries old. The Old Testament is full of stories of people working together and advice for how to treat coworkers. Jesus used various workplaces in his parables; farmers, fishermen, builders, and housewives could all tell he knew about their lives. His teachings in the Gospels and in the Church tell us he knows about our lives, too. There is no job we can do, no person we can work for or with, nor a workplace we can go to that doesn't need us to be a faithful member of the Body of Christ. There is no situation to which the teachings of the Gospel don't apply.

Many Catholic thinkers and writers have addressed the subject of faith at work. One present-day writer is Gregory F. Augustine Pierce wrote *Spirituality@Work: 10 Ways to Balance your Life On-the-Job* (ACTA Publications, 2003). Springing from this book is an ongoing online dialogue about the meaning of what to do about unfair wages, and how outward faith should be at work.

GO online Visit www.osvcurriculum.com for a link to the website for the online dialogue associated with this book.

GROUP TALK

1. Discuss some specific ways that faith influences jobs that you may have now or in the future.

2. Are some professions more inclined to be influenced by faith?

3. What are some concrete ways that faith could contribute to the way in which someone does his or her work?

Single with Others

❝ Single young adults have very different needs and interests from those who are engaged or married, with or without children. These single men and women work to identify what gives meaning to their lives in a way that is different from those who are married or have a religious vocation. The quest for close friendships and participation in small groups or communities of like people is particularly important. Young adults form these relationships even while realizing that they may be temporary, due to the transient nature of young adult life. ❞

Sons and Daughters of the Light, United States Catholic Conference, p.11

When God pronounced in Genesis 2:18, "It is not good that the man should be alone," he knew this because *God* is three Persons in one God, a Holy Trinity. God created a woman to be the companion to the man. We also recall the Trinity when we speak of families, and we see that in families it is impossible to be alone.

How can the single life be a Christian vocation if being alone is not good? Single people are not called to be loners, recluses who avoid contact with other people. Single people are called to commitments and friendships, as is everyone. The single life is sometimes one of solitude—the pleasurable, preferable experience of being alone—not loneliness, the painful undesired experience of aloneness. But coping with loneliness and a sense of belonging are challenges that lay single people face. This is why, within the single vocation, friendship takes on special importance.

The Importance of Friendship

The laity—married and single alike—have the prophetic mission "to be witnesses to Christ in all circumstances and at the very heart of the community of mankind"[2] (*CCC*, 942). For married people, the center of their community is in their Marriage and their family. For single people, the center of their community is often in their friendships and their connections to their family of origin.

Certainly married people can and do have strong, meaningful friendships. However, in living out their marriage vows they give their attention and energy first to their spouses and to attending to their families before anyone else. Single people have more freedom to devote time and energy to others, without specific obligations from an exclusive relationship with another person or a family of their own children. But it is definitely not realistic or fair to assume that single lay persons do not have strong familial ties. Many single lay people dedicate a lot of energy to caring for elderly family members or those with specific needs. Single persons may take an active role in the lives of nieces and nephews, or they make an effort with grandparents, aunts, uncles, and siblings that others are not able to. On the other hand, it's not right to expect single persons to bear more than their fair share of family obligations. We can't assume that because someone is single, he or she has more time or ability to shoulder all the responsibilities that an entire family should share. Single lay people have to find balance in their lives, just as people in all vocations do. The flexibility of the single life allows each individual to prioritize work, relationships, family obligations, and activities in a way that brings him or her happiness and fulfillment.

GROUP TALK

Spend some time thinking about single people you know. Describe how they make a difference in the lives of others. What roles do they have in other people's lives? How could faith be a part of those roles?

The Virtuous Life

Whether or not you commit to the dedicated lay single life in the future, you will need to build meaningful relationships and work at being a part of a community of friends and family. These relationships will bring you happiness, for it is through them that you will encounter a dimensions of God's presence that you will experience in no other way.

What about romantic relationships, dating, and intimacy in the lay single life? No matter whether you are entering into a friendship or a romantic relationship that has the potential to lead to Marriage, you will want to be with someone who shares your values. It is vitally important that potential spouses share each other's respect for human sexuality.

Our human sexuality is one of God's greatest gifts. Our sexuality is part of what makes us the people we are. It's more than whether you are a biologically a male or female. Sexuality affects everything about you, body and soul united. It includes the way you think and feel about things, the way you pray, the way you are inclined to act, the interests you have. Each of us should acknowledge and accept our sexuality. With our gift of sexuality comes responsibility. *Every* baptized person is called to lead a chaste life. Jesus himself is our model of perfect chastity.

Chastity is the virtue by which sexuality is integrated within a person. It comes under the cardinal moral virtue of temperance, which calls for a balanced use of all our gifts.

FAITH ACTIVITY

Read Sirach 6:14–17.

1. Have you ever had a faithful friend like the one described in this passage from Sirach?

2. Do the friends you have now live up to this description?

3. How important do you think friendships are for a person?

4. What do you think are some of the hardest parts about having and keeping good friends?

Leading a chaste life means leading a life in which we are not driven by our sexuality and sexual desires, but instead have mastery over them. This mastery doesn't happen overnight or without failures. The *Catechism* explains that chastity includes "an apprenticeship in self-mastery" which is a "long and exacting work" that one can never consider finished once and for all. (See *CCC* 2338–2345, and 2394–6.) It is essential to consider how your relationships now prepare you for faithful, honest, committed relationship in the future.

A Chaste and Modest Life A person practices the virtue of chastity according to his or her state in life. It sometimes surprises young people to learn that married people must also lead chaste lives. Certainly they are sexually active, but they must still have self-mastery over their sexuality and sexual desires. People who are married, single, ordained, or in the consecrated life can be tempted to grave sins against chastity—sins like masturbation, fornication, adultery, pornography, and homosexual practices.

We can see how each of these sins and any others against chastity deny one basic, God-given value: the dignity of the human person. It is possible to turn any person into an "object" if we choose to. We can even use ourselves as objects rather than express the dignity of our individuality. Treating anyone—ourselves, a friend, a spouse, a stranger—as an object for sexual pleasure rather than as a person, who is a sexual being that is to be respected, denies their human dignity.

Because it seems so difficult at times, society often seems to tell us not to even try to master our sexuality. Christ in his Church, however, treating us with human dignity, teaches that we *can* lead chaste lives, and offers guidance to help us.

The guidance begins with the Law of God given as Ten Commandments. There are two commandments that have to do with our sexuality. The Sixth Commandment, among other issues, addresses adultery, which will be addressed in the chapter on Marriage. The Ninth Commandment helps guide us to live a chaste life whether married or single. It states, "You shall not covet your neighbor's wife."

The key word in this commandment is covet, which means to want something that belongs to someone else, or to lust after something that belongs to someone else. In the Ninth Commandment we are told not to covet *people*. In other words, we are not to view people as objects we can use or own in some way; that is, we are not to lust after their bodies. This commandment also addresses purity and modesty.

We read in the Beatitudes that Jesus speaks directly to sins against our sexuality: "Blessed are the pure in heart, for they will see God" (*Matthew 5:8*). Purity of heart, like all virtues, can be cultivated and needs to be practiced. Like chastity, it comes under the cardinal moral virtue of temperance. One of the best ways to increase purity of heart is to practice the virtue of modesty. Modesty includes patience, decency, and discretion. It oversees how we dress, share our thoughts, and speak about ourselves and others. The *Catechism* describes modesty this way: "Modesty protects the intimate center of the person. It means refusing to unveil what should remain hidden" (*CCC*, 2521).

Single and Chaste Chastity is a powerful support to the single life. Chastity expresses itself in friendship, which is an integral part of the single life. Chastity enables us to develop friendships between persons of any gender. We can see in the Gospels how Jesus had good friendships. His friendships led to spiritual communion, and so should ours.

The virtues of chastity and modesty help us to see our sexuality, and the intimacy of sexual union, in the proper light. In future chapters we will discuss the sacredness of sexual intercourse and why it is an expression of love that belongs only to married couples. However, any presentation of the single life requires mention of cohabitation (living together as a couple outside of marriage) and premarital sex. Both of these practices are grave offenses against the dignity of marriage because as the Church teaches, the sexual act can only take place within marriage. Cohabitation and premarital sex weaken fidelity and undermine the value and nature of family.

Whether or not the dedicated lay single life will be your chosen life's vocation, you are and will continue to be challenged to master your sexuality, to be chaste and modest, to form good friendships that are not based on sexual activity, and to find in yourself your core dignity.

FAITH ACTIVITY

Challenges and Fulfillment List the top three challenges you think you'll face as a single person. Briefly explain how you might be able to handle each. Then list the top three things that can bring you fulfillment as you experience the lay single life. Use both lists as a tool for considering if you might be called to the live the lay single life permanently. Spend some time in quiet prayer asking God for strength to live out your vocation now and in the future.

GROUP TALK

- What makes a chaste and modest life possible?
- What do you think are some of the biggest challenges to chastity and modesty in life? How can these be overcome?
- Who helps you to remain faithful to the life God calls you to live?

Organizations and Affiliations

Single Catholics can join with others for spiritual and organizational affiliation. The spiritual gifts of saints who founded religious orders, such as Saints Benedict, Francis of Assisi, Dominic, Birgitta, and Ignatius of Loyola, attract some people to join a vowed religious community. Others, often single laypeople, are attracted by the gifts and message of the founder, but do not feel called to the consecrated life. Many religious orders have programs for affiliate members. Such associations allow lay people to be affiliated with members of religious orders without taking vows. They share in the spiritual benefits bestowed on members of the religious order, participate in the mission of the order in some fashion compatible with their daily lives, and help support the order through prayer, financial donations, and donations of time and talent.

Some religious orders identify lay members as members of a secular "Third Order." The title comes from the traditional designation of men who have taken vows in a religious order as members of the "First Order," and women who live vowed cloistered lives in the order as "Second Order" members. Third Order members can be single or married.

Third Orders are officially recognized by the Church, and their members are formally received by making promises. They meet for prayer, service projects, support, ongoing education, and socializing. They promise to live as witnesses to the Gospel of Christ and the charisms of their founder.

Many religious orders and religious service organizations also invite lay volunteers to actually join their mission for a period of months or years. Volunteers can be found doing everything from fighting forest fires to running soup kitchens to serving those who are poor, sick, or otherwise needy in the community. In these ways, lay Catholics—single or married—can witness that they are vital, contributing members of the Body of Christ, the Church.

Quick Check

1. What role does friendship have in the lay single life?

2. What commitments might describe those in dedicated lay single life?

3. Why are chastity and modesty important to living the lay single life?

4. How can dedicated lay people participate in religious communities?

The National Fraternity of the Secular Franciscan Order

The Secular Franciscan Order (SFO; formerly the Third Order of Saint Francis), founded along with the First and Second Orders by Saint Francis of Assisi in the thirteenth century, is an official order within the Catholic Church. Members do not live in community, like the First and Second Orders do, but they gather on a regular basis for prayer, formation, and service. They are professed by promising to follow the SFO Rule of Life, which was revised, approved, and confirmed by Pope Paul VI in 1978.

In the United States, the SFO is divided into thirty-one geographic regions, with a total of 741 local fraternities where approximately 17,000 lay men and women are professed members and approximately 1,400 more people are studying and preparing to be members. Members meet monthly at their local fraternity for prayer, discussion, and ongoing education. Additionally, there are also regional, national, and international SFO events that members can attend. The members can be single or married lay people.

SFO members focus their apostolic action in four areas: Ecology, Family, Peace and Justice, and Work. In each of these important realms, SFO members consciously bring the message of the Gospel of Jesus and the spiritual legacy of Saint Francis to bear in their actions, involvement, and decision making.

In the area of Ecology, SFO members bring Saint Francis' love for creation to bear in their concern for the environment. Their stated goals include a call for simple, less materialistic living and for greater respect for the earth. In the area of Family, recent SFO work has focused on the aging population and the needs of families and caregivers who have aging or handicapped members. The role of parents as spiritual guides of their children is always stressed, but also, SFO fraternities are called on to be like families for all members, especially those living alone. The Peace and Justice goals of the SFO call for all members to be prophetic voices calling for peace and for human rights for all. The SFO goals concerning Work challenge members to bring the spirit of Francis to their own places of work and also to stand in solidarity with workers throughout the world whose dignity and rights are denied.

All members of the Secular Franciscan Order are adults, but there is also outreach to youth in high school to introduce them to Franciscan spirituality and living and to encourage them to consider a Franciscan vocation to the First, Second, or Third Orders in their adult lives.

FAITH ACTIVITY

Researching Saint Francis Do some brief research about Saint Francis of Assisi to recall the basic story of his life. How does today's Secular Franciscan Order seem to bring his message to today's world? Research the locations of SFO fraternities and find which ones are closest to you. If possible, contact a local fraternity to find out what information they can share with you, or if you have some skills that can assist them in attaining their goals of apostolic action in Ecology, Family, Peace and Justice, and Work.

▼ *St. Francis of Assisi Preaching to the Birds* **by Giottodi Bondone**

We caught up with two single Catholics at a post-Hurricane Katrina distribution center on the Gulf Coast of Mississippi.

Jean B. is a woman in her early sixties who calls herself "a South Dakota farm girl." She spent a few years as a religious sister, but came to know that God was calling her to the lay single life. She has been a teacher and director of religious education, and is currently volunteering to help find and bring assistance to hurricane survivors.

Malcolm R. is a single man in his mid-thirties who hails from St. Louis, Missouri, where he's now a doctor but says that he started out, "as a feisty little black boy with a very *big, mean* grandma." He's staying for six months in the Gulf Coast region, providing medical care from a clinic set up in a trailer home.

INTERVIEWER: I found the two of you in here drinking coffee together. How long have you been friends?

JEAN: (laughs) We just met this morning, but I bet we'll be friends for a long while.

MALCOLM: Yeah, I came here to see what supplies they have for some of my patients. As you can see, they have a lot of some things, but they're seriously lacking in stuff we really need.

JEAN: You're new to this missionary work, aren't you, Malcolm? You'll learn that's how things usually are. We sometimes don't have enough of the things we think we need. But then we find out we can improvise or get along without them. At the very least, we certainly have enough love to go around.

INTERVIEWER: Is that why you came down here, then? To give love?

MALCOLM: Well, I didn't think of it as "love" at first, but the longer I stay down here, the more sure I am that love is why I stay. I came with some other folks from my parish. Our priest knows a priest from down here and he decided to get a group of us together to come help. The whole team stayed two weeks—that was the parish commitment. But I could see they needed a doctor for a bit longer. I'm staying for six months, for now, anyway.

INTERVIEWER: Malcolm, you mentioned your grandma as a great force in your life. How has she influenced you?

MALCOLM: Oh, you picked up on how important she is to me? Well, she raised me. Thanks to her I'm a good man, a good Catholic, and a good doctor. If it was up to her, I'd also be a good husband and dad. But she doesn't get to decide everything about my life.

INTERVIEWER: Don't you plan to get married?

MALCOLM: I don't believe I'm the marrying kind. Medical school was too busy for much dating, and I went right from there to work back in my old neighborhood hospital emergency room. Honestly, I have doubts I'd even be here helping out right now if I was married and had kids.

JEAN: No, you'd probably have your hands full at home!

MALCOLM: Probably. Where's your guy, Jean?

JEAN: I don't have one. I'm single, too. I never thought much of my ability to manage a husband and family. I've been single for a long time. I've found peace and stability in my friends and through my participation in the Church.

MALCOLM: I guess you could say that about me, too. I don't think I'm an overly holy person, but I initially came here with my Church group, so I guess I'm pretty involved.

INTERVIEWER: I think you both show your holy sides. It's a blessing that there are people like you to help make the world a better place.

JEAN: We do what we can—one person at a time.

who will you Become?

Look back at the statements you completed about values at the beginning of this chapter.

Privately consider the following questions.

Based upon what you discovered in this chapter, would these values be different if you were a married or single lay person, a member of a religious community, or an ordained minister? Why?

In the upcoming months, I would like to place more value on

Something I wish my friends valued more is

I could contribute to my family relationships by placing greater value on

My faith can help me consider what's really important in life by

When you read over the things you said you value about yourself, family, and friends, what might they tell you about the vocation God is calling you to?

Leader: Let us recall that God is one God in three Persons, The Father, the Son, and the Holy Spirit, as we pray the Sign of the Cross, the Sign of our Faith.

All: In the name of the Father, and of the Son, and of the Holy Spirit.

Leader: When we were baptized we were called to share in Christ's threefold mission to be prophet, priest, and king. Each of us has an individual vocation by which we will live out our baptismal call. Let us stand and renew our baptismal promises.

Do you reject sin so as to live in the freedom of God's children?

All: I do.

Leader: Do you reject the glamor of evil, and refuse to be mastered by sin?

All: I do.

Leader: Do you reject Satan, father of sin and prince of darkness?

All: I do.

Leader: Do you believe in God, the Father almighty, creator of heaven and earth?

All: I do.

Leader: Do you believe in Jesus Christ, his only Son, our Lord, who was born of the Virgin Mary, was crucified, died, and was buried, rose from the dead, and is now seated at the right hand of the Father?

All: I do.

Leader: Do you believe in the Holy Spirit, the holy catholic Church, the communion of saints, the forgiveness of sins, the resurrection of the body, and the life everlasting?

All: I do.

(All wait in silence as leader passes a small bowl of holy water around. As each person takes it, he or she dips fingers into it and makes the Sign of the Cross on oneself. Then pass the bowl to the next person. When all have blessed themselves, continue.)

Leader: Let us now give our assent to these promises we have made:

All: This is our faith. This is the faith of the Church. We are proud to profess it, in Christ Jesus our Lord.
(*Rite of Baptism for Children*, 57–59)

Study Guide

▶Check Understanding

1. Identify how values and priorities influence our lives.

2. Describe what makes the dedicated lay single vocation fulfilling and significant.

3. Distinguish between being transitionally single and the dedicated lay single life.

4. Summarize what makes the dedicated lay single life a radical Christian calling.

5. Explain the importance of Baptism and Confirmation to the lay single life.

6. Tell how the Eucharist can benefit dedicated lay single persons.

7. Describe why the Sacrament of Penance is important for living out one's vocation.

8. Give examples of how intentional living and conversion can help people on their path to God.

9. State what is common in the discernment and living out of any vocation.

10. Point out some of the societal expectations of people who have not yet committed to a particular way of life.

11. Name some of circumstances that might lead people to choose to remain single?

12. Describe how a person's attitude toward work and money can affect his or her vocational choices.

13. Recall the importance of friendship in the lay single life.

14. Name some commitments that dedicated lay single adults might have.

15. Define chastity and modesty.

16. Name ways dedicated lay people participate in the work of religious communities.

▶Apply and Develop

17. Prioritize the four areas of basic needs based upon how much time and energy you dedicate to each. Explain how these needs are met in your life now. How might the priority of these needs, and how you meet them, change as you grow older?

18. Propose several ways that single lay people can participate in the mission and offices of Christ in which they share through Baptism.

19. List some advantages to being a single lay person and explain why someone might choose this vocation for life.

20. Tell why it is important for members of all states of life to be chaste, with special consideration to the unique challenges of being chaste in the lay single life.

▶Key Words

See pages noted for contextual explanations of these important faith terms.

baptismal grace (p. 76)   conversion (p. 80)

character (p. 77)   covet (p. 91)

chastity (p. 89)   modesty (p. 91)

▶ A Franciscan Sister of Perpetual Adoration walks with a student from Chileda, a program in La Crosse, Wisconsin, based on a develpmental approach to the treatment of children with developmental disabilities.

CALLED TO CONSECRATED LIFE

CHAPTER 4

CHAPTER GOALS

In this chapter you will:

★ learn about the evangelical counsels and how they are lived by religious women and men today.

★ consider the rich and diverse history of religious orders of men and women in the Church.

★ find out about life in cloistered religious orders.

★ find out about life in active religious orders.

★ meet a religious brother and read about his vocation to consecrated religious life.

WHO ARE YOU?

Take a few minutes to consider the questions below.

When do you pray?
  Your best time(s) of the day for praying
  Your best day(s) of the week for praying
  Your best season(s) or special day(s) for praying

Why do you pray?
What life situations often bring you to pray?
What good does it do for you to pray?

What prayers do you pray?
What is your favorite formal or memorized prayer?
What are one or two of your favorite hymns?
When you pray in your own words, what do you
  usually talk about with God?

You'll revisit these at the conclusion of this chapter. See how prayer can help you hear and respond to God in your life.

Now spend some time thinking about these questions.

Do you consider yourself a person of faith? How is your answer reflected in this profile of your prayer life?

Who taught you how to pray? Is there anyone you pray with now?

Have you ever asked anyone to pray for you? Why?

Have you ever prayed for someone? Why?

How have you prayed for direction as you decide future steps?

Have you ever prayed for your own vocation or that of others? Why?

The Evangelical Counsels: Counsels of Perfection

Our contemporary culture tends to emphasize the things we own, the way we look and dress, the people we know, the school or university we attend, or the job title we have. But a trip to a local bookstore will show that people are yearning for a deeper experience in their lives.

This desire to connect to something beyond ourselves is part of our human nature. When God created us, he made us to be in relationship with him and others. To be in relationship with someone, you have to get to know him or her. You have to share your thoughts, hopes, and dreams. You have to trust the person with your fears and needs. You have to talk to them, and you have to listen. God wants us to do the same with him, and he continually calls us to encounter him through prayer. Throughout salvation history we see God calling his people and their response to him taking place through prayer.

Through prayer we can come to know God's will for us. Our hearts can be opened, our minds focused. Prayer can quiet us so that we can hear and experience God in our lives. We've discussed how important prayer is in the discernment process, and we know that every vocation is a sacred opportunity to witness to God's love and goodness. This chapter will concentrate on the way in which those in the consecrated life witness to God's love and work for his kingdom. We'll discover how important prayer is to their life calling.

The Consecrated Life A vocation to consecrated life is a very special call from God. Love for God sometimes impels people to stretch and to strive to model their lives after Jesus in as complete and perfect way as possible. They are filled with a desire to do more for the Father, to live completely for him, and to come closer to spiritual perfection with the help of the Holy Spirit. They find fulfillment and joy in giving themselves fully so that they can be Christ to the world in powerful and transforming ways.

66 All the sons and daughters of the Church, called by God to 'listen to' Christ, necessarily feel a *deep need for conversion and holiness*...In fact the vocation of consecrated persons to seek first the Kingdom of God is first and foremost a call to complete conversion, in self-renunciation, in order to live fully for the Lord, so that God may be all in all. Called to contemplate and bear witness to the transfigured face of Christ, consecrated men and women are also called to a 'transfigured' existence. 99

Pope John Paul II, *The Consecrated Life*, 59

FAITH ACTIVITY

Gospel Advice The word *evangelical* means pertaining to the Good News of the Gospel. The word *counsels* refers to recommendations or advice. Make a list of the different types of advice Jesus gives us and give some examples of how followers of Christ can follow that advice in their families, with their friends, at school and at work, and in the wider community.

Members of the consecrated life transfigure themselves to Christ most especially through the **evangelical counsels—poverty**, chastity, and **obedience**—which they vow to live by. These counsels are **vows** made in imitation of Jesus as a means of living his Gospel message. As Jesus invited the rich young man to do, those in the consecrated life:

- sell their possessions and own nothing in their name giving their money to the poor and following Jesus

- give themselves to God completely by living a **celibate life** for the sake of the kingdom

- give complete obedience to God, the community, and the Church through their religious communities.

We find in the Church a variety of forms of consecrated life, some lived with others in community and some lived in solitude. Among these forms are eremitic life (hermits may or may not publicly profess the evangelical counsels, but they live by them), consecrated virgins and widows, women and men in the religious life (brothers, sisters, nuns, monks, priests), and those in secular institutes (lay people living in the world, striving for perfection in love and working to make the world holy). In conjunction with these forms of consecrated life, we have societies of apostolic life, whose members do not take religious vows but live by the specific mission and purpose of their society.

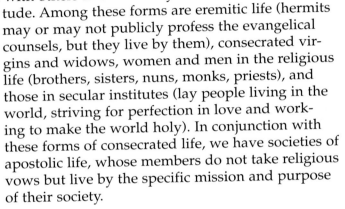

▼ A Franciscan Sister of Perpetual Adoration and one of the Tertiary Sisters of St. Francis work together as part of the Common Venture. The Common Venture involves the collaboration of four Franciscan congregations on projects related to health care and social issues.

In the consecrated life, we find a variety of ways people can live out their commitment to Christ, either in solitude, in community with others, and even in their families. For instance, there are women religious and women in the dedicated lay single life who are also consecrated virgins. and there are married women and men who belong to secular institutes and societies of apostolic life. While all these forms of consecrated life are essential to the life of the Church, in the rest of this chapter we will concentrate on women and men in religious life.

The consecrated religious publicly vow to live in poverty, chastity, and obedience as these are taught by Christ and his Church and as they are lived out in the particular religious communities to which the consecrated religious belong. Their vows are binding for the length of time stated when they make them. Some consecrated religious make vows for a year and renew them every year. Others make final vows—promises to God that they keep for life.

Just as the Holy Spirit has given great diversity in the Church, there is also diversity in how the evangelical counsels are lived.

<blockquote>
"From the God-given seed of the counsels a wonderful and wide-spreading tree has grown up in the field of the Lord, branching out into various forms of the religious life lived in solitude or in community. Different religious families have come into existence in which spiritual resources are multiplied for the progress in holiness of their members and for the good of the entire Body of Christ.[1]

Dogmatic Constitution on the Church, 43
</blockquote>

Poverty: Treasure in Heaven

The story of the Rich Young Man from the Gospels tells us when the rich young man heard what Jesus invited him to do, "he went away grieving, for he had many possessions" (*Matthew 19:22*).

When Jesus put forth his plan for God's Kingdom, he stated eight Beatitudes. The first of these teachings is "Blessed are the poor in spirit, for theirs is the kingdom of heaven" (*Matthew 5:3*). Saint Paul, the four Gospel writers, and nearly every spiritual thinker since then has written, prayed, or talked about what this first beatitude means. It has its roots in the Ten Commandments—"don't steal; don't covet"—but Jesus took being "poor in spirit" well beyond that. He told us to give things away, to share with others, and to stop obsessing about material possessions. This beatitude focuses on a spirit of detachment from material things. It does not mean that all Christians must give away what they own, but that they have the proper attitude toward and about what they own.

However, if you want to be closer to spiritual perfection, embrace poverty for the sake of the common good: sell everything; forfeit the ownership of your property. Give it to your family, friends, or the poor, and become like Jesus, who had "nowhere to lay his head" (*Matthew 8:20*).

Vowing Poverty There is nothing holy about dire poverty brought upon a family, community, or region by natural disaster, war, unemployment, or exploitation by wealthier people. That poverty is destitution, and no one vows to embrace that kind of poverty. Indeed, Catholic social teaching calls all of us to work against it and the structures from which it resulted. The vow of poverty is actually a vow to stand against poverty and stand in solidarity with the poor.

People who take a vow of poverty choose to own nothing in their own name. They realize everything comes from God, and they vow to not get caught up in wanting and owning material possessions. Instead, they hold everything they need in common with

FAITH ACTIVITY

Called by Jesus Read these Gospel passages on how Jesus called others to live as he did—and the kinds of people he invited: Matthew 4:18-22 and 19:21, Mark 1:16-20 and 10:21, Luke 5:1-11 and 18:22. Imagine you're one of those individuals, write a one-page letter to Jesus telling him how you've decided to respond and why.

everyone else in their religious community. They choose to live simply, with few or no extra material things around them, and not personally to own any of them. Money they earn is turned over to their religious community to be used by all members, used for the community's various ministries, and shared with the needy of the world.

With God's grace and continual help, people who vow evangelical poverty are freed from the distractions and possible preoccupations that can come from owning possessions and wanting more. By living with community they can also be freed from the concern and anxiety that come from the sole responsibility of providing for themselves or a family. Instead, they are able to focus on their relationship with God and strive for spiritual perfection, and through prayer assist with meeting the spiritual needs of the larger community.

▲ A Sister making her Final Vows in which she professes to live by the evangelical counsels.

GROUP TALK

Discuss the following with others in a small group:

- How important are your personal possessions to you? How would not owning them affect you? Is it possible you might be more free in some ways without them?
- Imagine pooling all your resources with a group of people and sharing everything in common. What would be some advantages of this arrangement? What would be some disadvantages? Could the advantages outweigh the disadvantages?

Celibate and Chaste

When his Apostles asked Jesus if it wouldn't be better to remain unmarried, he answered, "Not everyone can accept this teaching, but only those to whom it is given" (*Matthew 19:11*). Clearly, the vow of chastity is not a requirement for salvation. It is an invitation only given to and accepted by some.

Perhaps to an outside observer, vowing chastity may seem to be about everything a person must give up; it may seem to be negative. To the person making the vow, chastity is a positive, joyful choice.

As we saw in Chapter Three, the virtue of chastity is required of all Catholics. With Christ as the model of chastity, every baptized person—married, ordained, single, or consecrated religious—is called to lead a chaste life, integrating one's sexuality, and mastering one's sexual desires.

The vow of chastity is made as a life of celibacy in an unmarried life. A person who promises celibacy promises not to marry. The vowed religious choose not to marry in order to help build the Kingdom of God and to be in a more intimate relationship with God. Vowing chastity isn't to be done out of fear or selfishness. People take the vow of chastity for the sake of the Gospel, in order to more freely participate in the Church's mission to bring Christ to the whole world. They don't reject their sexuality, but realize that part of their personal dignity is the way God created them as a man or woman, and that chastity is an expression of that dignity.

GROUP TALK

No matter what vocation we choose, all Christians are called to chastity. Explain how this is so. Yet not all Christians are called to lifelong chastity as celibacy for the sake of the kingdom. How is God's kingdom advanced by those who accept this calling?

Signs of Christ's Bride, the Church The love God has for his people and the love Christ has for his Church are often compared in Scripture to the love a husband has for his wife. Religious men and women who make a vow of chastity are signs of that total giving of love to Christ, the bridegroom of the Church. Those who are celibate and chaste for Christ's kingdom are signs of hope who point to the future—to eternity in heaven, where we are assured, "they neither marry nor are given in marriage" (*Matthew 22:30*).

> Religious life derives from the mystery of the Church. It is a gift she has received from her Lord, a gift she offers as a stable way of life to the faithful called by God to profess the counsels.
>
> *Catechism of the Catholic Church*, 926

Obedience: Listening to God's Will and Keeping It

The word obedience comes from the Latin *obaudire*, meaning "to listen attentively." This is important for understanding the evangelical counsel of obedience. Consecrated religious who take a vow of obedience promise to obey the laws of God and the Church, the rules of their religious order, and the directives of their religious superiors.

Some may view this vow as asking adults to behave like children who must obey their parents without question. But most children question their parents. And since obedience is rooted in listening, asking questions is part of it. The evangelical counsel of obedience is not "blind obedience."

FAITH ACTIVITY

To Whom Are You Obedient? Make a list of the people who have authority over you in some way right now. Reflect on how you obey each of them. Does your obedience to any or all of them include active and attentive listening to what is needed and wanted from you? If not, how could this dimension of obedience affect the way you obey and how you relate to those in authority?

Quick Check

1. What are the characteristics of the consecrated life?

2. Which evangelical counsel's name comes from the Latin word for "listen attentively?" Why is listening an important part of this counsel?

3. Which evangelical counsel requires us to be poor in spirit? How does this differ from being in financial need?

4. Which evangelical counsel do consecrated religious always practice in a life of celibacy? Why?

All Christians are called to obedience, by which we can make conscious choices to do God's will and keep God's Law because we have "listened attentively" to know what they are. The Christian virtue of obedience is not blind.

True obedience requires active, attentive listening, not only to what someone says they want, but also to their unspoken wants and needs. True obedience requires the freedom to give a person what they ask for or to do what they ask of us.

Religious Obedience Religious obedience is the obedience to God's Law expected of every Christian, plus the voluntary submission to the authority of a religious order as it is expressed in the rules of the order and in the people who govern the order. This obedience is always freely given by an individual who wants to follow a way of perfection—as Jesus was perfect in his obedience for and love of the Father—defined by a religious order. However, a consecrated religious is not bound or permitted to obey the command of religious superiors if the action is immoral or sinful in any way.

The religious vow of obedience is a continuation of the Christian virtue of obedience. It starts with adherence to God's Law, but leads to a free sacrifice of one's independence in order to more closely follow the way of perfection.

Jesus models such obedience in his relationship with the Father. For, as Saint Paul wrote, Jesus "though he was in the form of God, did not regard equality with God as something to be exploited, but emptied himself, taking the form of a slave, being born in human likeness. And being found in human form, he humbled himself and became obedient to the point of death—even death on a cross" (*Philippians 2:6–8*).

It is this complete giving of self to God that the consecrated religious seek when they vow poverty, chastity, and obedience. As Pope John Paul II wrote,

The Church has always seen in the profession of the evangelical counsels a special path to holiness. The very expressions used to describe it–the school of the Lord's service, the school of love and holiness, the way or state of perfection–indicate the effectiveness and the wealth of means which are proper to this form of evangelical life, and the particular commitment made by those who embrace it.

Pope John Paul II, *The Consecrated Life*, 35

GROUP TALK

1 Describe contributions that those who live the consecrated life make or have made. How have these contributions touched your life?

2 How is the way you are responding to God's call now a blessing for others? How is it a holy path to God?

Religious Orders in the Church

There are approximately 54,000 religious brothers in the world today. Of that number, approximately ten percent are in the United States. Worldwide, there are approximately 775,000 religious sisters, with just shy of nine percent of them living in the United States. Forty years ago there were over 80,000 religious brothers and one million religious sisters in the world. So is vowed life in a religious community disappearing from the Church?

No, those numbers do not tell the whole story. A statistical "snapshot" of forty years is a mere scrap of data in the two-thousand year history of the Church. All through the ages, leaders have emerged to fill a particular need or to help address a particular issue in the Church of their time. They founded religious orders to do a ministry in the Church. Some of those orders have lived and died, their ministries no longer needed. Others have stayed alive by adapting their ministries to changing times.

The extraordinary people who founded these orders had specific **charisms**, or spiritual gifts, that made them the right people to start an order to fill a need. The religious orders in the Church today strive to be faithful to the original call and gifts of their founders. What compelled those founders to work so hard to serve the Church? What compels religious men and women today to stay faithful to the visions of their founders? All of them could answer using words from Saint Paul: "the love of Christ urges us on" (*2 Corinthians 5:14*). They want everyone to come to know God and experience his transforming love.

▲ Mission Helpers of the Sacred Heart celebrate at a community gathering.

GO online Visit www.osvcurriculum.com to learn more about the Mission Helpers of the Sacred Heart and for a link to their website.

GROUP TALK

Do you know or have you ever met any religious brothers or sisters? Compare notes with your classmates. What vowed religious people do you know? Are they of various ethnicities? What religious orders have you heard of? Discuss the following questions:

• What gifts do religious orders in the Church bring to the world today?

• How can communities of vowed religious contribute to the world in ways that differ from others?

The Church's Missionary Mandate Consider the widespread results of this missionary command from Jesus:

Go therefore and make disciples of all nations, baptizing them in the name of the Father and of the Son and of the Holy Spirit, and teaching them to obey everything that I have commanded you.

Matthew 28:19–20

That missionary mandate from Christ our Head has echoed down through the centuries, kept alive by the Holy Spirit speaking to people's hearts and souls. Only the Holy Spirit could build up a Church from such beginnings. Poured out on the Church by Christ, the Holy Spirit builds the Church, brings her to life, and makes it holy. In fact, the *Catechism* calls the Holy Spirit "the principal agent of the whole of the Church's mission"[2] (*Catechism of the Catholic Church*, 852). From the first small group of Apostles, came a Church that, in spite of many obstacles and crises, has lived, thrived, and sanctified its members and reached out to the whole world for over two thousand years.

The mandate included no detailed plan of action or list of needed credentials. Yet from it came a united Church of diverse members who have grouped and regrouped into families, parishes, and religious communities devoted to Christ's command to bring the Gospel message to everyone.

GROUP TALK

Discuss with a small group of classmates: If the missionary mandate has been given to the whole Church, it has been given to you. What does it mean to you that you have been told to "go make disciples of all nations?" How are the Catholic adults around you carrying out this mandate? In what ways do you think you might carry it out in your life?

▼ *Saints John the Evangelist, Scholastica and Benedict* by Master of Liesborn

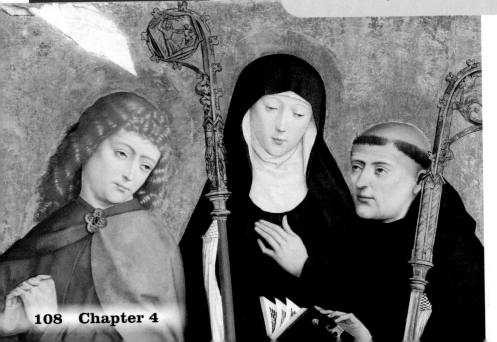

The History of Religious Life

Monasteries and convents did not instantly spring up on the day of Pentecost, but the Holy Spirit inspired many women and men to seek Christian perfection in ways that developed into the religious orders that greatly influenced the Church throughout the ages. The chart below indicates several religious orders. However, there are many, many more in addition to these.

FAITH ACTIVITY

Monastic Rules Research one of the five saints whose rules are the basis for most religious orders today. Why did the saint found their religious order? What are some of the main points of the rule?

Centuries A.D.	Groups	Famous Members	Lifestyle	Purpose
1st	Female virgins and widows	Saint Agnes, Saint Perpetua	Remained unmarried, lived simply, not set apart from the rest of the world	To draw closer to Christ, witness heroic sanctity during times of persecution
3rd	Solitary monks	Paul of Thebes, Saint Anthony of the Desert, Saint Basil, Saint Pachomius (who formed the first monastery)	Set apart from the world, gathered near each other or together in a monastery	To escape from persecution, seek perfection, live in proximity of other monks for support and encouragement
5th	Nuns gathered under one roof	Saint Augustine of Hippo wrote rules for their life together	Set apart from the world in monasteries, vowed chastity and poverty	To Gather with like-minded women seeking Christian perfection and mutual support
6th–8th	Irish monasteries of men, Benedictine monasteries and convents	Saint Columba in Ireland, Saint Benedict and his twin sister Saint Scholastica in Italy	Systems of several monasteries all following the same rule	To reach personal perfection by living by vows and by following prescribed rules, practice charity within a community
9th–12th	Restructured and reformed Benedictine monasteries	Saint Bruno, Saint Bernard of Clairvaux	Rise of larger monasteries as prominent centers of learning, stricter rules	To work the land to support the community, gather for prayer and study, live apart from the world
13th	Mendicant orders of holy beggars and preachers	Saint Francis of Assisi, Saint Dominic, Saint Clare of Assisi	Owned no property, subsisted by begging	To assist in the reform the Church, call to return to the Gospel and simpler living
16th	The Society of Jesus (Jesuits)	Saint Ignatius of Loyola	Community life without monastic enclosure	To assist in the reform of the Church, to educate others

**Friar Paul with Pupils at
Glenstal Abbey's Computer Room** ▲

Visit www.osvcurriculum.com for
some links to sites about vocations
to religious life and various religious orders.

GO
online

The Rules of Saints Augustine, Benedict, Francis,
Dominic, and Ignatius of Loyola have been the basis for
most of the religious orders that proliferated for centuries, some of which have endured into or were founded
during the twentieth and twenty-first centuries.

Monasteries kept learning alive over centuries of
destruction, plague, war, and revolution. Missionaries
traveled the world bringing the Gospel message to
distant neighbors while other religious orders brought
it to those close by, running parishes and schools.
Some monasteries offered hospitality to travelers; this
led some monasteries to expand to run hospitals for
the sick and the dying. People who were poor came to
the doors of convents and monasteries to beg, which
led some religious men and women to leave their enclosures and start orders that live and work among the
poor.

To this day, the Jesuit Order runs high schools and universities to educate Catholic youth and to contribute to both
Catholic and secular research and scholarship. The Alexian
Brothers, formed seven hundred years ago in Germany by a
group of men assisting victims of the Black Death when few
others would do so, still run hospitals and clinics and now
assist victims of HIV/AIDS who find themselves similarly
ostracized. Many of the schools and hospitals which Saints
Elizabeth Ann Seton and Francis Xavier Cabrini founded in
the United States in the eighteenth and nineteenth centuries
still operate today, and more have been built and operated
by members of the religious orders that these two American
saints founded.

Saints Alive!

Saintly men and women—many of them officially canonized saints of the Church—founded hundreds of religious
orders. If they could come back now, what would they think
of their orders? Our belief in the communion of saints tells us
they are still present to their religious communities, still able
to influence them, and still united to all of us in the Eucharist.
Surely these saints can be proud and happy because of the
activities their followers are engaged in today.

Founders of religious orders who first traveled to mission
outposts on ships, on horseback, or on foot, have followers
today who drive cars, pilot airplanes, and collect frequent-fly-
er miles. Founders who took patients' vital signs by measuring temperature and pulse rate by hand now have followers
using complicated telemetry to monitor everything from pulse
rate to blood oxygen levels. Founders who built orphanages
now have members serving as social workers in the homes of
the poor.

✔ Quick Check

1. What are charisms and why are
   the charisms of their founders
   so important to members of religious orders today?

2. What is the Church's missionary
   mandate? Who is supposed to
   carry it out?

3. What role does the Holy Spirit
   have in the Church today?

4. Name three things religious
   orders in the Middle Ages did that
   affected history.

Religious Habits

When your grandparents were young, they could identify priests, religious brothers, and religious sisters by the clothes they wore. Not only would the special clothing–called a **habit**–identify the person wearing it as a member of a religious community, but the style and color of the habit would identify exactly to which religious community that person belonged.

Gradually, fewer and fewer members of religious orders could be identified by the clothes they wore. Recognizing that their habits had originally been the clothing of laity in the place and era when their orders were founded, most religious orders opted for a much simpler habit or even regular street clothes with some sort of religious insignia worn to show their membership in their religious order.

This concept of a type of uniform worn by all members is certainly not unique to religious life. Until a few years ago, nurses' caps identified which nursing schools they attended. All branches of the military have different uniforms and different insignia on them to designate a person's rank.

A common part of some habits in the past and of some today is the **scapular**, a piece of cloth fourteen to eighteen inches wide, long enough that it reaches close to the feet both in front and behind when the head is put through. It has an opening in the middle of the cloth so that it hangs front and back from the shoulders. The word "scapular," in fact, is derived from *scapula*, the Latin word for shoulder.

The scapular symbolizes the "yoke" which Jesus speaks of when he invites us to follow him. Of course, the large wooden yoke worn by oxen when they are hauling something is reminiscent of the cross. But a yoke, like the cross, isn't just a burden to carry. It's worn in order to accomplish something.

Come to me, all you that are weary and are carrying heavy burdens, and I will give you rest. Take my yoke upon you, and learn from me; for I am gentle and humble in heart, and you will find rest for your souls. For my yoke is easy, and my burden is light.

✝ Matthew 11:28–30

FAITH ACTIVITY

Your Personal Yoke It's possible you were given a small cloth scapular around the time you received your First Communion. Or perhaps you have received a scapular medal. Each of us is called to bear the sign of Christianity, a "yoke" carried in union with Christ on the cross.

- How do you visualize your own burdens, your own strengths, and your faith that God will help you?

- On a scapular-shaped piece of paper, draw symbols of the burdens you carry and what you are to accomplish because you carry them.

- How does the scapular connect with your search for your vocation?

Cloistered Religious Life

As you read in the previous section, separation from the world was a hallmark of religious life from the third century on. At first, however, the separation was not in the form of a **cloister**, or an enclosure.

The idea of a cloistered life—enclosed so that occupants were totally separated from the outside world—first arose in the eleventh and twelfth centuries. In this way, members of cloistered communities could be **contemplative**—that is, focused entirely on prayer, Christian perfection, and union with Christ. For a time, this sort of enclosed monastic life was the main form of religious life in the Church. Even when the mendicant orders of Franciscans and Dominicans began, with the men preaching and begging and living outside a cloister, the women who followed Saints Francis or Dominic still lived in cloistered monasteries. Saint Clare of Assisi sometimes objected to this, longing to go about the countryside begging and preaching alongside the brothers. But in the thirteenth century, this was not considered proper nor safe behavior for women.

St. Meinrad Archabbey ▲

We more properly call religious who are not cloistered "brothers" and "sisters." Men in cloistered monasteries might be priests or brothers and would be addressed that way, but when we speak about them we call them **monks**. Cloistered sisters are actually called **nuns**; a term too often incorrectly used for women religious both in and out of the cloister or monastery.

As we'll see in the next section of this chapter, in the twenty-first century there are religious women and men serving in active ministries all over the world. One might wonder why, then, are there still cloistered monasteries where people voluntarily live in quiet seclusion or even total silence?

For the Good of the Whole Church When a new diocese is formed by the Pope and a bishop has been assigned to lead it, often a bishop invites an order of contemplative nuns or monks to establish a monastery in that diocese. The bishop, in this way, helps to focus on the spiritual needs of his new diocese by inviting a community of religious women or men to be present from the beginning, praying for this new endeavor.

This was not always the case in the United States. When the first Poor Clare nuns arrived here from Italy in the 1890s, several bishops rejected them when they asked to establish a monastery in their dioceses. They were told that the contemplative way of life was incompatible with the American way of life. It took three years for them to establish their first monastery in Omaha, Nebraska.

This early skepticism has largely been eliminated among Catholics today. Some, however, still question the validity of contemplative religious life in a world where so much work needs to be done to bring the message of the Gospel and to strive for justice and peace. They wonder if the cloistered monks and nuns might serve the Church better if they left their enclosures and worked directly in some apostolate.

This question was clearly answered by the Fathers of Vatican Council II when they promulgated the decree *On the Adaptation and Renewal of Religious Life.*

> [contemplative communities] retain at all times, no matter how pressing the needs of the active apostolate may be, an honorable place in the Mystical Body of Christ, whose 'members do not all have the same function' (Rom. 12:4). For these offer to God a sacrifice of praise which is outstanding. . . . their apostolate which is as effective as it is hidden. Thus they are revealed to be a glory of the Church and a well-spring of heavenly graces.

On the Adaptation and Renewal of Religious Life, 7

While the rest of the world is working, playing, sleeping, and sometimes praying, monks and nuns in cloistered monasteries are always praying for us. It is as simple and amazing as that.

FAITH ACTIVITY

Prayer Requests Most cloistered monasteries have some way for people to ask them for prayers. Check the directory of your diocese to see what contemplative orders are near you and find out if they take requests for prayers. Or, if no monastery is nearby, find one on elsewhere that will receive prayer requests. Make a prayer request now or plan to do so when something important comes up.

Our Call to Encounter God

The Vatican instruction on contemplative life says that it is "a unique sign of the entire Christian community's intimate union with God" (*Verbi Sponsa*, 6). The Church blesses and reveres those who live in the closest union with God because that is the union to which we are *all* ultimately called. A simple definition of prayer is "the raising of one's mind and heart to God or the requesting of good things from God"[3] (CCC, 2590), but there is a much more profound dimension to prayer. The *Catechism* calls prayer a "mysterious encounter" with God, a true exchange between God and a human. We are all called to this encounter; nuns and monks make it their life's work to reach this level of communication with God.

Life in a cloistered community centers around prayer. Meditation, Scripture reading, and contemplation help people recognize God's intimate presence around and within them. Monks and nuns have time for solitude each day. Silence is an important element of contemplative life. There is very little talking outside of the time of evening recreation in most monasteries. During work hours people only speak when they need something. There is no workplace chatter in a monastery and there are no radios and TVs playing in the background. Some contemplative orders, like the Cistercian branch of the Benedictines, observe total silence, even using hand signals to make requests or give information.

Liturgy of the Hours The official prayer of the Church, the Divine Office, is called the Liturgy of the Hours. It is called *liturgy* because it is the part of the public prayer of the Church. It is called *hours* because it is divided up into sections that are to be prayed to mark the passing hours of the day and night. This prayer aims at consecrating and making holy the whole day and night. Many Catholics pray the Liturgy of the Hours; all priests are required to do so. But they are not required to pray the different sections at special times of day. Contemplative communities, on the other hand, schedule their lives around their gatherings together in the chapel to pray, including rising in the middle of the night. Page 250, in the back of the this book, lists the hours that are prayed today.

Contemplative prayer centers around the Eucharist. Contemplative religious celebrate the Liturgy of the Eucharist every day, when a priest is available. Many groups also have times when the Blessed Sacrament is exposed so they may pray in adoration before Christ. Some groups even have **perpetual adoration**, requiring members to take turns praying before the Blessed Sacrament day and night.

FAITH ACTIVITY

Contemplative Prayer Spend some time alone thinking about your own personal call to encounter God and to be in a relationship with him.

- Could you ever imagine yourself praying this way or choosing this way of life?
- What does God seem to be saying to you about your prayer life right now?
- How does your prayer life help you clarify your vocation or life's calling?

Pray and Work

Saint Benedict set the motto "Pray and work" before his followers back in the eighth century, and it stands as a motto for Benedictines and other contemplative religious today. Benedict was striving for a balance between quiet prayer, contemplation, and the daily activity needed to live.

People don't become monks or nuns so they can live an easy life. Life in a cloistered community is not easy. Besides uniting with Jesus in prayer, members also try to unite with him in his suffering. Most contemplative orders practice some types of penance. Often members fast

from food, perhaps eating only one meal a day. Many meals are meatless. Typically, monastery beds have thin mattresses; bedrooms (often called cells) are sparely furnished; clothing is simple and there are no luxuries to be found. Monks and nuns strive to keep their entire focus on God.

However, they are not hermits. A cloister is also a community. Each individual who answers God's call to a contemplative life joins a number of other individuals who now make up one's religious community. It is here that members continuously practice Christian charity. They live in close proximity to each other, often without leaving the cloister. In fact, some monks and nuns only leave their cloisters for serious reasons. For some nuns, their only contact with the outside world is through a "grille" set up in a visiting room so someone can speak directly to her, though unable to touch her and often unable to see her clearly. Some orders have "extern" members who do not vow to remain enclosed on the grounds as the regular members do. These externs do the shopping and other business of the community.

Cloistered convents and monasteries have to be self-sustaining. Some bishops help support groups in their dioceses. The orders also rely on donations from lay benefactors. But most also engage in work that can provide some income. Many have a large garden that supplies them with food, and sometimes they sell produce at local farmers' markets. Some groups even run small farms to provide income from crops, meat, and dairy products. Many convents bake altar bread and sell it to parishes. Some make liturgical vestments and decorate them with embroidery. You can find some food products produced at monasteries and convents: There are communities that make and sell wine, candy, fruitcake, cheese, jams, and jellies. Some communities sell the artwork done by members. Others produce recordings of ancient and newly composed Church music.

Preservation of Scripture and of Christian scholarship continues to be an important aspect of cloistered life, as it has been since early times. Now, the quill pen has been replaced by the computer. Nuns and monks continue to translate texts, conduct research, and write their own books.

Some orders are "semi-cloistered" so that they can do some direct ministry for people outside the cloister while still remaining cloistered themselves. One such group is the Order of the Visitation, whose members run schools for girls. Another is the Sisters of the Cenacle, who provide retreats and spiritual direction for adults.

FAITH ACTIVITY

Visiting a Cloister or Monastery
Go "shopping" at some local convents and monasteries. Or, consider using the Internet to search for cloistered orders and the products they produce. From these Web sites, many groups reach out to the rest of the world. Whether you visit in person, or search online, record what your impression is of these men and women who live contemplative lives.

Poor Clare Sisters of the Second Order of Saint Francis

When Saint Francis of Assisi formed his band of brothers, a young woman, Clare, heard him preaching and knew God was calling her to follow the way of life Francis was proposing. So, as Francis was establishing his Order of Friars Minor for his male followers, he worked with Clare to establish the Order of Poor Ladies. From those thirteenth century beginnings over 20,000 Poor Clares now live in seventy-six countries around the world. The Poor Clares do not have one central governing body. Rather, each local monastery is autonomous, though linked by the Rule of Saint Francis. Sixteen different "observances" or versions of the Poor Clare Order exist today, due to the passage of time and the great distances between different monasteries. Some observances are stricter than others; some are less cloistered. Habits differ among observances, with some Poor Clare groups wearing a very traditional habit with a full veil and wimple (a cloth that usually covers the head and is worn around the neck and chin) and others wearing a modified habit. Most have a brown habit, though a few wear black. All wear the rope cord worn by all Franciscans, with three knots tied in it to signify poverty, chastity, and obedience.

Like many groups of nuns, some Poor Clares support themselves by making hosts (altar breads), specialty foods, and vestments; writing books; and doing artwork. What strikes anyone visiting a strictly cloistered Poor Clare monastery is the feeling of joy that comes from the sisters. Poor Clare Sisters are quick to laugh, and show genuine love for each other. Their convents are joyful places.

Clare of Assisi instructed the women from the beginning to adopt their schedule according to their needs. Their daily praying of the Liturgy of the Hours varies according to the needs of the community. Their life is balanced by solitude and community.

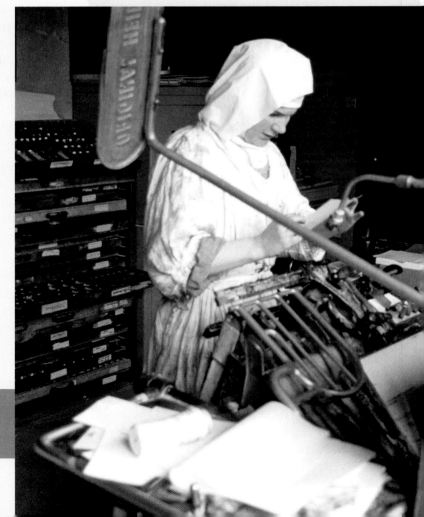

A novice of the Poor Clares in the printing room ▶

Formation of New Members

Sometimes a young person thinking about whether religious life is right for him or her feels attracted to a life he or she sees as so difficult and so spiritually perfect that it would be impossible to succeed in it. If you or anyone you know finds things about a contemplative religious life appealing, look into it. Pray about it, talk about it, and find out all the information you can about it. If you find the life of an active religious sister or brother attractive, find out more. Writing to a few religious orders for information or checking out their Web sites doesn't mean you've made a final decision.

When you talk to monks, nuns, brothers, or sisters, or read what they have written about their vocations, often they will tell you of their own uncertainties as they explored the communities they now live in. No one is "holy enough" and no one lives any life perfectly. In religious life, the time of **formation** is very important. A person doesn't take on all the responsibilities of a full community member until he or she has gone through a period of training in which he or she is introduced to the many prayers, practices, rules, and traditions of that religious order.

Formation periods in all religious orders, both contemplative and active, usually last several years, with members joining as **postulants** or candidates, who observe and learn while often living somewhat separate from the professed members of the community. Following that level, members become **novices** for one or two years. They begin to participate more fully in the community's life of prayer and sacrifice. They sometimes receive a habit or the insignia of their religious order. After their novitiate is completed, they take temporary vows or first vows. Only after these years of formation do religious profess their final (or permanent) vows and become full members of the religious order. During the time of formation, the postulant or novice is free to decide to leave the community and return to secular life. The community's authorities, or superiors, are also able to suggest that a potential member not proceed with formation if he or she sees fit to do so.

✓ Quick Check

1. What is the contemplative life and who is called to lead it?

2. What is Saint Benedict's motto?

3. What are the Liturgy of the Hours?

4. What type of formation does a person seeking to be a consecrated religious undertake?

Active Religious Life

Religious brothers and sisters are not ordained, so technically they are members of the laity. Early religious orders were often founded by a lay person or group of lay people in conjunction with a priest or bishop, and in response to some need in the Church or the wider world at the time. Because they were lay people, they were in the world where they could see what was needed. Because they were not married, they were free to give themselves to provide a needed service or serve an important cause. Joining a community would be practical and economical. They couldn't join already-existing cloistered religious communities because that would make working in the outside world impossible. In order to be recognized as official religious orders by the Church, each new community had to have a stable state of life with an established place to live, and its members had to publicly profess vows of poverty, chastity, and obedience. Also, the bishop of the diocese in which each new order or community existed had to petition Rome to receive approval from the Pope.

The first active religious orders were the Franciscans and Dominicans in the thirteenth century. These were the First Orders who went about preaching and witnessing to the Gospel, some as ordained clergy and some as religious brothers. Women followers were always cloistered nuns, who were in the Second Orders. But early on, there were already lay men and women who wanted to live by the principles set out by Saint Francis or Saint Dominic. They evolved into the Third Orders. There are still secular Third Orders today, to which single and married lay people can belong while remaining in their homes and jobs. Lay women who wanted to follow Francis or Dominic without living in a cloister were gradually accepted as members of what came to be called the Third Order Regular because they lived together in a community and followed a Rule ("regula").

From those early beginnings, many active religious orders arose, not enclosed in a monastery, but bound by vows and rules. The Church's missionary mandate was lived out in more diverse ways as that "great tree" of communities professing the evangelical counsels continued to branch out in new directions.

Visit www.osvcurriculum.com for links to the Franciscan Brothers of Brooklyn and other sites.

GO online

▼ Priests and Brothers of the Missionaries of the Poor care for mentally and physically handicapped people in their mission center in Kingston, Jamaica.

Women and Men Religious

Controversy continued between those who felt religious women should be in cloisters and those who felt they should work outside their monasteries and convents to serve the poor and spread the Gospel. While both groups seemed to have a place in the Church, there were Church leaders who wanted only one or the other, but not both. In 1545, the Council of Trent tried to suppress all active religious communities of women by requiring them all to become cloistered.

At that time, some hospitals and schools had to close for lack of personnel and some orders went out of existence. As was mentioned earlier, some religious communities tried to compromise by becoming semi-cloistered. They brought those they wanted to serve into close proximity with the cloister they lived in.

Over the next two hundred years there was great disagreement among the hierarchy about the nature of religious life for women. Meanwhile, women who felt called to the cloister went there, and those who felt called to address some problem in the world while still professing the evangelical counsels found each other, formed communities, and fought to have the rule about enclosures changed.

Religious Sisters The power of the Holy Spirit shines through the stories of every active religious order of women. These women with a mission moved relentlessly forward, convinced that God wanted them to be part of the Church's missionary mandate in more ways than praying for the missions.

The reluctance to allow women religious to leave their enclosures was a sign of the times. Doing the things these sisters proposed to do—heal, feed, clothe, and shelter the poor; teach children outside of the home; and so on—was not considered proper for any woman. The needs of the poor around them, and the realization that women, too, have a missionary mandate from Christ, led to a gradual—and subsequently total—lifting of the suppression of religious women in active communities. It was clear that their gifts were needed to help carry out the Church's mission. The seventeenth and eighteenth centuries saw the proliferation of new active religious orders of all kinds both in Europe and in the New World.

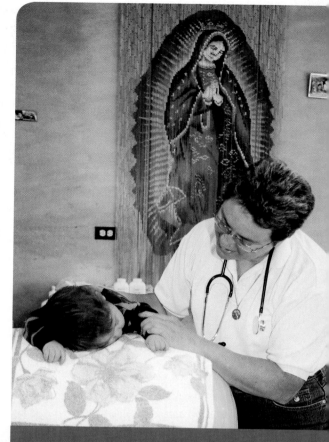

▲ Sr. Janet Gildea, SC, MD, works with a special needs child in a clinic in Mexico. Sr. Janet is featured in the Catholic Communication Campaign's "You Could Make a Difference," a video/DVD featuring three religious sisters, a religious brother, and priest, as they live out their vocations across the country.

GO online Visit www.osvcurriculum.com to learn more about the DVD and for a link to the U.S. Bishops' website.

FAITH ACTIVITY

Founding a Religious Community Write a proposal for founding a religious community based on what Jesus would do to meet the needs in your local area. State a particular ministry to which the religious community would be dedicated.

Often it was a priest or bishop who, when faced with some population of people in great need, would look for lay women to come nurse, teach, or distribute food.

When Saint Vincent de Paul needed someone to help train young women to assist the poor he turned to a young, wealthy widow, Louise de Marillac, who had been donating money and service to his extensive work in France. Together they founded the Daughters of Charity in 1663. Both Vincent and Louise were canonized saints, and their order continues today all over the world in many forms and branches.

In the 1820's, Catherine McCauley was convinced of the need to help those who were poor in Dublin, Ireland. She was a wealthy, single woman who used her money to build a center called the House of Mercy in which she could teach poor children, care for orphans, and provide housing for poor Irish young women who came to the city to work as maids. She dreamed of starting a corps of Catholic social workers, not of starting a religious order.

But the people of Dublin were suspicious of her center and of the women who came there. It was Archbishop Murray of Dublin who suggested Catherine found a religious order so her work could go on after her death. Since religious orders in Ireland were still cloistered, the archbishop got permission from Rome for her to establish a religious order of sisters who would profess vows but not have to remain cloistered. This was so novel to the people of Dublin that they called Catherine and her sisters "walking nuns," because they went out about the city serving the poor. Catherine called herself and her companions "Sisters of Mercy" when they were formally professed as sisters in 1831.

Both the Daughters of Charity and the Sisters of Mercy have communities all over the world serving the Church in the fields of healthcare, social work, and education. Many orders have multiple ministries; others specialize. An interesting example is the congregation of the Dominican Sisters of Hawthorne. Founded in 1900 by Rose Hawthorne, who was the daughter of American novelist Nathaniel Hawthorne, the Hawthorne Dominicans' sole ministry is the care of poor people who have incurable cancer.

Religious Brothers Male religious did not face the same challenges that women did in being accepted outside the cloister. Priests, as we shall discuss further in the next chapter, can also be members of religious orders and live in religious communities. Some religious orders of men, especially the Franciscans and the Dominicans, have both ordained priests and non-ordained brothers as members. In fact, Saint Francis himself was a religious brother and ordained deacon, realizing his call was to rebuild the Church spiritually and to live among the poor as a poor man, but not to be ordained a priest.

FAITH ACTIVITY

Religious in Your Area What do you already know about religious sisters? Find out what sisters live and work in your own diocese. Research some orders of active religious.

• What do you notice these different groups of sisters have in common?

• What seems to be unique about each group you investigate?

• Do you find any of them particularly attractive to you because of their spirituality, their mission, their culture or the areas where they serve?

While most male religious orders have both priests and brothers as members, there are several orders of only brothers. Like their female counterparts, these religious orders of brothers vow poverty, chastity, and obedience; live in community by a rule; and serve the Church in some specific way. Both the Alexian Brothers and the Hospitaller Brothers of St. John of God are international religious orders of men who provide health care. These brothers are doctors, nurses, hospital administrators, addiction counselors, and researchers. Their hospitals, clinics, nursing homes, and rehabilitation centers are among the finest in the world.

Religious brothers have made contributions in the fields of education and youth ministry, too. The Christian Brothers, Marist Brothers, and Xaverian Brothers all have established and staffed Catholic schools throughout the world for over a century. Their schools are among the finest in the world with graduates going on to college and meaningful careers.

GROUP TALK

- If you were interested in becoming a consecrated religious, which type of religious community would you be most interested? Explain why.

- What do you think would be most rewarding about the religious way of life? Most difficult or challenging? Explain.

Missionaries to the Ends of the Earth

The Catholic Church is a missionary Church. Some members may be called to work in foreign missions, traveling miles from home, but the entire Church is missionary. Saint Thérèse of Lisieux knew this. From her Carmelite cloister in France, she prayed and reached out to missionaries all over the world, aware that she, too, shared the missionary mandate to "Go, teach all nations." Her participation in the missionary activity of the Church led her to be named the Patron Saint of missionaries when she was canonized a saint.

The missionary spirit of religious orders fit well with the adventurous spirit of early explorers in the New World. There were Franciscan Missionaries traveling with Christopher Columbus. Jesuit Missionaries not only brought Christianity to North America, but also helped explore and map the continent.

The founders of many American religious orders were priests, brothers, and sisters from Europe. The young immigrant Church in America needed pastors and teachers who could speak their native languages and understand their culture. Every European founder of an American branch of a

FAITH ACTIVITY

Missionaries from Your Parish You have probably seen and heard missionaries speak at your parish each year. Missionaries usually come to parishes to ask for prayers and donations, but they also hope to attract young people to join them in their missionary work. Look for some missionary literature or search for their Web sites. Check your first reactions as you read. What kind of mission appeal gets your attention? What sort of missionary work could you see yourself doing, if not for life, at least for a time?

Mother Teresa with children from the orphanage she operated in Calcutta ▼

religious order was, in a sense, a missionary. Even nuns who had vowed to live in a cloister had to set that vow aside in order to sail across the ocean to establish cloistered communities. The first Poor Clares, for example, came over from Italy and spent nearly three years traveling around the United States before finding a diocese in which to settle.

Some religious orders were founded and continue today as missionary orders whose members are all sent to work among people who are not Catholic, and often not Christian. Maryknoll Missioners and the Divine Word Missionaries are priests, brothers, sisters, and lay people who work in foreign missions. The Glenmary Home Missioners, on the other hand, work to bring the Gospel to small towns and rural areas of the United States.

Advocates for Social Justice Active religious have not only worked to help people in need; they have also been at the forefront of those trying to end the injustices and bring about social change.

Saint Katharine Drexel was a wealthy young woman from Philadelphia who was appalled when she saw the rampant racism around her. She put her own financial resources to work, and in 1891, also gave up her life as a socialite to found the Blessed Sacrament Sisters, whose mission focuses on ministry to African Americans and Native Americans. She died in 1955 and was canonized in 2000. Her order of sisters continues to serve and thrive in the Church today.

Blessed Teresa of Calcutta was a religious sister from Albania, who taught wealthy girls in India until she could no longer ignore the plight of the poor she saw outside the school walls. She left her religious order in 1948, became an Indian citizen, and began to work alone to aid the poor and dying of Calcutta. In 1950, she founded the Congregation of the Missionaries of Charity. She died in 1997, and was beatified in 2003. Her religious order now has sisters in thirty countries serving the poorest of the poor.

These and countless other groups of religious sisters and brothers work in virtually every possible venue to help bring Christ's peace to our world. They are present in places such as Palestine and Israel, Ireland, and Central and South America, quietly working and witnessing to the Gospel values that are needed in the face of war, poverty, and racism. Hospital brothers and sisters hold out against government pressure to offer abortions or engage in embryonic stem cell research in their health care facilities. They choose to risk financial and professional damage rather than destroy human life.

These religious men and women profess poverty, chastity, and obedience. They live in the support system of their religious community. Prayer and the celebration of Mass are a regular part of each of their days. Thus, they bring a spiritual dimension to everything they do.

FAITH ACTIVITY

Prayer in Your Daily Life Spend some time reflecting on how you could include or increase a faith dimension in your life. Have you ever seen faith and prayer make a difference in someone's life and how they do things? Does prayer enter into your daily life in any way?

✔ Quick Check

1. What are some reasons that active religious communities developed?

2. What is meant by the term "semi-cloistered"?

3. What are some contributions religious in active communities have made in the Church?

4. How do people living religious life as a brother or sister participate in the missionary work of the whole Church?

The Christian Brothers

There is an ancient tradition of religious men educating young people; however, the monks in monasteries were teaching the children of the wealthy and the titled in Europe. Perhaps that ancient practice contributed to the attitude that education was only for the rich. Whatever the reason, this was the case in seventeenth century Europe. One well-educated son of wealthy parents wanted to change that. His name was John Baptist de La Salle.

He was ordained a priest in 1678, and, because of his family ties, he had a lucrative position as Canon of the Reims Cathedral. He valued his own excellent education so much that, when he saw the conditions of the poor in Reims who had no access to education, he wanted to do something to change that.

John Baptist de La Salle gathered a group of young men and began training them to be teachers. He left his family home and his position as Canon and moved in with these teachers so he could put his own education to work. In this way he formed the community of the Institute of the Brothers of the Christian Schools, more commonly known as the Christian Brothers. Originally, their primary mission was to provide free quality education to poor children. Today they teach over 900,000 students in eighty countries.

John Baptist de La Salle was more than just a well-intentioned person willing to try his hand at teaching. He was an innovative educator. In fact, the educational establishment in France resented his new methods such as grouping students according to ability, demanding well-prepared teachers, and getting parents involved. He also founded training colleges for teachers, reform schools for delinquents, technical schools, and high schools. He was canonized in 1900, and in 1950 he was named Patron Saint of educators.

Christian Brothers continue to be innovators in education. A man interested in becoming a Christian Brother would also want to become a high school teacher, youth minister, campus minister, or college professor. The headquarters of the order are in Rome and there are regional offices throughout the world. The brothers live together in community and profess the Evangelical Councils. They no longer offer free education, but they continue to reach out to the poor and provide affordable education. The Christian Brothers have over forty formally associated high schools in the U.S. including Hudson Catholic Regional High School, Jersey City, New Jersey; La Salle Academy, Providence, Rhode Island; De La Salle Institute, Chicago, Illinois; Calvert Hall College High School, Baltimore, Maryland; Totino-Grace High School, Minneapolis, Minnesota; and Christian Brothers College High School, St. Louis Missouri. Each one strives to offer rigorous academics, numerous activities, and a strong moral and spiritual atmosphere for students to become fully educated. A high percentage of their graduates matriculate to many different colleges. They also operate seven colleges—including Christian Brothers University in Memphis, Tennessee.

GO online Visit www.osvcurriculum.com to learn more about the Christian Brothers

Here I Am Lord:
A Conversation with. . . a Religious Brother

When we were put in contact with Brother Al Rivera, FMS, a member of the Marist Brothers, we saw the word "chef" in part of his e-mail address. He has spent parts of his life doing very different things. We caught him just before he left to run a weekend youth ministry conference in New York.

INTERVIEWER: Before I ask you anything else, Brother Al, is the word "chef" in your e-mail address a sign that I'm missing a great lunch?

BROTHER AL: (laughing) Well, before I became a brother I got a degree from a culinary school, became a chef, and worked for a hotel. About the great lunch—everybody around here loves it when it's my turn to cook.

INTERVIEWER: A chef who became a brother. . . how did that come about?

BROTHER AL: Well, it didn't happen overnight. I didn't wake up in the kitchen at the hotel one day and say, "Wow! I think I'll be a brother!" I went to a Marist high school, so I knew the brothers and their spirituality. But at that time I had never thought being a brother was what God had planned for me. I was just a Puerto Rican kid from New York. My parents were good Catholics, but certainly not overly pious, and religious vocations aren't especially encouraged in my culture.

INTERVIEWER: It sounds like almost all the cards were stacked *against* you becoming a brother.

BROTHER AL: But there's more! I had a girlfriend, and we were engaged to be married.

INTERVIEWER: Okay, *all* the cards were stacked against you.

BROTHER AL: Except—I think I was always drawn to the Marist way of life. I was impressed by the brothers at my high school. They radiated a sense of life and vitality and showed a genuine interest in young people. They helped all the kids, including me, recognize our gifts and talents and also consider how we could use them to make a difference in the world.

Also, my girlfriend was always as interested, as I was, in how we could serve God, how we could make a difference in the Church somehow. In fact, she is now a religious sister. So I think you could say we influenced each other's vocations.

INTERVIEWER: You say you didn't just decide to be a brother overnight; how long did it take you, and how did you decide?

BROTHER AL: Like most people, I needed personal contact. While I was in college, one of the brothers from my high school invited me to join the Contact Program. It's for college-age men who are open to the possibility of a vocation to the Marist Brothers. He saw something in me that I didn't see. As I went through that program, I gained some insight into the life and mission of the brothers and how I might fit into that life. I didn't join them immediately. I went on to finish school and get engaged. But I couldn't shake the sense that God wanted me to do something else—to become something more.

INTERVIEWER: What was it that attracted you to the Marists?

BROTHER AL: One big factor was the life of our founder, Saint Marcellin Champagnat. He observed a classmate being beaten by a teacher when he was a boy so he dropped out of school, but continued to study on his own until he went to the seminary to study for the priesthood. As a young priest in nineteenth century France, he was called to the deathbed of a teenager who had had very little religious instruction. With his own bad school experiences and this meeting with a dying boy, Saint Marcellin felt called to do something about the illiteracy and spiritual emptiness of the youth around him. He formed a group of brothers devoted to Mary, who were dedicated to teaching and ministering to youth. And that's what we Marists still do today.

INTERVIEWER: You're all packed up and ready to go to a big youth rally. You look very happy to be doing what you do.

BROTHER AL: I am! Working with youth has challenged me to redefine my notions of who I am and what a brother should be. And young people are a constant reminder to me of God's presence in my life. Someone once said that brothers are "a hidden surprise of the Church." I like that! I like to be part of the surprise.

who will you become?

Reflect on your prayer life.

Look back at the questions about prayer you answered at the beginning of this chapter.

Do you picture yourself as an adult with prayer as a central part of your life?

What do your responses tell you about your faith and your prayer at this time in your life?

What do you believe about the power of prayer?

How do you plan to handle your participation in liturgy when you are out of high school, away at college, or working? How can you make participation in the Mass part of your week?

Do you think you will be an active parishioner when you are on your own?

What prayers and religious practices from your youth will you bring with you into adulthood?

What prayers and religious practices will you probably leave behind?

How can continued prayer help you to discern what vocation you have in life?

❯Prayer

Leader: Today let's reflect on God's call to each of us, as we pray Psalm 25 in the style Psalms are recited by those who pray the Divine Office (Liturgy of the Hours) in a community setting. We'll begin with the Sign of the Cross . . .

Leader: O God, come to our assistance.

All: O, Lord, make haste to help us.

Leader: Glory be to the Father, and to the Son, and to the Holy Spirit,

All: As it was in the beginning, is now and ever shall be, world without end. Amen.

Leader: (reads the Psalm antiphon) Happy are the people the Lord has chosen to be his own.

Left Side: To you, O Lord, I lift up my soul.
O my God, in you I trust;
do not let me be put to shame;
do not let my enemies exult over me.
Do not let those who wait for you be put to shame.

Right Side: Make me to know your ways, O Lord;
teach me your paths.
Lead me in your truth, and teach me,
for you are the God of my salvation;
for you I wait all day long.

L: Be mindful of your mercy, O Lord,
and of your steadfast love,
for they have been from of old.
Do not remember the sins of my youth or my transgressions;
according to your steadfast love, remember me,
for your goodness' sake, O Lord!

R: Good and upright is the Lord;
therefore he instructs sinners in the way.
He leads the humble in what is right,
and teaches the humble his way.
All the paths of the Lord are steadfast love and faithfulness,
for those who keep his covenant and his decrees.

L: Glory be to the Father, and to the Son, and to the Holy Spirit,

R: As it was in the beginning, is now and ever shall be, world without end. Amen.

All: Happy are the people the Lord has chosen to be his own. Amen.

Study Guide

▶Check Understanding

1. Describe the life that consecrated persons are called to live.

2. Express in your own words the meaning and significance of the evangelical counsel of obedience.

3. Name the ways consecrated religious live the evangelical counsel of poverty.

4. Explain the significance of the evangelical counsel of chastity.

5. Define charism and explain why the charisms of founders of religious orders are important to members today.

6. Describe the Church's missionary mandate and who is supposed to carry it out.

7. Identify the Holy Spirit's role in the Church today.

8. Summarize the activity of religious orders in the Middle Ages and how it affected history.

9. Explain the contemplative life and who is called to lead it.

10. Recall Saint Benedict's motto and explain its importance in the development of religious communities.

11. Give an explanation of the purpose and role of Liturgy of the Hours.

12. Outline the formation a person seeking to be a consecrated religious undertakes.

13. Name some reasons that active religious communities developed.

14. Explain what is meant by the term "semi-cloistered."

15. Summarize some contributions religious in active communities have made in the Church.

16. Give some examples of how people living religious life as a brother or sister participate in the missionary work of the whole Church.

▶Apply and Develop

17. Formulate a message for people your age about the value of and fulfillment in living in the "school of the Lord's Service."

18. Compare and contrast the purpose and characteristics of the major groups of religious communities formed over the centuries. You may choose to focus your attention on Saints Augustine, Benedict, Francis, Dominic, and Ignatius of Loyola.

19. Distinguish between cloistered religious communities and active religious communities. Why are both important to the life of the Church?

20. Select three religious women or men who had an impact on the growth of the active religious life. Evaluate the similarities and differences in their contributions. Describe how the people you selected can be role models for people living out any vocation.

▶Key Words

See pages noted for contextual explanations of these important faith terms.

celibate life (p. 102)

charisms (p. 107)

cloister (p. 112)

contemplative (p. 112)

evangelical counsels (p. 102)

habit (p. 111)

monk (p. 112)

novice (p. 117)

nun (p. 112)

obedience (p. 102)

perpetual adoration (p. 114)

postulant (p. 117)

poverty (p. 102)

religious formation (p. 117)

scapular (p. 111)

vows (p. 102)

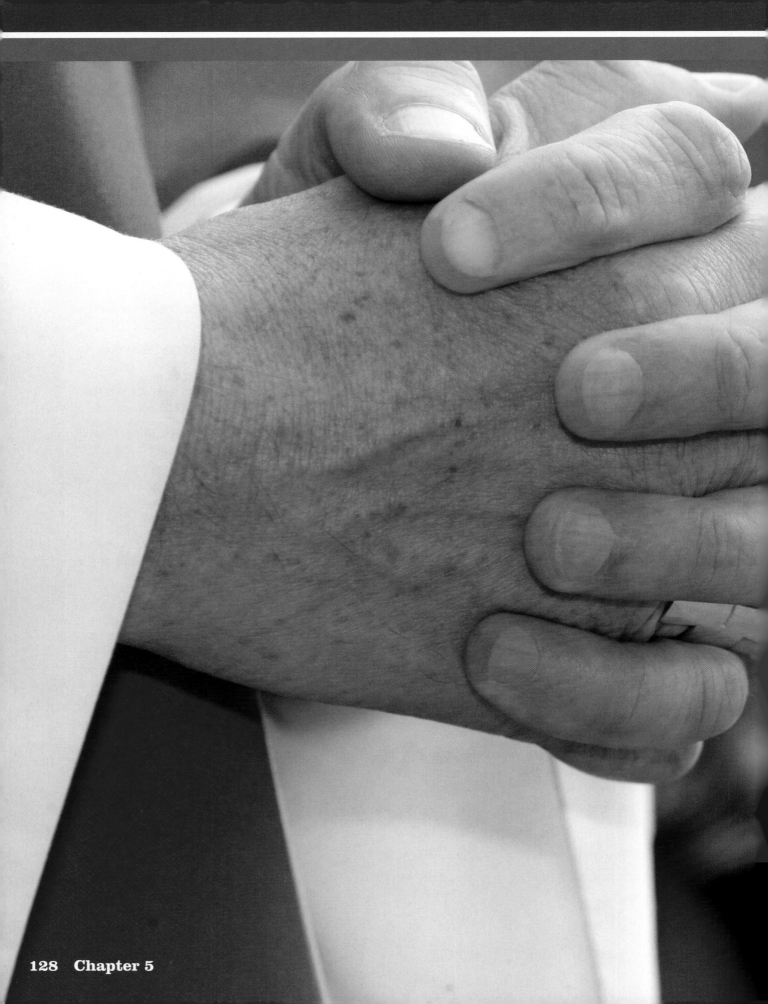

CALLED TO THE ORDAINED LIFE

CHAPTER 5

CHAPTER GOALS

In this chapter you will:

* consider the importance of service for of all baptized Catholics, in particular for those who receive the Sacraments at the Service of Communion.

* learn about the three degrees (or orders) of the Sacrament of Holy Orders.

* discover elements of the Rite of Ordination and investigate the practice of priesthood in the Catholic Church.

* consider the ministry of the bishop, and the line of apostolic succession.

* meet an ordained priest who is a member of a religious order and a missionary.

who Are you?

Complete the survey below

Mark each statement below on a scale of 1 (strongly disagree) to 5 (strongly agree).

I often participate in school-sponsored service projects.	1	2	3	4	5
I often volunteer to help at my parish.	1	2	3	4	5
Neighbors in need can count on me to help them.	1	2	3	4	5
I have refused money offered when I've helped out.	1	2	3	4	5
I feel people should pay me for things I do for them.	1	2	3	4	5
It feels good to help people in need.	1	2	3	4	5
I like helping "behind the scenes" (setting up, packing food boxes, cleaning up, etc.).	1	2	3	4	5
I like to give direct service to someone in need (serve food, child care, hospital work, etc.).	1	2	3	4	5
If someone isn't a "people person," there's not much service they can really give.	1	2	3	4	5
I've had some great experiences when I've given service as a volunteer.	1	2	3	4	5

Now spend some time thinking about these questions:

Do you think giving service should be part of a Christian's life? Is it part of yours now?

What kinds of service do your parents and other family members give? How have they influenced you?

To which kinds of service projects are you most attracted? Why do you think this is so?

Serving Others

There are many ways to serve others, and you might be surprised at how many people make a career out of doing so. Hundreds of thousands of men and women serve their country in the military service, as judges, in the diplomatic corp. Elected officials serve their constituents; customer service representatives and technicians serve their clients; waiters serve their customers; hotel staff serve their guests; governing boards of organizations serve their members. But serving others isn't limited to these roles. Many people see the work they do as a service to others. Doctors and nurses care for their patients; lawyers advocate for their clients; teachers educate their students; child care providers take care of children entrusted to them.

What do the people in all of these positions have in common? In many instances those serving focus on meeting the needs of those being served, in some fashion. In some cases those serving put the needs of others, their community, or their country before their own. For some, their service is a form of leadership.

The Catholic understanding of service encompasses all of these principles, but it has a specific starting and ending point: love, of God and of neighbor. We see serving and helping as a way of ministering to others, as a way of responding to God's love and offering it to others, as a way to help others in the everyday occurrence of our lives and in the significant events of the broader society. Jesus gives us a concrete example of how love, service, and giving of self are connected.

And during supper Jesus, knowing that the Father had given all things into his hands, and that he had come from God and was going to God, got up from the table, took off his outer robe, and tied a towel around himself. Then he poured water into a basin and began to wash the disciples' feet and to wipe them with the towel that was tied around him. . . .

After he had washed their feet, had put on his robe, and had returned to the table, he said to them, "Do you know what I have done to you? You call me Teacher and Lord—and you are right, for that is what I am. So if I, your Lord and Teacher, have washed your feet, you also ought to wash one another's feet. For I have set you an example, that you also should do as I have done to you."

✝ John 13:2-5, 12-16

Jesus gives his followers a concrete model for leadership: service motivated by love. Jesus shows us what love is really about by his relationship with his Father and by the way he interacts with others. In fact, he gives us his new commandment to love one another as he has loved, and that love is all about relationships. He loves us as his Father first loved him, and the Holy Spirit brings to life that love so that we can all share in it. Jesus' love is active, does not discriminate, is not concerned about societal expectations, does not limit itself to a select few. Jesus models unconditional love, which is divine love. The Father loves us so much that he gave us his own Son so that we might know that love; that is unconditional, completely giving love. We all long to experience unconditional love from parents, family members, and possibly a lifetime spouse, but the love of God is needed in those relationships so that we can hope to achieve unconditional love.

GROUP TALK

1. What does Jesus' action in the passage show us about the relationship between love and service?

2. How do you think relationships would change if more people really understood and practiced what Jesus meant by loving others?

3. Name three things that give you a glimpse into God's total and unselfish love.

We all Serve No matter what career you choose, no matter what state of life God calls you to, no matter what jobs you have now and in the future, love is a part of your life. And you are called to serve God in any life situation. How do you serve God? By working to build his kingdom on earth, spreading the message of his love, living based upon the values Jesus modeled, participating in the sacraments and the prayer life of the Church, joining the work of the Church in many ways. When you make just decisions, stand up for those who need a voice or whose voice is ignored, promote peace, and acknowledge God's priority and role in your life, you work to build up his kingdom. All of the baptized share this mission, but they live it out differently depending upon the state of life they are called to.

Among other things, your Baptism commits you to share your gifts and talents, your time and your energy with the Church and to benefit others. You can help people meet physical, spiritual, and emotional needs, serving those who are most in need, whether near or far. As we have discussed in previous chapters, all baptized people of any state in life share in the priesthood of Christ. Each of us ought to be able to identify how we are called to share in the common priesthood of the faithful in our particular circumstances. We are called to give of ourselves to God and others. In this chapter we will consider how the ministerial priesthood serves the common priesthood and how it is fundamentally and essentially different from the common priesthood by nature of the sacred power given in ordination. We will explore how the clergy—deacons, priests, and bishops in the ordained ministry—use their gifts and talents to respond to God's call to serve him and his People through teaching, divine worship, and pastoral governance.

FAITH ACTIVITY

A Royal Priesthood Read 1 Peter 2:9 and discuss what this verse says about the role of all Christians. Give examples of how all Christians can fulfill that role every day. Then name ways you think deacons, priests, and bishops fulfill that role.

> While the common priesthood of the faithful is exercised by the unfolding of baptismal grace—a life of faith, hope, and charity, a life according to the Spirit—, the ministerial priesthood is at the service of the common priesthood. It is directed at the unfolding of the baptismal grace of all Christians. The ministerial priesthood is a *means* by which Christ unceasingly builds up and leads his Church. For this reason it is transmitted by its own sacrament, the sacrament of Holy Orders.
>
> *Catechism of the Catholic Church,* 1547

> Deacons share in Christ's mission and grace in a special way.[1] The sacrament of Holy Orders marks them with an *imprint* ('character') which ...configures them to Christ, who made himself the 'deacon' or servant of all.[2]
>
> *Catechism of the Catholic Church,* 1570

The ordained minister is called to exercise his responsibility and authority as Christ did, out of love. Jesus told his disciples, "…but whoever wishes to become great among you must be your servant, and whoever wishes to be first among you must be slave of all. For the Son of Man came not to be served but to serve…" (*Mark 10:43–45*).

This is clear in passages like this one from Paul's Letter to the Philippians:

> *Let the same mind be in you that was in Christ Jesus,*
> *who, though he was in the form of God,*
> *did not regard equality with God*
> *as something to be exploited,*
> *but emptied himself,*
> *taking the form of a slave,*
> *being born in human likeness.*
> *And being found in human form,*
> *he humbled himself*
> *and became obedient to the*
> *point of death—*
> *even death on a cross.*

✝ Philippians 2:5-8

FAITH ACTIVITY

The Humility of Christ Find Philippians 2 in your Bible and read the verses 1–11 to learn more of what Paul says about Jesus. Spend some time quietly reflecting on these words. Write your own thoughts and questions to God in the form of a prayer, poem, or song.

Those in the ordained ministry are specifically devoted to loving, serving, and praying for others as Jesus did. Their ministry often makes them more aware than most people of real human conditions and needs. Their focus on and faith in Jesus' teaching helps them deal with social and global problems.

At the Service of Communion

You remember that the seven sacraments of the Catholic Church are divided into three groups.

- **The Sacraments of Initiation**—Baptism, Confirmation, and Eucharist—establish our relationship with the Father, Son, and Holy Spirit, call all of us to holiness, and consecrate us to be part of the Church's mission to evangelize the whole world.

- **The Sacraments of Healing**—Penance (or Reconciliation) and Anointing of the Sick. These sacraments continue Jesus' ongoing ministry of healing and salvation; they offer God's forgiveness and a way to experience and celebrate ongoing spiritual growth and conversion.

- **The Sacraments at the Service of Communion**—Holy Orders and Matrimony (Marriage). These sacraments are given to foster the good of others, and they focus on the salvation of others, and also enhance personal salvation through serving others. (See *Catechism*, 1533.)

Why are Holy Orders and Marriage linked? The *Catechism* explains that the other five sacraments are directed toward a person's personal salvation: one's own forgiveness of sins and restored friendship with God. Holy Orders and Marriage, however, "are directed towards the salvation of others" (*Catechism*, 1534). What does this mean? Those who receive these sacraments receive the grace to help others come to know, love, and serve God. The primary emphasis of their vocations is bringing others into relationship with God and encouraging their faith within God's family, whether in the home or in the local and universal Church. This doesn't happen in isolation, but by welcoming people into the life of the Church community and by nurturing the communion that exists among all those who are part of Christ's Body.

During the Sacrament of Holy Orders, deacons, priests, and bishops are consecrated "to nourish the Church with the word and grace of God in the name of Christ" (CCC, 1119)[3] This sacrament is given to promote and nurture the good of the spiritual family, the Church. And through the grace of the Sacrament of Matrimony, "Christian married couples help one another to attain holiness in their married life and in accepting and educating their children" (*Dogmatic Constitution on the Church*, 11). This sacrament is given to promote and nurture the good of the human family.

GROUP TALK

Discuss in small groups:

- What are some ways that ordained ministers and married couples encourage and form other persons' relationships with God?
- How do ordained ministers and married couples foster the good of the family, human and spiritual?

✔ Quick Check

1. What did Jesus teach us—by word and example—about service?

2. Who are the clergy?

3. What is the difference between the common priesthood and the ministerial priesthood?

4. What does the Church mean by Sacraments at the Service of Communion?

One Sacrament, Three Degrees

You've noticed the use of the word *orders* when reading about this sacrament. Because of our modern use of that word, many people think that Holy Orders are religious "commands" that some men follow. The word *orders* actually comes from the Latin word *ordo*, which means "an established governing body."

In the Church there are three established governing bodies, or orders, into which men can be integrated. Through **ordination**, a baptized man receives special grace that will enable him to carry out the duties and responsibilities of his state in life. The sacred powers that he receives come from Christ through the Church. Through the consecration he receives at Ordination, the ordained man is set apart and invested with the authority that comes with his office.

There are three degrees in the Sacrament of Holy Orders—**bishops**, **presbyters** (priests), and **deacons**. Like Baptism and Confirmation, Holy Orders confers an imprint, or "character," on the ordained minister, which configures him to Christ:

- the *deacon* to Christ who made himself the servant of all

- the *priest* to Christ the high priest

- the *bishop* to Christ who calls him as a successor of the Apostles

These three degrees (or orders) of the Sacrament of Holy Orders are part of the Church's organic structure and are irreplaceable. Without them, we cannot speak of the Church.

GROUP TALK

Discuss in small groups the following questions:

- Why do you think the *Catechism* quotes Saint Ignatius of Antioch who says that we cannot speak of the Church without bishops, priests, and deacons? (See *Catechism*, 1554.)

- What would be missing without each of these three orders?

Overview of Ministries

The Order of Bishop: Pontiff and Pastor The **episcopacy**, or Order of Bishop, is the highest degree of Holy Orders—a degree not reached by most men ordained to the priesthood. When a man is ordained a bishop, he receives *"the fullness of the sacrament of Holy Orders"* (*Catechism*, 1557). The bishops are in a direct, unbroken line from the Apostles who received their mission from Jesus, as well as the power to act in his person.

The Pope selects and names certain priests to become bishops. The Pope is the bishop of Rome. He, too, has reached the same Third Degree of Holy Orders that all bishops reach. Additional honorary titles such as "archbishop," or "cardinal," give a bishop more responsibility and more honor, but in terms of sacraments, these titles do not add anything to the position bestowed on a bishop by his ordination. A cardinal is a bishop who is a special advisor to the Pope, can vote in the election of a new Pope, and sometimes is in charge of a larger archdiocese. An auxiliary bishop is assigned to assist the archbishop or bishop who is responsible for an archdiocese or diocese.

Each degree of Holy Orders is conferred by the imposition of the hands of a bishop onto the men receiving the sacrament and through the prayer of consecration. It is significant that in order to be ordained a bishop, a priest needs to be appointed by the Pope. In addition, from the earliest of years of the Church, at least two other bishops must accompany the principal ordaining bishop in ordaining a new bishop. When a man is ordained bishop, he joins the **College of Bishops**, that is, the community of all those who are bishops. College is from the Latin word *collegium*, which means "a collection or society." He is called to be in cooperation with the Pope other dioceses in the Church, as well as to guide his own diocese and community.

We will return to examine the bishop's apostolic role more closely later in this chapter.

The Order of Presbyter: Coworker of the Bishop Priests form around their bishop a presbyterium— "an intimate sacramental brotherhood" (*The Decree on Priestly Ministry and Life*, 8).—that helps him serve and govern the local Church, or diocese. Each presbyter, what we also call priest, receives from the bishop the charge of a parish community or is appointed to a special ministry to serve God's People, for example, a teacher, canon lawyer, diocesan official.

The priesthood is a way that a baptized man can respond to God's call to grow in holiness, to become more like him, and to love and serve him. If a man feels drawn to this ministry and feels God is calling him to this life, what are the first steps he would take? He would follow the discernment process we talked about earlier in this book—explore opportunities; seek direction; ask advice; pray for guidance; and assess needs, abilities, gifts, experiences, and relationships. Many parishes, most dioceses, and several national organizations have vocation outreach programs and initiatives to help males of a discerning age determine if God is calling them to the unique, special service of ordained ministry.

Candidates for ordination undergo extensive formation, which will be considered later in the section. However, some fundamental requirements exist to help potential candidates for priesthood and those who will evaluate them determine if the priesthood is the right place for them.

> "...those...have integral faith, are moved by the right intention, have the requisite knowledge, possess a good reputation, and are endowed with integral morals and proven virtues and the other physical and psychic qualities in keeping with the order to be received."
>
> *Code of Canon Law, Can. 1029*

In the Person of Christ and the Name of the Church In some ways the role of the priests, as that of all ordained ministers, comes down to one essential truth: they are Christ to us in a unique, special, and much needed way, and Jesus wanted this to be the case. Jesus wanted his followers in all times and places to be able to experience his welcoming, nurturing, healing, forgiving, life-giving presence. Jesus desired that any person open to his teachings and his way of life would have to be a teacher, leader, and example of service. We know from the Gospels and other New Testament books that Jesus chose his Apostles, the predecessors of our bishops, to make all of this possible. In turn, through history, the bishops appointed priests to help most especially in this sacramental role and appointed deacons to help in the ministry of service.

While the history is far more detailed than this, the bottom line is that ordained ministers represent Christ to us based upon their consecration in the Sacrament of Holy Orders. Their share in the ministerial priesthood—Christ's priesthood—unites priests and bishops to Christ in a special way, and Christ shares his authority and sacred powers to guide and build up his Church. They are "to serve in the name and in the person of Christ the Head in the midst of the community" (*Catechism*, 1591). They accomplish this by the Holy Spirit acting in and through their lives. So Christ is with us always as he promised, and he continues to teach, lead, and shepherd us, his flock, and be present as the head of the Church, which is his Body.

Notice that the *Catechism* stresses that the ordained man serves "in the midst of the community."

- How is that different from serving apart from the community?
- What does it say about community recognition of a man's vocation?
- What does it say about the need to be part of a community?

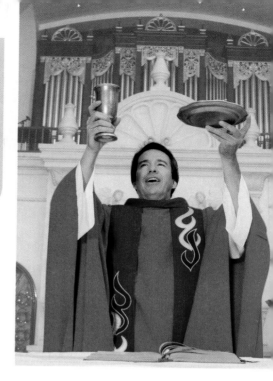

By virtue of their ministerial priesthood, bishops and priests represent Christ to the whole Church. They also act in the name of the whole Church when presenting to God the Church's prayers and when celebrating the Eucharist. This does not mean that ordained ministers are mere delegates of the Church community. They act in the person of Christ, as servant leaders of the Christian community. The Church's prayers and offerings are inseparable from the prayers and offerings of Christ. That's why during the Mass, at the end of the Eucharistic Prayer, the priest prays: "Through him, and with him, and in him, O God, almighty Father, in the unity of the Holy Spirit . . ." (*The Roman Missal*)

The priest, then, stands in a unique position. He acts in the person of Christ, representing him to the assembly of faithful members gathered to pray. He also acts in the name of the whole Christian community when presenting their prayers to God. In the words of the *Catechism* "It is because the ministerial priesthood represents Christ that it can represent the Church" (*Catechism*, 1553).

The Diaconate: To Be the Servant Christ Deacons have been a part of our Churches since coming onto the scene in the early part of the Acts of the Apostles. The Apostles needed help meeting the material needs of the new community so that they could better concentrate on spiritual needs. Seven men were chosen from among those in the community to help with distribution of food and other material needs. (See *Acts 6:1–6*.)

The word *deacon* means, "servant." The deacon's ministry is symbolized by Christ's washing the feet of his Apostles. Deacons participate in Jesus' work and grace in a special way. They model their ministry after Christ, who was a servant to all. They are ordained to assist the bishop in his works of service. They accomplish this in numerous ways, focusing their work on the needs of the community. They are ordained not to the ministerial priesthood but to the ministry to do works of service for the Church.

The grace of the sacrament of Holy Orders strengthens the deacon to serve God's people through the ministries of the word of God, of the liturgy, and of charity and justice. The deacon is called to be an evangelist and teacher, a sanctifier, and a witness and guide. And their service is a sign of their faithfulness to God and love for others. (See *The National Directory for the Formation, Ministry, and Life of Permanent Deacons in the United States*, Chapter One.)

And the amazing thing about deacons is that they live out these roles in every day life, among their families and friends, in the work place, and within the parish community, helping us to respond to God's call to conversion and holiness. By giving witness to the Gospel message in their own lives, deacons empower others to be led by Christian values. You can see the vital and important role deacons have in the faith life of all of us in the Church.

A very apt description of the role of the deacon comes from the Rite of Ordination when the bishop presents the newly ordained deacon with the Book of Gospels, saying,

> Receive the Gospel of Christ, whose herald you
>   have become.
> Believe what you read,
> teach what you believe,
> and practice what you teach.

Ordination of Deacons, #210

Quick Check

Review Questions

1. What are the three degrees (or orders) of the Sacrament of Holy Orders?

2. What is the College of Bishops and how is it symbolized at the ordination of a bishop?

3. What is a presbyter and what does he do in the Church?

4. What are the three main areas of service that deacons undertake?

Deacons assist the bishop and priests in the celebration of the Eucharist and the distribution of Holy Communion. They also bless marriages, proclaim the Gospel, preach, baptize, preside over funerals, and engage in various ministries of pastoral governance and of charity. There are two types of deacons: **permanent deacons** and **transitional deacons**. Since Vatican Council II, the Latin (Roman Catholic) Church has returned to her earlier practices of having permanent deacons. Single and married men are both called to this important ministry in the Church to serve in various roles in the diocese.

Some individuals are called to be married, pursue a job or profession, and serve the Church as an ordained minister. As a permanent deacon, these men can do that. Some permanent deacons serve the Church full time as their profession.

The term transitional deacon refers to the role served by those preparing for the priesthood. About a year before ordination to the priesthood, a man is ordained a deacon. A man selected to serve in a diocese ordinarily is ordained a deacon by the bishop of that diocese. After that, he begins to exercise his diaconate until he is ordained a priest.

GROUP TALK

1. What rewards and challenges do you think would be involved in
   - being a permanent deacon
   - being married to a permanent deacon
   - being the son or daughter of a permanent deacon?

2. Do you know a person who would make a good permanent deacon? What is the person like?

3. What qualities do you think are most important for the ministry of the permanent deacon today?

4. Is this something you might be called to do? How would you respond if your future spouse were called to this way of life?

The Road to Priesthood: Seminary Training

There are several stages of preparation for priesthood; it doesn't begin in the seminary. It begins with a calling from Christ. The first point of contact for a man who thinks he might want to be a priest is often another priest, such as a parish priest, the pastor, or a friend. Otherwise, he may visit the vocation office of his diocese. Most dioceses have retreats, social events, or summer programs to meet prospective seminarians, pray with them, and help them discern whether they are called to be priests.

After this time of getting acquainted, men who decide they want to pursue seminary studies, and whom the diocese decides are good candidates, go to a seminary that is approved by the diocese.

There are 229 seminaries in the United States. Seminaries are not all alike, and they are not all for every potential priest. Much depends on a man's age and level of education. Each diocese has a list of college and major seminaries that it helps to sponsor. The diocese generally chooses which seminary it will send a man to, if it chooses to sponsor him.

GROUP TALK

Discuss these questions with a few classmates:

- Why do you think it's important that a man go to a seminary approved by his diocese?
- Do you know someone who God might be calling to be a priest?
- What would you ask someone thinking about being a priest?

General Information about Seminaries		
College Seminary	**Major Seminary**	**Late-Vocation Seminary**
For: Recent high school graduates or college graduates who need more hours of philosophy	**For:** Men with college degrees and enough hours of philosophy	**For:** Older men coming to priesthood after lifelong careers in other fields
Studies: All undergraduate coursework leading to a Bachelor's degree in philosophy or liberal arts. Classes about priesthood, Scripture, and Church Doctrine	**Studies:** Graduate studies leading to a Master's degree in Theology (MA or MDiv); Specific training in celebration of Mass and the sacraments and pastoral guidance	**Studies:** Philosophy and theology courses based on past education; Specific training in celebration of Mass, the sacraments, and preaching
Location: Frequently near the campus of a college or university where seminarians take regular classes	**Location:** Usually a separate, somewhat secluded campus so students can more easily reflect and pray	**Location:** Usually a separate, somewhat secluded campus so students can more easily reflect and pray
Other activities: Daily Mass and prayer; Spiritual direction; Sports and other campus activities; Regular campus social life, some include co-ed activities, but no dating	**Other activities:** Daily Mass and prayer; Spiritual direction; Ministry experiences—teaching, social work, hospital work, special ministries; Assignments to diocesan parishes for various experiences	**Other activities:** Daily Mass and prayer; Spiritual direction; Ministry experiences—teaching, social work, hospital work, special ministries; Assignments to diocesan parishes for various ministry experiences

Living Out the Sacrament

Ordination is a big event for everyone in a diocese. Many Catholics attend an ordination, for it is a special time. During this celebration, God gifts the whole Church with new ministers. Most dioceses celebrate ordinations at the cathedral on a Saturday or Sunday.

There is one essential rite of the Sacrament of Holy Orders for all three degrees—the laying on of hands by the bishop and the solemn prayer of consecration. Surrounding that rite are other beautiful prayers and rituals.

Differences in the Ordination of the Three Orders					
Who is being ordained?	**Who is conferring the sacrament?**	**Is there an anointing?**	**Vestments given?**	**Other items given?**	**Configured to:**
Deacon	Generally, the bishop of the new deacon's diocese	No	Yes, stole (worn over only one shoulder) and dalmatic (outer vestment)	The Book of the Gospels	Christ the servant
Priest	The bishop of the new priest's diocese	Yes, hands anointed with the oil of chrism	Yes, stole (worn over both shoulders) and chasuble (outer vestment)	Chalice and paten (cup and plate used at Mass)	Christ the high priest
Bishop	The principal bishop accompanied by at least two other bishops	Yes, head anointed with the oil of chrism	Yes, miter (ceremonial hat) and crosier (shepherd's staff)	Also given: the Book of the Gospels, ring, and pectoral cross	Christ, as a successor of the Apostles

The Sacrament of Holy Orders shows us a lot about the role and mission of the ordained ministers.

Only a bishop can validly ordain baptized men, and—in keeping with Christ's selecting only men as Apostles and the Church's continued practice of following this divine constitution of the Church—only baptized men can be ordained. There are other forms of ministry that can be exercised without ordination by a bishop. For a priest to be able to preside licitly and publicly at the Eucharist, he must be ordained by a bishop and receive faculties to do so in the diocese where he serves. Priests also have the power to absolve a person of sin in the name of Christ, but only after they have received that faculty from the bishop, religious superior, or the Pope.

FAITH ACTIVITY

Symbols of Orders Based upon what you've learned about the role of deacons, priests, and bishops, create a mural that reflects their various ministries. You might want to use some of the signs and symbols from the Rite of Ordination as a starting point. Consider how these symbols speak about the meaning of ordination.

Working with a parish, which is a part of a bishop's diocese, the priest represents his bishop and takes upon himself some of the bishop's duties for the local parish. Priests can only serve in a diocese with the approval of the bishop and in union with him. When diocesan priests are ordained they promise obedience to the bishop and they renew that promise each year on Holy Thursday. This is not the same vow that consecrated religious take; we will explain the difference between diocesan and religious order priests below.

GROUP TALK

Discuss with a small group:

- What are some of the things that your parish priests do?
- How do the people of your parish collaborate with the priests ministering there?
- What are some things you can do to assist your parish priest in serving the community?

To Serve God's Holy People

As the Rite of Ordination indicates, bishops and priests have a significant responsibility for building up God's Kingdom through their celebration of the sacraments. It is through the sacraments that all baptized Catholics, regardless of their state in life, meet Christ and receive his grace. The sacraments make it possible, they share God's life with us and lead us on the path to happiness and fulfillment. Priests and bishops celebrate the Eucharist to feed our souls, to unite us with Christ, and to forgive our venial sins. They lead us in the Sacrament of Penance and Reconciliation and absolve us of our sins. They serve God's people in other non-sacramental ways to help the community respond to God's call.

The power to consecrate bread and wine, changing it into the Body and Blood of Christ is a unique and important aspect of the priesthood. Christ told his Apostles to take and eat the bread and drink the wine; he also told them to continue to do it in memory of him. Christ gave the power to forgive sins to his Apostles, and it remains in the Church through bishops and priests who preside in the Sacrament of Penance and Reconciliation with the community. Through the ministry of the bishops, and the shared work of their priests, Christ and his sacrifice continue to be present to us. In this way Christ's followers are strengthened to be nurturing, healing, and forgiving people who bring to life his message.

However, priests are human men subject to the human condition of sinfulness just like all human beings. The very fact that priests are humans who are tempted and face many of the same challenges we do is another proof of the power of Christ's Spirit, who works through priests to bring Christ to the world even when they are struggling to cooperate with the grace in their own lives.

At times of great darkness and division in the Church, there are also opportunities for conversion and new dedication. The *Catechism* quotes Saint Gregory of Nazianzus, a doctor of the Church during the fourth century, writing to his brother priests: "We must begin by purifying ourselves before purifying others [St. Gregory of Nazianzus, *Oratio* 2, 71, 74, 73: PG 35, 480–481]" (*Catechism*, 1589). Through everything, the Church has continued, not only to survive, but to grow, to produce holy saints, and to bring the Gospel to more and more places and people in the world.

Celibacy For the first thousand years of the Church's history, there were some priests, bishops, and even popes were married. Gradually, celibacy began to be more widely practiced until it was enforced as a requirement for ordination in the Western Church and remains so today. (See Second Lateran Council, 1139 and the Council of Trent, 1545–1563)

As part of being configured to Christ who himself was chaste and celibate, priests in the Roman Catholic Church typically are not permitted to be married. There is an exception to the celibacy rule in the Western Church. If married Protestant clergy become Catholic they may feel God is calling them to serve as priests in the Catholic Church. If Holy Orders is a possibility for them and they are ordained after a careful discernment and a thorough evaluation process, they can remain married. Though they may not remarry if they are widowed. If a single Protestant minister is received into the Catholic Church and becomes a priest, he may not marry after he is ordained.

Permanent deacons can be chosen from among single or married men. Hence there are ordained deacons who have also received the Sacrament of Matrimony. However, if an unmarried man is ordained a deacon, he cannot marry after his ordination; and if a married deacon is widowed, he is not permitted to remarry.

In the Eastern Catholic Church, while celibacy is held in high esteem, and many ordained men choose to be celibate, married men can be ordained as deacons or priests. Bishops can only be chosen from among celibate men, however; and once a man is ordained he is not permitted to marry.

Priests understand that they are to be celibate "for the sake of the kingdom." Celibacy allows them to serve God with an undivided heart and to focus on the needs of God's people. By joyfully accepting celibacy, "They give, moreover, a living sign of the world to come, by a faith and charity already made present, in which the children of the resurrection neither marry nor take wives."[4]

▲ A Catholic priest serving as a military chaplain to soldiers.

Everyday Mission of a Priest

In large and small parishes, in cities, suburbs, or rural areas, priests are called on to minister to people in a variety of ways. Because there is a shortage of priests, many of them are overworked—sometimes in charge of two or three small parishes, or alone in a large parish that formerly had two priests. Their duties can be as varied as counseling married couples, running a soup kitchen, piloting a plane, teaching school, or serving as chaplain in an emergency room. They collaborate with parishioners, working with parish councils to coordinate the functioning of the parish and to make sure the parish ministries are as effective and inspiring as possible. There is also much paperwork associated with working in a parish, and quite a few bills to pay. While the tasks that make up a priest's "job" vary greatly, priests are grounded by the constant and consistent spiritual dimensions of their lives, especially in their primary task of celebrating Mass. All priests pray the Divine Office every day along with other prayers, devotions, reading of Scripture, and meditation. The commitment to spiritual growth helps them maintain their relationship with Christ and overcome the challenges and struggles they face.

Diocesan priests get a salary for their work in the diocese. A priest may not be rich in money, but is always rich in the love of God, good friendships, and the satisfaction that comes from helping people, presiding at the sacraments, and working for God and the Church.

GROUP TALK

1 What advice would you give to priests today about the best way to reach out to families?

2 What advice would you give to priests today about welcoming and including young adults in parish life?

3 What kinds of advice would you give a friend who feels called to the priesthood?

Diocesan Priests and Religious Order Priests In Chapter Four we read about religious orders that include priests among their members. Men who have a vocation to be a member of a religious order might be called to be brothers or priests. When a man joins a religious order, he usually professes his vows of poverty, chastity, and obedience in his order before he is ordained. He lives community life with other vowed priests and brothers. Because of his vow of poverty, he owns nothing of his own, but shares everything in common with everyone in his religious community. He often wears a distinctive habit or pin that identifies him as a member of the order.

A male religious' ordination might be conferred by the bishop of the diocese where he lives, by a religious order bishop or, who is a bishop, by an **abbot** if his religious superior is an abbot. A priest who is a member of a religious order must be faithful to the bishop of the diocese where he ministers in matters that pertain to teaching faith and morals and observing liturgical directives, but his first fidelity is to the superior of his religious order to whom he has made a vow of obedience. He is assigned priestly work by that superior which is then approved by the bishop of the diocese where he will be working.

Diocesan priests are not members of religious orders. At their ordination they promise to be obedient to their bishop and to remain celibate. They do not take a vow of poverty and are permitted to own their own property, although they are encouraged to live simple lives. They do not wear a religious habit, but most wear a black suit or a cassock (robe) with a Roman collar to identify them as priests.

The Society of Jesus

If you know a priest or a religious brother who writes the letters "S.J." after his name, he is a member of the Society of Jesus, commonly called the Jesuits. The Jesuit Order is one of the largest religious orders in the world. From its headquarters in Rome, the Jesuit Order fans out to 112 countries on six continents. There are over 20,000 members in the Society of Jesus.

Currently the Jesuits are divided into ninety-three provinces throughout the world. Of these, at present ten are in the United States. Each province has many communities within a defined geographic region, headed by a Provincial Superior. All provinces are connected to and obedient to the Father General and his Council in Rome.

It takes many years to reach final vows as a Jesuit, whether as a priest or as a religious brother. The first two years of every Jesuit's training are his novitiate training. The unique part of Jesuit formation is the thirty-day retreat during which each novice makes the Spiritual Exercises of Saint Ignatius, a step-by-step process of prayer and meditation that draws a person closer to Christ. This important religious experience is a central event in each Jesuit's early training that he will take with him into the future. He will have the opportunity to make the Spiritual Exercises again during another thirty-day retreat before he makes his final vows, many years later.

Saint Ignatius of Loyola, who developed the Spiritual Exercises, was the founder of the Society of Jesus. Born in 1491 in Spain, he was a nobleman and soldier who experienced a profound conversion while he was recovering from a battle wound in 1521. He came to see God in all things and to have a burning desire to do everything for the honor and glory of God. Over the next years he gave up his nobleman's life and sought to learn what God wanted him to do. He eventually gathered a community of fellow graduate students around him for prayer and to do the Spiritual Exercises he was developing. These men made vows together in 1534, and in 1540 the Society of Jesus was officially founded and approved by Pope Paul III.

The Jesuit Order has been present and influential in many events throughout history, and its members continue to be active today. Jesuits were missionaries in the New World when it was first being explored. They were on expeditions on the Mississippi River and in Indian missions in Canada and the northern United States. Jesuits maintain twenty-nine colleges or universities in the United States today and fifty high schools. Jesuit priests are parish pastors, university professors, doctors, lawyers, journalists, spiritual directors, and foreign missionaries, to name just a few of their careers. All are called by God and to the Jesuit Order. Jesuits live together in communities where they share their ministries and material possessions.

▲ Detail from *The Vision of St. Ignatius of Loyola* by Peter Paul Rubens

GO online You can find information on the Jesuits' international and U.S. websites at www.osvcurriculum.com.

FAITH ACTIVITY

Changed Perceptions Spend some time in quiet reflection on what your view of being a priest is and how that view has changed since starting this course. Record your thoughts in your notebook.

The Bishops in Union with the Pope

Today's bishops are the successors of the Apostles. But what does that actually mean?

While Jesus was with them on earth, he prepared the Apostles to lead the Church after he ascended into heaven.

- He gave them authority to cast out unclean spirits and to heal the sick.

- He sent them out two by two to preach and heal.

- On the night before he died, Jesus gave his Apostles his Body and Blood and the power to "do this in memory" of him, and thereby make him present once again, changing bread and wine into his Body and Blood.

- When the risen Christ came to the Apostles in the upper room, Jesus said "Receive the Holy Spirit. If you forgive the sins of any, they are forgiven them; if you retain the sins of any, they are retained" (*John 20:23*).

- He directed Peter, as the first bishop and pope, to lead his sheep. This began the succession of Apostles in the episcopacy and lent great stability to the early Church.

- As he prepared to ascend into heaven, he gave them the mandate to "Go therefore and make disciples of all nations" (*Matthew 28:19*).

- On Pentecost Sunday, he sent his Holy Spirit to empower them.

FAITH ACTIVITY

Research Pope Benedict XVI What do you know about our present pope? Look up information about his personal history and his election. What is his motto? Has he written any encyclicals or apostolic letters yet? Find some quotations from recent speeches he's given. How is he using his power to care for souls? If you could write a letter to him or have a talk with him, what would you say?

▼ Pope Benedict XVI delivers his speech during the opening session of the Synod of the Bishops

The Church was born on Pentecost Sunday; but unless the Apostles found successors for themselves, the Church would die when they did. It was clear from everything Jesus did and said that the Church was meant to live on into the future; so the Apostles not only baptized new members for the Church, but identified and raised up new leaders just as Jesus had done. **Apostolic succession** is guided by the Holy Spirit. This assures us that today's bishops are successors of the Apostles in a direct, unbroken line.

Pope, Successor of Peter When Jesus asked his disciples who he was, he received various answers. Finally, Peter said, "You are the Messiah, the Son of the living God" (*Matthew 16:16*). Afterwards, Jesus said, "I will give you the keys of the kingdom of heaven, and whatever you bind on earth will be bound in heaven, and whatever you loose on earth will be loosed in heaven" (*Matthew 16:19*).

In that story we also hear Jesus say, "And I tell you, you are Peter, and on this rock I will build my church, and the gates of Hades will not prevail against it" (*Matthew 16:18*). These words indicate that Jesus intended Peter to be the visible foundation of the Church, the keeper of the keys of the Kingdom of Heaven.

Peter was first among the Apostles. Later he was the Bishop of Rome. The Pope, his successor and the bishop of the Church of Rome, is the head of the college of bishops today. We also call the Pope the Vicar (agent) of Christ and, as we saw earlier in this chapter, the universal Pastor of the Church on earth. The Dogmatic Constitution on the Church from the Second Vatican Council states that the Pope enjoys, by divine institution, "supreme, full, immediate, and universal power in the care of souls [CD 2]" (*Catechism*, 937).

The College of Bishops As we read earlier, ordination as a bishop makes a man a member of the episcopal college, or College of Bishops. He is the visible head of the diocese entrusted to him, and with the other bishops around the world he shares in the apostolic mission of the whole Church—not just his particular Church, his diocese—under the authority of Peter's successor, the Pope.

When working with the Pope, the College of Bishops has full authority over the whole Church. The College of Bishops from all over the world working with the Pope is a sign of the unity of the Church, as well as its diversity and universality.

The Local Ordinary:
Teacher and Pastor

The local ordinary is the residential bishop who has immediate responsibility for and jurisdiction over his own particular Church (diocese). In that Church he is the "visible source and foundation of unity" (*Catechism*, 938). In each diocese, with the help of the priests and deacons—and when present, the auxiliary bishops—the bishop has the responsibility to:

- authentically teach the faith

- celebrate divine worship, especially the Eucharist

- oversee the spiritual ministry of all Catholic parishes, schools, or other ministries in the diocese of the bishop.

- guide his Church as a true pastor

- work with the diocese's presbyterium, religious communities, and laity

The Second Vatican Council Decree on Bishops in the church states: "Bishops, therefore, have been made true and authentic teachers of the faith, pontiffs, and pastors through the Holy Spirit, who has been given to them."[5]

You may have read or heard the Pope is called "pontiff," but his title is rightfully "the Supreme Pontiff." The word **pontiff** literally means "a bridge maker." The Church uses the word for all bishops, who act as a "bridge" between God and the Body of Christ, the Church.

The word **pastor** refers to a bishop's role as the shepherd of his people. From early Christianity, Jesus was regarded as a pastor. This flows from his own calling of himself, the "good shepherd," the one who "lays down his life for the sheep" (*John 10:11*). There can be no mistaking the connection of the title of pastor to the words Jesus spoke to Peter and the other Apostles on the seashore after he was raised from the dead. On the shore, Jesus asked Peter:

"Simon son of John, do you love me more than these?" He said to him, "Yes, Lord; you know that I love you." Jesus said to him, "Feed my lambs." A second time he said to him, "Simon son of John, do you love me?" He said to him, "Yes, Lord; you know that I love you." Jesus said to him, "Tend my sheep." He said to him the third time, "Simon son of John, do you love me?" Peter felt hurt because he said to him the third time, "Do you love me?" And he said to him, "Lord, you know everything; you know that I love you." Jesus said to him, "Feed my sheep."

✝ John 21:15-19

Bishops as God's Stewards In his letter to Titus, Saint Paul called the bishop "God's steward," for he is responsible for God's people. Paul then gave Titus a list of the qualities a bishop needs: He must be blameless, not arrogant or quick-tempered, not addicted to wine, not violent, and not greedy for gain. He must be hospitable, love goodness, be prudent, upright, devout, and self-controlled. He must have a firm grasp of the word of God in accordance with the teachings of the Church, and must be able to preach with sound doctrine and to argue effectively anyone who refutes God's word. (See *Titus 1:7–9*)

A steward is a servant who cares for someone else's property or household. We are all called, for example, to be good stewards of the earth, for it doesn't belong to us; it is a gift from God. Humankind has been given dominion over the earth. Christians in particular are called to be stewards for the glory of God and the building up of his Church. Thus, God has led specific ministries to be formed within the Church to help the faithful exercise good stewardship over his creation.

✔ Quick Check

1. What is apostolic succession?

2. What is the role of the Pope?

3. What is a local ordinary called to do for his diocese?

4. How are bishops God's stewards?

GROUP TALK

Discuss with two or three other students:

- Which two qualities on this list do you think are most needed by a bishop today? Why?

- From research on your bishop, which qualities, most especially, do you find in his life and ministry?

- Who else might benefit from living by this list of virtues?

Serra International

For people interested in learning more about ordained or religious life, and parishes interested in promoting these vocations, the organization Serra International can help. Serra International is one of a handful of prominent lay Catholic groups dedicated to increasing vocations to the ministerial priesthood, vowed religious life, and encouraging all people to live out the universal call to holiness. Members focus on priorities such as spiritual growth, education in Christian principles, service projects, and social activities.

Named after Junípero Serra—the eighteenth-century Spanish missionary to North American Indians in California—Serra International was founded in 1934, in Seattle, Washington, by four men meeting informally over lunch. It now has over 19,000 Serrans in 800 clubs in 36 countries worldwide, including over 12,000 men and women in 332 clubs within the United States alone. Its purpose is to invite all Catholic men and women to follow their baptismal call, promote, encourage, and affirm specific religious callings, and to inspire leaders at all levels of its organization through spiritual and practical faith formation.

Pope John Paul II wrote that the fostering of vocations must be fully incorporated into the life and work of the community. The Holy Father also wrote of the Church's "lay vocation arm," and recognized the Serra Club for this purpose. He even granted them their own day during the Great Jubilee of 2000, and granted them a private audience in December of that year.

Serra activities are numerous and quite varied. One program, Called by Name, involves personal invitations from bishops to consider a Church vocation. Another, the Travel Chalice, is where a chalice goes from home to home within a parish as a reminder for families to pray for Church vocations. Through prayer and through works—such as sending them greeting cards on their birthdays, and on anniversaries of ordination and vows—Serra supports those who have answered their vocational call.

Joining Serra is one way to respond to the universal call to holiness. The Eucharist is key and essential element to growing closer to Christ and becoming more like him. Priests are needed for the Sacrament of Eucharist. So, Serra members work and pray for "the Lord of the harvest to send out laborers into his harvest" (*Matthew 9:38*).

For more information on Serra, visit www.osvcurriculum.com. **GO online**

a Missionary Priest

Meet Father Ignatius Saverimuttu, SSS. The three S's stand for three Latin words that translate to "Congregation of the Blessed Sacrament," an international order with headquarters in Rome and provinces and communities all over the world. Father Ignatius, a short, dark-skinned, sixty-two-year-old man with a wide smile, hails from Sri Lanka. But he's currently serving for two years as a hospital chaplain in New York City, living at St. Jean Baptiste Parish, which has been served by the Blessed Sacrament Fathers since 1900. We caught up with him at the parish rectory.

INTERVIEWER: As an American Catholic this seems sort of backwards to me. You're a native of Sri Lanka and were ordained a priest there, and now you're a missionary in the United States.

FATHER IGNATIUS: (laughing): Yes, Sri Lanka is a mission country–seventy-percent of the population is Buddhist. But the world has changed! Really, isn't every country in some way a mission country?

I: Is that how you became a priest, through the work of missionaries in Sri Lanka?

FR. IG.: Oh, no! I was born to Catholic parents in a village that was mostly Catholic. Native Sri Lankan priests served our parish. However, the bishop of our Sri Lankan diocese was an American from New Orleans. When he met me in our village at my Confirmation, he asked if I was interested in becoming a priest. I was fourteen years old and he invited me to the diocesan seminary and made arrangements so I could go.

I: But that was a diocesan seminary. How did you end up in the Blessed Sacrament Order?

FR. IG.: My path to the priesthood had many twists and turns. I went through the diocesan seminary, but I had not had much schooling in our village and knew very little English. I failed my final exams and could not graduate. I studied some more, but failed again. Though everyone was encouraging me to study even more, I didn't want to! I went home to live with my mother.

I: And she sent you off to join the Blessed Sacrament Fathers?

FR. IG.: No, not at all. She encouraged me to think about getting married as my brother had done. While I lived with her, I built her a house, so she was very happy with that. I went to Mass and prayed the Rosary with her every day. I worked for the parish in my village as a trained catechist for seven years. All that time, she hoped I might marry, but I knew God had something different in mind for me. I just didn't know what. Then I went to study catechesis in India for two years. It was there I met the Blessed Sacrament Order and was invited to consider joining them as a religious brother. I joined the community in Sri Lanka so I could be close to my family. I was very happy as a brother in the order for fifteen years. I became a superior of a house of priests and brothers and worked in the formation program. By then my English had gotten quite good, and I was no longer afraid I'd fail any courses, so my superiors encouraged me to study for the priesthood along with the young men in our community. I was forty-seven years old when I was ordained in 1991!

By then my brother had died at a young age, leaving five children. My mother lived to see me ordained and living a happy life as a priest before she died a few years ago. I've also been able to help my nieces and nephews materially and spiritually. I presided at the marriage ceremonies for the three that are married. My niece has told me she is postponing her wedding until I get back home to Sri Lanka.

I: When will that be? Do you plan to be in New York a long time? How did you end up here anyway?

FR. IG: Last year I came to the States for three months to do mission appeals in parishes in the South and the Midwest. Not to brag, but I did very, very well, and I think people really liked meeting me and hearing me preach. After I returned to Sri Lanka, thinking I'd be there forever, my superiors asked me to serve for two years here in New York City so that another community member from Sri Lanka wouldn't feel so alone while he is studying here. We have a nice community here. There are ten Blessed Sacrament religious here–five of us are priests, and there are three brothers and two novices. I am very happy to be here.

who will you become?

Consider your call
to service.

Will volunteerism and service be part of your life in the future? Review your answers to the survey at the beginning of this chapter. How has learning about Jesus' model of love and service influenced your attitudes toward serving others?

How has learning about the ordained life changed your attitude?

Many high schools require students to complete one or more service projects before they can graduate. If your high school has such a requirement, what types of service have you done? What value does this requirement have for your school? For you? If you don't have that requirement, what do you think of it?

There are many ways to be of service. Some deal directly with people. Others are more behind the scenes, perhaps preparing materials, entering data, or making repairs. All types of service are of value and are needed. Based on your survey responses, what types of service do you think you would be most likely to give?

Some jobs, though done for pay, are very service oriented (and usually not very high paying). What types of jobs might fall into that category? Do you feel called to live out your commitment to Gospel values in any of those types of jobs?

How might God be calling you to serve others now and in the future?

A Prayer Based on Saint Ignatius Loyola's Examination of Consciousness

Leader: As we pray in the spirit of Saint Ignatius Loyola, remain seated with your feet flat on the floor, your back straight, and your hands either folded or turned with palms opened facing up. Close your eyes or focus on your hands.

Recall that you are in the presence of God. You are here with God, who loves you, welcomes you, and guides you. Spend some moments in silence greeting him.

(Pause for about a minute.)

Leader: Give thanks to God now for the many gifts he's given you. Thank him in the silence of your heart for what you have received from him this day, the pleasant and the difficult alike.

(Pause for about a minute.)

Leader: Examine how you have lived this day so far. What has happened to you in your life and in your relationships? (brief pause) What has God asked of you today? (brief pause) Have you been generous today? (brief pause) Have you been honest today? (brief pause) Is there anything you regret doing or saying today? (brief pause)

Leader: We can always turn to God and ask forgiveness. Let us pray a prayer of contrition, pray for each other, and ask for prayers. Let us pray together:

All: Almighty God, we confess, to you and to one another, we have greatly sinned in our thoughts, words, actions, and by failing to do good. We confess all our sins as our own fault. We ask the Blessed Virgin Mary and all the holy saints, to pray for us. May God have mercy on us through our Lord Jesus Christ.

Leader: May Almighty God forgive and bless us all.

All: Lord, Jesus, you are friend, brother, role model, and inspiration to us. In Baptism, you called us each to be priests, prophets, and kings. Show us how to answer your call in the ordinary circumstances of our lives. Send your Holy Spirit to help us discern how you would have us serve others, help build the kingdom, and bring your Gospel to the world. Renew us and renew our faith. Amen.

Study Guide

▶Check Understanding

1. Give examples of how Jesus modeled service.

2. Name some ways that all baptized Christians can serve God.

3. Identify the difference between common priesthood and the ministerial priesthood.

4. Describe how Holy Orders and Matrimony are Sacraments at the Service of Communion.

5. List the three degrees (or orders) of the Sacrament of Holy Orders and name how each relates to Christ.

6. Explain the College of Bishops and how is it symbolized at the ordination of a bishop.

7. Describe who a presbyter is and what he does in the Church.

8. Identify the three main areas of service that deacons undertake and give an example of each.

9. Summarize how priests and bishops help build up God's Kingdom through the celebration of the sacraments.

10. Tell how the practice of celibacy in the priesthood differs between the Roman Catholic Church and the Eastern Catholic Churches.

11. Describe what a priest's daily life might include.

12. Distinguish between a diocesan priest and a religious order priest.

13. Define apostolic succession.

14. Name some of the Pope's titles and explain how they describe his role in the Church.

15. List the fundamental responsibilities a local ordinary has in his diocese.

16. Describe how bishops are to be God's stewards.

▶Apply and Develop

17. Propose five ways that the ministries of deacons and priests "are directed toward the salvation of others."

18. Based upon the description of the permanent diaconate, recommend four things your parish can do to encourage vocations to this ministry.

19. Compare and contrast the role of and relationships among bishops, priests, and deacons, using information from the celebration of the Sacrament of Holy Orders.

20. Examine the ways that the Pope and bishops continue the work that Jesus first entrusted to his Apostles.

▶Key Words

See pages noted for contextual explanations of these important faith terms.

abbot (p. 147)

apostolic succession (p. 150)

bishop (p. 136)

College of Bishops (p. 137)

deacon (p. 136)

episcopacy (p. 137)

ordination (p. 136)

pastor (p. 152)

permanent deacon (p. 141)

pontiff (p. 151)

presbyter (p. 136)

Sacraments of Initiation (p. 134)

Sacraments of Healing (p. 134)

Sacraments at the Service of Communion (p. 135)

transitional deacon (p. 141)

CALLED TO MARRIED LIFE

CHAPTER 6

CHAPTER GOALS

In this chapter you will:

★ reflect on the importance of loving relationships in our lives and consider how the love shared in marriage makes it a Sacrament at the Service of Communion.

★ learn why marriage is the union of a man and a woman in a sacred covenant.

★ explore the civil and Church requirements for marriage, including how the Sacrament of Marriage is celebrated.

★ consider the life of faithfulness that all married couples are called to, and how the Church supports those who struggle in their marriages.

★ meet a couple engaged to be married.

who Are You?

Use this scale to evaluate
how you are at relationships:

A—Always/Almost always　　　**D—Not often**
B—More than half the time　　**F—Never/Not at all**
C—Sometimes/About half the time

____ When spending time with a person, do you notice how they seem to be feeling?
____ How often do you tell family members or friends what you think or how you feel about something?
____ How often do you tell family members or friends that you love them?
____ How often do you give little gifts (not necessarily things that cost money) to
　　　a friend for no reason except that you thought of them?
____ Do you remember what other people like to eat, watch, or listen to?
____ Do you look directly into someone's eyes when talking to them?
____ Do you thank people for things they do for you?
____ Do you feel happy for good things that happen to another person?
____ Will you change your plans to accommodate a friend who wants to do something
　　　other than what you planned?
____ Will you ask another person to change their plans to do something you really want
　　　to do?
____ Are you honest?
____ Do you feel safe disagreeing with close friends?
____ Do you pray with people you are close to?
____ Do you ever talk about your faith and your thoughts about God with close friends?
____ Are you interested in other people's lives?
____ Are you a good listener?
____ Are you able to bring humor to a tense situation?
____ Are you open to trying new things?
____ Are you comfortable being alone?

Now think about close friendships and relationships in your life right now. You'll revisit these at the conclusion of this chapter to consider how your relationships now and in the future can have an impact on the way you live as a disciple of Christ.

• What do your responses above tell you about how your current relationships are going?
• What are your best qualities or assets for relating to others?
• What qualities or assets do you need to improve on?

Relationships of Love

As you have seen in prior chapters, living out our baptismal call is all about relationships, in each and every state of life. The nature of our God is relational, for our God is a communion of three Persons: Father, Son, and Holy Spirit. The love and communion among the Father, Son, and Holy Spirit model for us how to love and live in relationship with others.

Jesus' word and actions revealed how much God the Father cares for us. They also showed us what it means for us to love someone. To truly love another is to care unselfishly about the other person's total welfare in the context of that person's real life circumstance. Genuine love always desires good and not harm. These principles are fundamental to every relationship, be it with family members, friends, or the person who may become your spouse for life.

Right now, you probably have many different types of friendships and family relationships. As you grow older and have an increased understanding of what it means to be a disciple of Christ in today's world, you will hopefully continue to experience a variety of relationships of different levels of significance. Most may be purely social, school-related, or professional. Others might evolve into deep friendships characterized by a greater connection, shared respect, and mutual effort. Some might be of a more affectionate or romantic nature. You will have to put time and energy into maintaining such close friendships and relationships. You will need to be mature enough to know how deeply involved to let yourself become.

Your current ideas and experiences of relationships have been influenced by society, your faith, and most of all your personal history. All of us tend to pattern our relationships on the ones we've grown up experiencing in the home. You can always improve on and adapt your ideas about, and ways of relating to, people. You need to be aware of your views on female-male relationships, and how those who have raised you have profoundly influenced the ways you typically respond in close relationships. You need to have a sense of what these influences are before you can change them. Each personal relationship is as unique as the persons are! And any relationship must be re-created constantly if it is to grow.

FAITH ACTIVITY

Expectations In small groups, list images and expectations of how men and women relate with each other in marriage. Put a "+" in front of each positive image or expectation and a "–" in front of each negative or destructive one. Compare your list with the other groups and discuss alternative images or expectations as a way to counter the negative ones.

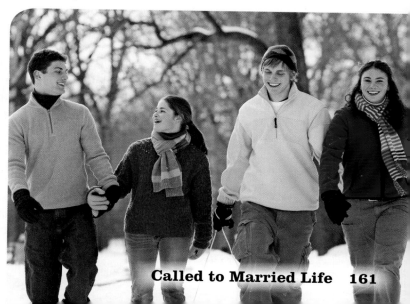

The Choice to Love

If relationships with others are part of being a single or married lay person, an ordained minister, or a member of the consecrated life, how can the way you relate to others be an indication of whether God is calling you to the married life?

Whether you stay single or you marry, what's important is how you love—in the everyday little ways. For true happiness and meaning in life don't occur suddenly when one marries the right person, enters a religious community, or is ordained. It's unfair and unrealistic to expect anything or anyone else to fulfill in us what God alone can satisfy. Your real fulfillment, then, will result from your constantly drawing closer to God, through the small daily choices to love, through participation in the sacraments and an active prayer life, and through being an involved member of the Church.

We bring to any relationship who we are, and that largely depends upon how we love ourselves and have learned to love others. If you feel God is calling you to share his life and love in the married life, the best way to prepare is to become a loving person now—to family, friends, acquaintances, and even strangers. If you strive to be a loving and caring person now, you will most likely evolve into a loving and caring person in whatever path you walk in life.

GROUP TALK

1 Why can't we separate being loving toward others in general from loving one particular person?

2 Name some ways people your age could be more loving at home and at school. Explain how this would also enhance their close personal relationships.

3 Who in your family—immediate and extended, community, school, or parish has helped you see or experience relationships based on love?

4 Name one important childhood ideal you were taught what you did not realize was important until later. What are some other factors that have influenced the way you live and relate to others?

Love Transforms Pope Benedict XVI wrote his first encyclical letter to the Church at Christmas of his first year as Pope. It is called *God is Love*, and in it the Pope writes about love in very beautiful, powerful, and practical terms. At one point he writes about how love changes in a Marriage. It begins as a "searching" love, as the new couple explores together what it means to be "one flesh" and a family within the Church. Eventually that searching love is replaced by a love that "involves a real discovery of the other, moving beyond the selfish character that prevailed earlier. Love now becomes concern and care for the other. No longer is it self-seeking, a sinking in the intoxication of happiness; instead it seeks the good of the beloved: it becomes renunciation and it is ready, and even willing, for sacrifice" (*God is Love*, #6).

The Longing for Communion

Holy Orders and Marriage are both Sacraments at the Service of Communion. The ordained ministers serve the Church by bringing the Body and Blood of Christ to our altars so that we can be united to the Son of God. They call us to unity and lead us in liturgies where we gather together as one Body of Christ.

Here is how Blessed Pope John Paul II described this aspect of being "at the service of communion" in a marriage:

> " All members of the family, each according to his or her own gift, have the grace and responsibility of building, day by day, the communion of persons, making the family 'a school of deeper humanity': this happens where there is care and love for the little ones, the sick, the aged; where there is mutual service every day; when there is a sharing of goods, of joys and of sorrows. "

On the Family, 21

In his Apostolic Exhortation on the family (See *On the Family*, 17), Pope John Paul identified four ways marriage and family are at the service of communion by:

1. forming a community of persons
2. serving life
3. participating in the development of society
4. sharing in the life and mission of the Church

We will look at these ways in this chapter and the next.

Forming a Community of Persons By promising to publicly join together to form a community of love, married couples are witnesses to the covenant between God and his people and to the relationship of Christ with his Church. They are at the service of this longed-for communion with God, for which we were all created by God the Father.

FAITH ACTIVITY

How Does Love Change a Couple?
Ask a couple you know well to share some wedding photos—perhaps your parents, grandparents, an aunt or uncle, or an older sibling. Put them next to some recent photos of the same people.

With these photos in front of you, reflect on Pope John Paul's words about sacramental grace and the quotation from Pope Benedict about how love changes. Write your thoughts about what you see and what it means.

By their witness of faithful love, they are actually witnesses to God's faithful love. Married couples do this in so many ways:

- through their communication and respect for each other

- by the sacrifices they are willing to make for their spouses

- by their willingness to grow in their understanding of themselves and the other

- by the priorities they place on the welfare, happiness and health of their spouse

- by the value they give to family—extended and immediate.

Those married couples blessed with the gift of children are called to all of the above along with the responsibility to share their faith with their children in small and large ways:

- creating special times or rituals of prayer in the home

- teaching their children the difference between good and evil, and right and wrong

- modeling choices made based upon Christian values

- making participation in the Mass a priority

- observing Church seasons and feasts in the home and parish

- creating an environment of trust and hope.

In all of these ways, parents mirror God's faithful love by being true and real to each other, and encouraging their children to be the same.

" Christian couples are, for each other, for their children and for their relatives, cooperators of grace and witnesses of the faith. They are the first to pass on the faith to their children and to educate them in it. By word and example they form them to a Christian and apostolic life; they offer them wise guidance in the choice of vocation, and if they discover in them a sacred vocation they encourage it with every care. "

Decree on the Apostolate of Lay People, #11

GROUP TALK

Discuss how you can share the message and the spirit of the vision of family as "a school of deeper humanity." Try to think of what you would like to convey to a person who has little or no concept of marriage as a sacrament or of family life as holy.

A Calling The great majority of people do walk the path of Marriage. But this doesn't mean that people should presume this is the way they will live without actually discerning whether God is calling them to this life. This is in no way a judgment on any given individual; the cultural expectation in our country—spoken or unspoken—is that single people will marry, and if they do not something isn't right. We addressed these stereotypes in the chapter on the lay single life.

In this chapter you will be encouraged to see that Marriage is a calling, as are the lay single life, the priesthood, and the consecrated life. Married life is a way of loving God and others that deserves a complete discernment process, not a presumption that this is the way for you. This involves exploring opportunities to get a real sense of what it takes to be successful in Marriage; seeking direction from Scripture, the Church Tradition and teaching; asking advice from those you trust to be honest with you; assessing your needs, abilities, and relationships in relation to what marriage entails with all its possibilities.

You may have started this discernment process already, and it is one that will probably last for many years. At different points along the way, it will be helpful to ask yourself these questions:

- Is this how I can best extend God's love to others?

- Is this how I can best share with others my talents and my deepest values, beliefs, and hopes?

- Am I convinced that I'll find the most fulfillment in this way of life, and be most able to give to others generously and joyfully?

We all know that feeling called to marriage does not automatically translate into finding the right marriage partner. All of the aspects of finding and building healthy relationships that give you life and joy, as well as ending or avoiding those that do not, could be the focus of an entire course. While that is not the purpose of this text, in this and other chapters, you are given the opportunity to reflect on different aspects of your life: what type of person you are, your talents, gifts, and interests, your values and priorities, your desire and ability to be in an intimate relationship, your sense of responsibility and commitment to family, the role of faith in your life, and the things that really matter to you.

When you know who you are, you can make conscious choices to enhance or better yourself. You can modify how you relate to others, and who you choose to have around you. As you grow older, meet other people, and deal with life's challenges and excitement, who you are and how you relate to others will evolve. Knowing who you are and where you want to go is key to finding fulfillment in any state of life.

FAITH ACTIVITY

Reflect Spend some time thinking about the questions listed next to the bullet points. Ask yourself whether marriage fits into your reactions to each. Record some of your thoughts so that you can go back to them later in this course. Consider how your thoughts and feelings about marriage might impact whether you feel God is calling you the married life.

✓ Quick Check

1. What does it mean that God is relational?

2. Why is how you love important?

3. What did Pope John Paul II say about marriage being a sacrament at the service of communion?

4. How do married couples witness God's faithful love?

Marriage: A Divine Covenant

The story of God is a love story. The story of God's love is manifested in the created world, in his Church, and in our relating to and caring about the people around us. The Old and New Testaments reveal the story of God's love in the fullest sense of revelation: God is love, and he created humans to love and to be loved.

The Book of Genesis gives us a glimpse of what God had planned for humanity. The book starts with two different creation stories, taken from two different Jewish traditions. Neither is meant to be a scientific treatise, so they don't tell the story as a biologist or an anthropologist would. Both accounts are stories of faith, so, different as they are, they are both included in our Sacred Scripture. Both reveal what God wants us to know about him; about the goodness, diversity, interdependence, and order that he willed for all his creatures; and about ourselves.

From the First Creation Story in Genesis:
Then God said, "Let us make humankind in our image, according to our likeness…
So God created humankind in his image, in the image of God he created them; male and female he created them.
God blessed them, and God said to them, "Be fruitful and multiply, and fill the earth and subdue it; and have dominion over the fish of the sea and over the birds of the air and over every living thing that moves upon the earth."

Modern-art depiction of Adam and Eve.

From the Second Creation Story in Genesis:
Then the LORD God said, "It is not good that the man should be alone; I will make him a helper as his partner." …
So the LORD God caused a deep sleep to fall upon the man, and he slept; then he took one of his ribs and closed up its place with flesh. And the rib that the LORD God had taken from the man he made into a woman and brought her to the man. Then the man said, "This at last is bone of my bones and flesh of my flesh; this one shall be called Woman, for out of Man this one was taken." Therefore a man leaves his father and his mother and clings to his wife, and they become one flesh.

✝ Genesis 1:26–28; 2:18–24

The first account indicates that we have been created *in God's image*, and *different from each other—male and female*. The second account indicates the close bond between *men and women*, who are different from all other creatures. Men and women are of the same dignity. Both are necessary to give glory to God and continue the human race. Both lead us to the understanding that God created humans not as solitary beings, but as beings called into relationship with him and with one another. We were created to get to know God, to be close to him, to love him, to serve him, and to share that love with others.

Marriage in Society From well before the time that the creation accounts were written, marriage as an institution existed. But we learn from continued reading of Genesis and our own experiences, despite the original state of communion and holiness in which humans were created, sin entered the world. Original Sin introduced doubt, weakness, jealousy, pride, and many other challenges to the ways men and women relate to one another.

While cultures both ancient and Western recognized marriage and family as important social units, their perceptions and practices about marriage certainly differ from ours today. There was marriage, but it was not often a union of equals nor a covenant of love. Wives were possessions in some cultures, political pawns in others. Men could have many wives to ensure they would have children.

During Jesus' time, marriage was seen as a vehicle for ensuring the birth and care of children and of transferring property to the next generation. Marriage and divorce were arranged matters. It was Jewish expectation that fidelity would characterize a marriage, for their marriage represented God's sacred union with his people. And adultery with or by a married woman seriously violated her husband's property rights. A husband could divorce his wife just by formally dismissing her, but a wife needed her husband's permission to obtain a divorce. Thus, as Jesus went on to teach, the intent of the Sixth Commandment, "You shall not commit adultery," had been distorted.

FAITH ACTIVITY

God's Response to Our Need
Read the second creation account in Genesis 2. What does this story show about the human need for companionship and God's response to that need?

GROUP TALK

1 What attitudes of Jesus' time do you think are still reflected today in views of marriage and male-female relationships?

2 How is marriage depicted positively in popular culture?

3 How would you describe an ideal marriage?

FAITH ACTIVITY

The Wedding Feast Look up the story of the Wedding Feast at Cana. (See *John 2:1–11.*) The bride and groom were unaware of Jesus' miracle. What are some ways God might work in a marriage even when the couple is unaware. Write your reflections or express them in a poem, song, painting, drawing, or other art form.

Jesus' Teachings Jesus brought us a new view of marriage. It is to be a sign of the new covenant with God. That covenant, entered into freely by both spouses, is based on faithful love. From then on, marriage was to be seen as indissoluble. Jesus reminded his followers, "What God has joined together, let no one separate" (*Matthew 19:6*).

This was a shocking statement at the time. The disciples asked why Moses had allowed divorce (see *Deuteronomy 24:1–4*) if what Jesus had said was true. He answered, "It was because you were so hard-hearted that Moses allowed you to divorce your wives, but from the beginning it was not so" (*Matthew 19:8*). Jesus went back to the beginning, when Adam and Eve were told to cling together as one flesh and to be fruitful and multiply. Jesus was showing us what God had planned in his original order of creation, before sin turned that order into chaos. The *Catechism* says:

> By coming to restore the original order of creation disturbed by sin, he [Christ] himself gives the strength and grace to live marriage in the new dimension of the Reign of God. It is by following Christ, renouncing themselves, and taking up their crosses that spouses will be able to 'receive' the original meaning of marriage and live it with the help of Christ.[1]
>
> *CCC*, 1615

Faith tells us that, through our sacramental participation in Christ's death and Resurrection, we receive all the graces we need to live out the universal vocation to holiness and to work to build the Kingdom of God. The fact that Jesus performed his first miracle at a wedding feast is a wonderful reminder of his presence and his saving grace in all marriages. (See *John 2:1–11*.) In the Sacrament of Marriage, Christ gives married couples the graces they need to remain faithful to each other.

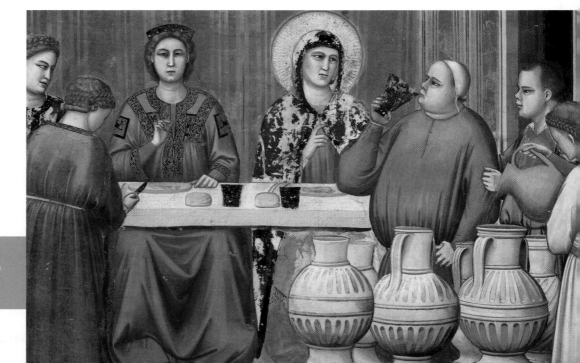

▶ Detail of the Virgin from *Marriage at Canna* by Giotto di Bondone

The Christian Perspective

Every culture has had some way to signify that a man and woman are united in a legally acceptable sexual union. Therefore, religious and civil laws about marriage are among the oldest on earth. They exist to protect women, children, and property; to establish patrimony; and to deal with questions about inheritance.

Christianity also needed to address the question of the sexual union of men and women. They had Jesus' teaching about love and the treatment of women to apply to the lives of those who were married. Jesus' teaching was revolutionary. He was born into a world where wives were considered property, and where women caught in adultery were executed while adulterous men were innocent of any crime.

For Jesus to stand in defense of an adulterous woman and say that only someone without sin had a right to stone her was unheard of. (See *John 8:1–11.*) His Apostles were thunderstruck when they found him talking with the Samaritan woman at the well, who ended up being one of the first to tell about him. (See *John 4:1–42.*)

At the wedding at Cana, as at all Jewish weddings of the time, women and men were in separate rooms for the feast. Early Christians reading or hearing this story recognized its social taboos. Mary crossed over to the men's side to speak with Jesus, and Jesus did what she asked him to do. Mary and Jesus violated these taboos in the name of charity toward a neighbor. In the kingdom Jesus had come to establish, women and men were seen as equals.

> ## FAITH ACTIVITY
>
> **Roles of Women and Children**
> Work in pairs or threes to create a "conversation" with Jesus about the way things are in today's world with regard to women and children. Decide together what you think he would say to us today. Create a comic strip, video, poster, or skit to depict this conversation.

Christ the Bridegroom The Old Testament has many allusions to God's love for his people being like the love of a bridegroom for his bride. The New Testament clearly brings that image forward to describe, under the New Law, the Church as the Bride of Jesus Christ whom he loved and whom he saved by handing over his own life.

In the Gospel according to Mark, when Jesus is asked why his disciples didn't fast as John the Baptist's disciples did, Jesus answered, "The wedding guests cannot fast while the bridegroom is with them, can they? As long as they have the bridegroom with them, they cannot fast. The days will come when the bridegroom is taken away from them, and then they will fast on that day" (*Mark 2:19–20*).

Jesus identified himself as the bridegroom, and his Church as the bride. What does this mean for Christian understanding of marriage? Paul explains in his Letter to the Ephesians:

Husbands should love their wives as they do their own bodies. He who loves his wife loves himself. For no one ever hates his

Quick Check

1. What do the creation accounts reveal about men and women and their relationship to each other?

2. What were the societal and religious understandings of marriage in the time of Jesus, and how did Jesus' teachings counter those understandings?

3. Why is the image of Christ as the bridegroom important to a Christian perspective of marriage?

4. Why is marriage a sacred covenant?

own body, but he nourishes and tenderly cares for it, just as Christ does for the church, because we are members of his body. "For this reason a man will leave his father and mother and be joined to his wife, and the two will become one flesh." This is a great mystery, and I am applying it to Christ and the church.

✝ Ephesians 5:28–32

In their 1994 pastoral message to families, the United States bishops offered further this insight: "Like the whole Church, every Christian family rests on a firm foundation, namely, Christ's promise to be faithful to those he has chosen. When a man and a woman pledge themselves to each other in the sacrament of matrimony, they join in Christ's promise and become a living sign of his union with the Church (cf. Eph 5:32)." (*Follow the Way of Love*, p 594 of compendium)

A Covenant of Love From Jesus' life and ministry we derive at the core meaning of **marriage**.

- Marriage is a solemn promise, a sacred covenant, like the one God has made with us in which a husband and wife create intimacy and unity in love and in all aspects of life.

- It is a bond of unity between one man and one woman, a bond that is of God from the very beginning of creation, a covenant that God has established with certain laws, such as it is a bond that should never be broken.

- It is mutual promise of a lifetime of faithful love, a shared commitment.

The fidelity and permanence of marriage are to reflect that lasting, faithful, complete way God loves each of us and wants us to love one another. In marriage, the husband and wife's mutual promise to love each other faithfully for life symbolizes and reflects God's complete, lasting love for us. We will see in the next section that the Catholic Church holds that every true marriage is freely chosen, permanent, and a sacred covenant whereby a woman and man choose each other above all others.

This type of commitment might seem beyond our grasp. However, we can trust that what God wants for us, he makes possible through his grace: his life, love, and action in our lives. Married couples will tell us that when they acknowledge the need for God in their lives, when they see God's love as the source of their own, they experience a comfort, joy, and strength that takes the ordinary and makes it extraordinary.

Natural Family Planning

Sexual union in marriage has two goals: the transmission of new life (procreative) and the well-being of both spouses (unitive). Both goals must be present in every act of sexual union between a husband and wife. Yet, there are times when it might be better to wait to have a child. What is a couple to do? The Church teaches that contraception is morally unacceptable because it removes the possibility of creating life from the sexual act and it takes away from the total self-giving to which the spouses committed themselves. The good intentions on the part of a couple for why they want to avoid a pregnancy don't give them the right to use birth control methods that are against Church teaching.

This dilemma has caused a great deal of controversy for Church members. This may stem from a confusion between *rights* and *gifts*. It is a common fallacy to believe that sexual activity is everyone's right, or even a necessity for a happy life. Here are some important distinctions: sexuality is a gift given to everyone; sexual temptations are the results of Original Sin; sexual intercourse is a gift reserved for married couples. Sexual activity is a gift to be accepted, not a right to be demanded.

The most effective way to prevent pregnancy is to abstain from all sexual acts; this is what all unmarried Catholics are called to do. Abstinence from sexual intercourse is also the way married couples are to prevent pregnancy. Of course, married couples should not abstain from sex all the time—if they did, they would be denying the goal of the marriage act, which includes the unity of the couple. If they want to prevent pregnancy, they need to abstain from sex when the woman is most likely to conceive a child.

Every woman's body is different and even the same woman has differences in her body from month to month, so couples need a reliable way to find the woman's fertile days each month. That "way" is called Natural Family Planning which protects both the procreative and the unitive aspects of conjugal love. Each couple learns the wife's signs that her body is in a fertile phase, and uses that information to either engage in or avoid sexual activity during that time. It is 97–99% effective when used correctly.

Over the years more and more parishes, dioceses, doctors, and hospitals have taught the method to married and soon-to-be-married couples. Since 1981, the United States Conference of Catholic Bishops officially endorsed Natural Family Planning and has had a Diocesan Development Program for NFP with NFP teachers and mentors present in virtually every diocese. In addition, organizations like the Couple-to-Couple League serve as grassroots, local support systems for couples who want to learn NFP.

GO online You can find a link about natural family planning at www.osvcurriculum.com.

Marriage as Institution

From the beginning God willed that man and woman would be partners, united in the mutual work of continuing his work of creation. We've considered how marriage is a sacred covenant, and this holds true for sacramental and non-sacramental marriages alike. What is the distinction between a sacramental and non-sacramental marriage? Can both be valid in the eyes of the Church? It's important to consider Church and civil regulations regarding validity before making the distinction between sacramental and non-sacramental marriages.

Not everyone is married in a religious ceremony, Catholic or otherwise. The Church acknowledges civil marriages as true and valid according to the civil legal sense. She acknowledges those spouses' legal status, rights, and obligations regarding each other, children, and society. When Catholics are married in purely civil way outside of the faith community, there's a lack of evidence that they intend and promise what Catholics believe and celebrate about marriage. They may in fact embrace all that the Church teaches about marriage, but since they have chosen not to be married in the Church, their marriage is not sacramental. On the other hand, if a couple doesn't believe in the permanent and religious dimension of marriage, they cannot promise to it.

Validity For a marriage to be valid, the man and woman must:

- both freely give their consent to be married to the other person

- intend to remain married for life

- be open to having and raising children

The *Catechism* says that this consent must be "an act of the will of each of the contracting parties, free of coercion or grave external fear.[2] No human power can substitute for this consent.[3] If this freedom is lacking the marriage is invalid" (*CCC*, 1628).

The man and woman must also (1) be free to marry, that is, they may not already be married to someone else; (2) be at least the minimum age required by the diocese and by the state; and, (3) not be close relatives.

GROUP TALK

1 What else do you think civil and Church authorities should require of couples before they marry?

2 What kind of freedom and maturity would you need before feeling ready to marry someone, if that is your calling in life?

The Sacrament of Matrimony

In the Sacrament of Matrimony also called Marriage, the couple celebrates not only the sacred union and covenant that God intended, but they also celebrate their belief in Jesus and their commitment to try to live as a couple what Jesus taught and lived. To celebrate and live together what that means, both spouses must believe it. That's why marriage can be a sacrament only for two baptized Christians.

When a baptized man and woman exchange their vows in the Sacrament of Marriage, they enter into the mystery of the union of Christ and the Church, which this sacrament signifies. They receive the grace to love each other with a love similar to the love with which Christ loves his Church. The sacramental grace of marriage:

- perfects their human love

- strengthens their indissoluble bond

- sanctifies them on their journey to heaven

- provides help so that they may carry out their privileges and responsibilities as spouses and parents.

The grace of marriage is not a one-time gift. Received at the time of their wedding, this grace is given to the couple all through their marriage. Grace is a free gift from God, which strengthens, enlivens, and renews a person in some way. Matrimonial grace assists the couple to do what they say as they exchange their wedding vows. In turn, each spouse says, "I (name), take you, (name), to be my wife/husband. I promise to be true to you in good times and bad, in sickness and health. I will love you and honor you all the days of my life" (*Rite of Marriage, 25*). It takes grace to do this for a whole lifetime.

In the Sacrament of Marriage, Jesus is also present to support and bless the couple. His assistance will help them live the Gospel message in their married life.

A Public Celebration Every celebration of marriage is a public act. This does not mean the wedding ceremony has to be a large one with many guests. It does need to be a public ceremony that takes place during a Church liturgical celebration before a priest or deacon, with authorized witnesses. The liturgical celebration should, if at all possible, take place during a Mass when two baptized Catholics are marrying.

The priest, or deacon authorized by the bishop to officiate at the wedding ceremony does not bestow the sacrament upon the couple. The bride and groom confer the sacrament upon each other. The priest or deacon, in the name of the Church, receives the consent of the spouses to give themselves to each other in marriage. He gives them the blessing of the Church. The presence of authorized witnesses is a visible sign that is required by both Church and civil law.

Sometimes couples think it would be fun, romantic, or unique to get married in a setting other than a church, such as a park or garden. The Church requires that baptized people marry according to correct ecclesiastical form because:

- Sacramental marriage is a liturgical act. It should be celebrated in the public liturgy of the Church.

- When they marry, a couple enters a covenant, blessed by Christ and the Church. It gives them certain rights and responsibilities in the Church.

- Since marriage is a defined state of life in the Church, witnesses are needed to certify the marriage has validly taken place.

- It will help spouses remain faithful to their "I do," because it was vowed publicly in the Church as a graced sacramental act.

The words and ritual actions of the Rite of Marriage signify and make present the sacramental graces described previously. These words and actions also symbolize the Christian meaning of marriage. They instruct and inspire the couple as they begin their life together, showing everyone assembled that these two people are going to share in the mystery of God's love.

Elements of Rite of Marriage Celebrated During Mass	
Entrance Rite	Procession (the ministers go first, then the priest, then the bride and bridegroom; local custom may provide for the couple or bride to be escorted by parents)
Liturgy of the Word	Scripture readings—one always from the Gospels; if three, one from the Old Testament as well
Rite of Marriage	Introduction Questions Consent (legal requirement; The couple must state that each is free to marry and freely chooses to marry this other person) Blessing of Rings Exchange of Rings General Intercessions
Liturgy of the Eucharist	Follows the Order of Mass with a special nuptial blessing before the Sign of the Peace
Concluding Rite	Solemn Blessing Dismissal

Other Requirements

The Church requires preparation by the couple before they marry—study, prayer, times for discussion, and discernment. Each diocese has different requirements, so it's important for a couple to contact their parish before they do anything else like rent a hall or hire musicians. First they need to find out what steps their diocese requires.

They also need to learn the regulations and expectations of the parish where they will marry. Dates and times need to be worked out to everyone's mutual benefit. Rules about music, flowers, or other decorations need to be discussed.

Sometimes there are ethnic or family traditions regarding weddings that seem more "binding" than any Church or state laws. Couples shouldn't assume their parish liturgical ministers know about their family tradition. They also, however, shouldn't assume that their parish won't allow them to do something traditional—such as laying flowers at the feet of Mary after the Eucharist—but outside the usual ceremony. Open conversation is needed just as much in preparing for marriage as it is in marriage itself.

FAITH ACTIVITY

Planning a Wedding If you were planning the liturgy for your Catholic wedding at a Mass, what Scripture readings would you choose with your husband- or wife-to-be? Which music selections would you make? The parish office may have handouts that outline for a couple which readings and musical selections are available. You may also wish to look at the Rite of Marriage. What do you think would be important to include at a wedding in your church?

Some of the traditions are so ancient that their original meaning has been lost while the action has remained. For example, when women were considered property, they were "given away" by their fathers to the bridegroom and his family. The priest or minister would even ask, "Who gives this woman's hand in marriage?" That question is not part of the Rite of Marriage, but brides often are still "given away" by being walked down the aisle by their fathers or other male relatives to be handed over to the groom who is waiting at the altar. However, some couples are choosing to walk down the aisle together at the beginning of the wedding, or to have the bride and groom each walk down escorted by both their parents, to signify the joining of two families.

GROUP TALK

Think about weddings you've attended or been part of. What customs did you observe at those weddings? Were any of them ethnic customs or customs specific to one family? What elements of a wedding do you feel are absolutely a requirement for it to seem like a "real" wedding to you? What elements do you think you'd want at your wedding if you get married?

Marrying a non-Catholic

A married couple's religious beliefs are extremely important to their life together. Our beliefs about God and the role of faith in our lives greatly influence what we value and how we behave and relate to others. Compatibility, if not complete similarity, in faith and morals is vital for happiness in marriage. Even couples of the same religious tradition can have such different understandings of what living their faith means that life together can become difficult. Many people in our society do marry someone of another religious tradition. It's even possible that you will, so it's important to understand the implications those differences can have for marriage.

A mixed marriage is one in which a Catholic marries a baptized non-Catholic. Disparity of cult refers to a marriage in which a Catholic marries a non-baptized person. The Church neither forbids these marriages, nor recommends them. This is indicated by the fact that for them to occur, a permission (for mixed marriages) or dispensation (for marriages with disparity of cult) is required. Nonetheless, when they occur, the Church blesses them. All valid sacramental or non-sacramental marriages are blessed by God. The Church recognizes the right for both baptized and non-baptized spouses in a marriage to be free to practice their own religion without interference from the other spouse. The Church does not pressure a non-Catholic person to become Catholic in order to marry. Though non-Catholics are always welcome to become members of the Catholic Church, they are usually counseled not to do so just before their wedding simply to please their future spouse.

When a Catholic marries a non-Catholic, the Church wants to protect and support the Catholic's freedom of religion and provide for the faith of any children who might be born of this marriage. So, before their wedding day, the Catholic person is required to make a promise reaffirming faith in Jesus Christ, stating the intention to continue living that faith in the Catholic Church and promising to do one's best "to do all in my power to share the faith I have received with our children by having them baptized and reared as Catholics."

Some important distinctions need to be made about the marriage of a Catholic to a non-Catholic Christian or to a non-Christian. When a Catholic marries a validly baptized Christian in the Catholic Church, or with Church permission, that couple receives the Sacrament of Marriage. Generally the marriage of a Catholic and a validly baptized non-Catholic Christian does not take place at Mass. When a Catholic marries a non-Christian in a Catholic wedding ceremony, or they are married in another ceremony with the Catholic Church's permission, their marriage is blessed by the Church and considered valid and indissoluble. They do not receive the Sacrament of Marriage, however.

Clearly, in both cases, the Church blesses the vows of love between these two people and recognizes them as truly married. But to have the Sacrament of Marriage, valid Baptism is required. Christian marriage is a sign of this couple's love for each other and for Christ and his Church; it is also a sign of Christ's union with his Bride, the Church. These signs are not complete when one of the parties is not validly baptized.

Quick Check

1. What is required for a marriage to be valid in the Church?

2. Why is it necessary for both bride and groom to be baptized in order for marriage to be a sacrament?

3. What is the sacramental grace of marriage?

4. What does the Church teach about marriage between Catholics and non-Catholics?

GROUP TALK

Discuss the following questions in small groups:

- Do you know any married couples who are in a mixed marriage or one with disparity of cult? If not, imagine a couple for the next few questions.

- What challenges have you observed because they do not share the same religion?

- How does the Catholic partner participate in the life of the parish?

- Is the non-Catholic partner active in any church, or religion?

- How do the couple's children view religion?

- In what faith are their children being raised?

Marriage Encounter and the Encounter Movement

The Marriage Encounter movement began with a priest and a married couple in Spain in 1952. It was their idea that was born then and eventually heard around the world, although that was not their plan. The couple, Mercedes and Jaime Ferrer of Barcelona, Spain, simply wanted some spiritual direction as a couple and they could find none. Up to this time, spiritual direction was geared, primarily, toward the individual, and usually a celibate individual in a convent or monastery. They approached Father Gabriel Calvo, and with their help he developed a method for guiding a couple's communication called an *Encuentro or "Encounter."*

Couples were given simple directions for how to talk, how to really listen to each other, and they were given dialogue questions to get them started. Couples were trained to speak to other couples about their experiences and their faith. From that simple plan, Father Calvo began to offer Encounter Weekends in parishes around Spain.

There was no official organization then, but as the movement grew in Spain, Father Calvo and trained couples were invited to other countries. In 1966, they came to the United States where they met with leaders of the Christian Family Movement and were endorsed by them. A Jesuit priest, Father Charles Gallagher, S.J., became interested in the movement, and it was his vision that led to the founding of Worldwide Marriage Encounter in 1968. A smaller group of similar-minded Catholic couples also met Father Calvo during his visit to the U.S., and they started the National Marriage Encounter Movement around the same time. Engaged Encounter began in 1975 as a Catholic movement to help couples learn to communicate better even before they married. It, too, is now used by many other Christian denominations in countries all over the world.

You might have seen bulletin announcements or posters at your parish inviting couples to attend a Marriage Encounter Weekend. You might know people who regularly meet with their Marriage Encounter group. Your diocese may encourage, or even require, engaged couples to attend an Engaged Encounter Weekend before they get married. The ads usually invite couples to make a good marriage even better, and to learn to really communicate.

The Encounter Weekend format is used by three groups–Worldwide Marriage Encounter, National Marriage Encounter, and Engaged Encounter. They all operate on the simple premise that people can change the world one family at a time, and that good communication is the key to change. All three groups began and continue to be headquartered in the United States, despite the concept's origin in Spain. WWME and Engaged Encounter now have groups all over the world. All three groups began as Roman Catholic movements; but now all three have Encounter programs for couples in dozens of Protestant denominations and for Jewish couples.

Encounter weekends are not group therapy, a support group, or a retreat. Couples who attend a weekend do not come to solve problems, nor do they attend in place of marriage counseling. In some cases, however, it is used as a substitute for Pre-Cana before marriage. At an Encounter Weekend, the couple focuses on each other, not on the whole group of attendees. As a couple, they focus on God and their relationship with him.

The Encounter Weekend is the main focus of the movement, but many people want to stay connected to the movement after they experience a weekend. They form marriage encounter groups that meet regularly in homes for prayer and discussion. Many former weekend attendees go back to serve as speakers and helpers at weekends for other couples.

GO online You can find links to the Marriage Encounter movement and Engaged Encounter movement at www.osvcurriculum.com.

Graced for Faithfulness

The celebration of the sacraments may begin in the church building, but they are meant to transform our lives as we live them out, receiving and sharing with others God's special gifts and love. Marriage is a sacrament that a couple gives each other—not just on their wedding day, but in every unselfishly loving thing they do or say for each other.

Just as God was present on their wedding day, so God is present when the spouses lovingly greet each, prepare the family meal together, listen to their children's stories about their day, quietly enjoy each other's company, or express their love and affection. All of these things are holy. When married relationships are characterized by care, sacrifice, and faithfulness, Christ is present in the couple's loving thoughts, words, and actions. This is what it means to live out the Sacrament of Marriage; it is this that the Church blesses and celebrates.

What is Fidelity?

We have seen in this chapter how crucial faithfulness is in the celebration and living out of marriage. Being faithful requires self-discipline and self-control. That means having the perseverance to stick it out when the going is difficult. It means working to fix problems rather than making excuses for or trying to escape them. It means exercising self-control and chastity, not dishonoring the marriage covenant by committing adultery.

Fidelity is about being loyal and keeping promises. Our faithfulness to our commitments should reflect God's faithfulness to us. In a marriage or other close relationship, being faithful means not doing something that will wreck the relationship's foundation.

Being faithful requires being determined to be true to the one you love. It requires the character and unselfishness to sacrifice your preferences to make that happen. That means keeping your priorities straight. If you marry, you will have to realize that your spouse and children are the most important people in your life, and choose and act with that in mind. It may involve putting your loyalty to your family before your desire to further your career. At times you'll have to be willing to give up a purely self-centered pleasure for the greater good of keeping your marriage and family commitments.

FAITH ACTIVITY

Holy Ways Work with a partner to list all the everyday activities that people might consider as a holy way of living their vocation. Compare your list with another group's, and discuss what else could be added to the list if people truly believed that holy is in the ordinary experience of life. Then discuss whether you view your daily activities in that way.

In a mutual relationship, your spouse is prioritizing his or her life, wants, and needs with the same goals in mind. And, the two of you aren't sharing the joys, hopes, and challenges of faithful living in isolation, but as part of God's family.

GROUP TALK

1 How much does fidelity mean to you in a relationship? Why?

2 Why do you think married couples remain faithful to each other?

3 Why might people your age have difficulty keeping promises and commitments? What can people your age do to be more responsible in their relationships?

Support In a perfect world, all spouses would be faithful to each other; all homes would be stress free; and there would always be enough money. But our world is not perfect, and all relationships will experience difficult times, frustrating situations, and life-changing events. All kinds of challenges can pound away at an individual marriage, until the couple thinks it might be best to separate or end the marriage. It is here that the sacramental graces of marriage are needed most. Oddly, it is in times of greatest challenge that a marriage can be its holiest, dipping into the grace, strength, forgiveness, and divine love that first helped forge the marriage. Couples that have weathered a storm in their marriage report that they have come out with deeper, stronger love and a more committed marriage on the other side of the crisis.

Some couples may think that to survive they should be turned inward to look only at each other. However, people who turned to the Church to celebrate their wedding hopefully noticed something important as they prepared to be married. The Church really cares about them and wants their marriage to succeed. The Church isn't holding out a long list of laws and a grim disapproval of them. The Church is the means by which they can get the grace they're going to need for the years and years to come. The Church is the place where there is a community of believers to pray for them, support them, even advise them. A couple must look at each other, certainly, but then together look out to the community, to friends, to family.

Serving Life Pope John Paul explained that marriage is at the service of communion by serving life. Married couples serve life by being open to the gift of children, caring for and loving children, showing affection and fostering positive relationships in the home, being forgiving and reconciling, affirming the dignity of all family members, and in many more ways. On several occasions the Pope wrote and spoke of the "culture of death" prevailing in today's world. The Sacrament of Marriage stands in defiance of that culture.

Our world is one where divorce, polygamy, and free union (cohabitation)—all grave offenses against the dignity of marriage—undermine the communion in marriage. Connected to this is the refusal to be open to fertility which removes the supreme gift God gives to a marriage—a child. Easy dismissal of such essential aspects of marriage have greatly contributed to this culture of death. In the face of these practices that would destroy the communion between God and his people, married couples who remain faithful to their vows stand as a beacon of hope to the whole Church.

FAITH ACTIVITY

Beacons of Hope Research different ways that married couples serve the community. In what ways do they promote and protect life in their homes and in their communities? In what ways can the love they share be brought into the lives of those around and the wider community?

When it Doesn't Work Out

It is often believed that the Catholic Church does not allow legal separation or civil divorce, and that a divorced person is automatically excommunicated from the Church. This is a misconception. Sometimes one spouse will even stay in a dangerous or unhealthy marriage situation under that very belief.

The Church recognizes that there are some situations that make it impossible for a married couple to stay together. The Church believes in the indissolubility of marriage, yes; but she also professes belief in the sanctity and dignity of human life.

The Church allows a married couple to separate and live apart if they cannot remain together. They are still married and they are not free to re-marry, but they do not have to live together. Outside of the Church divorce is often the decision in such a situation. Civil divorce will protect a spouse, the children, and the property the couple once shared. The Church permits **civil divorce** in some cases. A couple who gets a civil divorce is still married in the eyes of the Church.

The time after a divorce is a time Catholics need the Church and the sacraments very much. Divorced Catholics are not permitted to marry anyone else because they are still in a sacramental marriage, but they are encouraged to remain active in the Church for prayer, support, understanding, and encouragement. Parishes should welcome divorced Catholics who have not remarried into full parish participation. Often individual parishes or the diocese might offer support for divorced Catholics through programs like the Phoenix Program for divorced and widowed Catholics.

When a divorced Catholic enters into a civil marriage with someone else, the Catholic is still a member of the Church, but can no longer receive the Eucharist or other sacraments except in danger of death. Such a person is encouraged to continue to come to Mass, and to bring their children for religious education. Parish staff and members should welcome divorced and remarried Catholics with understanding and encourage them to participate as fully as they can in Church life.

FAITH ACTIVITY

The Effects of Divorce Write your thoughts about the effects of divorce. Have you experienced divorce in your own family? Do you have friends whose parents have divorced? How have your views about divorce changed as you've gotten older? How do you think your views and experiences will influence you if you get married?

Quick Check

1. How do couples live out the Sacrament of Marriage in their daily lives?

2. What is fidelity in marriage?

3. How does marriage serve life?

4. What is the Church's teaching on divorce, remarriage, and annulments?

What About Annulments? If a divorced Catholic whose spouse is still living wants to marry or has married someone else, they are encouraged to bring their case to their parish priest to find out if they can be declared free to re-marry by seeking a Church annulment. Investigation of each case sometimes finds that there are grounds for a Church annulment of the original marriage. Remember the list of requirements for a valid sacramental marriage—if it is discovered that one of those requirements was not actually met, the marriage can be declared null by the Church.

Annulments can be confusing. How can a couple that made vows to each other to stay married forever, receive an annulment that says they weren't really married? The process of seeking an annulment often is a complex one. Was the first marriage valid or not? Was it a sacrament or not? The annulment process seeks to discover the state of each person at the time of the first marriage. There are a number of conditions that would render the marriage null and void. Lack of due discretion, psychological issues, drugs, fear, alcohol, and other issues present at the time of the first marriage may be reasons for the Church tribunal to annul the marriage. If one of the spouses was under the influence of drugs or alcohol, for example, it's quite possible he or she didn't really consciously and freely consent to the marriage vows. If a person was very young at the time of the wedding, it's possible they didn't truly understand the indissolubility of the vows they were making. Sacramental marriages are handled differently than non-sacramental ones.

Common questions that arise about the annulment include, "Does this mean I was never married?" and "What about our kids? Does granting an annulment make them illegitimate?" When the Church grants an **annulment** (declaration of nullity) it doesn't mean the couple was not legally married, nor does it mean that their children are illegitimate. It means that their relationship at the time of their first marriage lacked the necessary conditions enabling them to enter a permanent sacramental bond lasting until death. The marriage was valid and legal in the eyes of the state, but the Church, when granting an annulment, declares that no real sacramental bond existed from the beginning of the marriage. The children of this union are the offspring of a legally married couple, and have all legal rights as such. The dissolution of the sacramental bond of marriage does not affect the legality of the marriage or the legitimacy of the children.

Rainbows Ministry

What do families do when they are suffering from the loss and grief of a divorce, a loved one's death, or the aftermath of a natural or man-made disaster? Twenty years ago not much was known about how to help children involved in such family crises. Thanks to one woman, all that has changed. Her search for help for her sons led to a worldwide success story.

Suzy Yehl was a divorced mother of three little boys looking for some help when she realized how much pain the divorce had caused them. She didn't find any. And she was in pain, too. Out of that pain and that need was born Rainbows, an international organization that provides a bridge to emotional healing for children, adolescents, and adults confronting death, divorce, or other painful family transitions. It is called *Rainbows* because it guides children and adolescents through family storms, and offers hope after the dark times of hurt. Children meet weekly in small Rainbows groups with a trained volunteer. Through games, stories, art-work, and conversation, children are helped to recover from loss and move forward with new hope.

Many children and teens blame themselves for their parents' divorce or have distressed feelings about it or other devastating losses. Rainbows' leader-guided peer support groups help them work through these issues. It is an international group open to children of all races and religions, dedicatd to facilitating emotional heal-ing for traumatized youth. It offers love, care, listening, hope, strength, knowledge, and a peaceful environment at no cost to the children or their families.

Inaugurated in Chicago, Illinois, in 1983, Ms. Yehl started Rainbows in four schools and quickly expanded to fifteen. Each year Rainbows provides training and curricula for 32,000 volunteers offering grief sup-port services. Since 1983, nearly one million children and their families in forty-nine states and seventeen countries have benefited from Rainbows. Youth and their families receive these services in churches, syna-gogues, schools, and social service agencies regardless of age or religious affiliation. The original curriculum for primary grade and middle school children has now expanded to include materials for teenagers and adults. Kaleidoscope is available for adults, and Prism is available for single parents and step parents. A special curriculum developed after 9/11, and another after Hurricane Katrina. Hence, Rainbows has grown to address the widespread personal tragedies of children and teens, whether resulting from natural disasters or man-made problems.

We went to New York this time, to visit with Lynn and Josh, who will be married in two months. Lynn is a twenty-four-year-old nurse who works in the intensive care unit at a nearby hospital. Josh is twenty-six, is also working at the hospital, and is in nurses' training.

INTERVIEWER: So your wedding will be in nine weeks! It looks like you're working on your invitations tonight.

JOSH: Aren't they great? We made them ourselves—on the computer, I mean. Anyhow, I think they look like us—homey and not-perfect, but nice.

LYNN: And it's just like us not to be finished too!

I: Is it stressful now before the wedding?

L: A little. We're both working on things, and we're paying for a lot of the wedding ourselves.

J: It's a joint project. We and both our parents are chipping in. We're keeping it affordable and fun.

I: It's going to be at a Catholic Church I see. Are you both Catholic?

JOSH and LYNN: Yes, we are.

L: Hey! Now we're starting to talk at the same time like old married couples do!

I: Did you look for a Catholic to marry?

L: I didn't, but now that I'm engaged to Josh and we've gone through the Pre-Cana classes, I'm really glad we're both the same religion. My parents weren't, and sometimes it was rough when they argued about faith.

J: It was really important to me to find a Catholic girl. I always said I'd only marry a Catholic. But then sometimes I wonder—because if I had fallen in love with Lynn like I did, and she wasn't Catholic, well, I think I would've still married her. I don't know.

I: But you actually were planning to marry a Catholic if you could? Why?

J: Because I really like the Catholic Church. My whole family is Catholic. This is probably going to sound corny, but it's true! I've always wanted to be the kind of dad my dad has been. He raised me to be a good Catholic, and I want to do the same for my children.

I: And your faith has a part in that?

J: It does! Being Catholic gave me a moral code to live by and a way to pray. It'll be good when we have children. We'll be carrying on our family tradition.

L: It's going to be so much easier sharing the same faith. I didn't think about that when we first met, but now I would not want it any other way.

I: Why did you decide to marry him? Have you known each other for a long time?

L: We met two years ago, and we got engaged eight months ago—he proposed to me right next to the Christmas tree!

J: We met because of mutual friends. I was just getting out of the Navy and had decided to go into nursing. My friends told me there was this nurse I should meet.

L: So that's what we talked about the day we met. We were at these friends' party, and we sat off in a corner and talked about nursing. It was amazing how much we had in common! We talked for hours.

I: And then you knew you were in love?

L: Not at all.

J: Me neither. I just was glad to have a nurse to talk to about my going into nurses' training. Then we found out we have a lot in common.

I: So you're marrying her because ...?

J: I'm marrying Lynn because she's funny, honest, has values similar to me, and because I love her deeply. It doesn't hurt that she's also very pretty! But that's not the important thing about her.

L: What I love most about Josh is that he's so kind. He's a very gentle, caring man. He's going to be a great nurse and a wonderful father for our children. His religious values will greatly enhance me and our home.

J: We want two kids. Or more. Or, well, whatever.

L: First, we need to get these invitations finished!

who will you Become?

Look back at the survey you completed at the beginning of this chapter. An informal survey can provide a good "snapshot" of what you are like now. It can help you identify the things you want to keep doing and the things you may want to evaluate or change about yourself.

What qualities did you like about the way you approach relationships of all types, and what qualities did you want to see yourself work on? What qualities are most important in a marriage?

Each of the boxes addresses an important aspect of close relationships–romantic ones, and those with close friends and families as well.

Write a few ways you can do these things based upon qualities you already have or would like to possess.

Build trust

Show empathy

Be mature

Express tenderness

Be aware

Be imaginative

Prayer

Leader: Let us pray today by reflecting on the words Saint Paul wrote in 1 Corinthians 13:1–13 about love.

All: "God is love, and those who abide in love abide in God, and God abides in them." (*1 John 4:16*)

Reader 1: If I speak in the tongues of mortals and of angels but do not have love, I am a noisy gong or a clanging cymbal.

Reader 2: And if I have prophetic powers, and understand all mysteries and all knowledge, and if I have all faith, so as to remove mountains, but do not have love, I am nothing.

Reader 3: If I give away all my possessions, and if I hand over my body so that I may boast, but do not have love, I gain nothing.

All: "God is love, and those who abide in love abide in God, and God abides in them." (*1 John 4:16*)

Reader 4: Love is patient; love is kind; love is not envious or boastful or arrogant or rude.

Reader 1: It does not insist on its own way; it is not irritable or resentful;

Reader 2: It does not rejoice in wrongdoing, but rejoices in the truth.

Reader 3: It bears all things, believes all things, hopes all things, endures all things.

All: "God is love, and those who abide in love abide in God, and God abides in them." (*1 John 4:16*)

Reader 4: Love never ends. But as for prophecies, they will come to an end; as for tongues, they will cease; as for knowledge, it will come to an end.

Reader 1: For we know only in part, and we prophesy only in part.

Reader 2: But when the complete comes, the partial will come to an end.

Reader 3: When I was a child, I spoke like a child, I thought like a child, I reasoned like a child;

Reader 4: When I became an adult, I put an end to childish ways. For now we see in a mirror, dimly, but then we will see face to face.

Reader 1: Now I know only in part; then I will know fully, even as I have been fully known.

Reader 2: And now faith, hope, and love abide, these three; and the greatest of these is love.

All: "God is love, and those who abide in love abide in God, and God abides in them." (*1 John 4:16*)

Study Guide

▶Check Understanding

1. Explain what it means that God is relational.

2. Tell why the way you love is important.

3. List the four ways Pope John Paul II explains marriage as a sacrament at the service of communion.

4. Give some examples of how married couples witness God's faithful love.

5. Express what the creation accounts reveal about men and women and their relationship to each other.

6. Describe the societal and religious understandings of marriage in the time of Jesus, and how Jesus' teachings countered those understandings.

7. Explain the importance of the image of Christ as bridegroom in the Christian perspective of marriage.

8. Recall why marriage is a sacred covenant.

9. Name the criteria for a valid marriage in the Church.

10. Point out why it is necessary for both bride and groom to be baptized in order for marriage to be a sacrament.

11. Identify the sacramental graces of marriage.

12. Explain the Church's teaching about marriage between Catholics and non-Catholics.

13. Detail ways couples live out the Sacrament of Marriage in their daily lives.

14. Define fidelity in marriage.

15. Describe how marriage serves life.

16. Summarize the Church's teaching on divorce, remarriage, and annulments.

▶Apply and Develop

17. Examine how the love we are called to have in all relationships is an indication of how married love forms a communion of persons.

18. Write a description of the Christian marriage based on Jesus' teachings and example and Pope John Paul II's apostolic exhortation, *On the Family*.

19. Differentiate between sacramental and non-sacramental marriages within and outside of the Church.

20. Illustrate ways that the grace of the Sacrament of Marriage assists couples in living faithful, permanent, life-giving marriages.

▶Key Words

See pages noted for contextual explanations of these important faith terms.

annulment (declaration of nullity) (p. 182)

civil divorce (p. 181)

Marriage (p. 170)

CHAPTER 7

CALLED TO FAMILY LIFE

CHAPTER GOALS

In this chapter you will:

* reflect on the blessings of family life, and consider how the way we communicate influences relationships within and outside of the family.

* learn what we mean by calling the family the domestic Church.

* consider the importance of Catholic families as schools of virtue and charity.

* discuss intentional living based on Catholic values and moral teachings.

* meet a married couple who has made a commitment to family values in a big way.

WHO ARE YOU?

There are no "better" answers to these questions. Your answers simply give clues about where you are on the communication spectrum.

1. When my parents or my siblings praise me for a job well done, I

shrug it off and
don't say anything. ———————————— thank them and talk about the
accomplishment.

2. When the phone rings at home, I

hurry to answer it. ———————————— let it ring and hope it's not for me.

3. At a party, I

move around and
talk to lots of people. ———————————— spend time with
one person or a few people.

4. When I need to call someone, I

just pick up the
phone and start talking. ———————————— mentally rehearse what
I'm going to say.

5. When working in a group at school and a point is being discussed, I

jump into the
discussion right away. ———————————— listen to what everyone
else has to say and hold my ideas
until the end.

6. When someone disagrees with me at home, I

dismiss them as
wrong. ———————————— assume I am wrong.

7. When one of my family members starts to speak about something very personal, I

change the subject
or make a joke to lighten the mood. ———————————— focus on the person and
listen carefully.

8. When I'm in a group of family members, I tend to

spend most of
the time talking. ———————————— remain silent and
make little or no contribution
to the conversation.

9. I fit in great with

loud, boisterous
family members. ———————————— quieter, more reflective
family members.

Look over your answers. Do you see any patterns that might indicate what kind of communicator you are in your family?

Communication and Today's Families

All of us need to communicate on multiple levels for our lives to have meaning. We communicate thoughts, feelings, needs, wants, information, ideas, hopes, dreams, goals, and beliefs. We can only get to know someone through communication. God wanted us to know him and to love him, so he made himself known to us through his Revelation in Scripture and in the Church Tradition. God the Son was sent as the ultimate communication of God the Father's love.

God continues to communicate with us through the liturgy and sacraments, in personal prayer, though the people around us, and through creation. And, he calls us to respond to his communication by sharing ourselves and giving ourselves to him and others. However we choose to respond to that call, in whatever state of life and in whatever job or career, communication is essential.

What Is Communication? It is far more than just the words we say. It's understanding each other through words and gestures, which allows us to share our thoughts and feelings. You can talk at a brick wall, but you can communicate only with someone who understands what you mean. Effective communication is a two-way street. Always remember that you are communicating with someone who's different than you.

People often think they're communicating when they're really just expressing themselves. They're thinking of the message they're trying to get across rather than how it's being understood by the other person. Or they're hearing but not really listening, concentrating more on what they are going to say next rather than on what the speaker is saying.

FAITH ACTIVITY

In Your Life Spend some time reflecting quietly on the following questions: With what person do you feel you communicate well? Who do you think understands you the best? With whom do you communicate poorly, or with whom you would like to communicate better?

We learn to talk early in life, but we can always learn to better communicate. Most tension in relationships results from poor communication. If you want your relationship to grow and last, learn to communicate more effectively. When communication fails, so do marriages, relationships between **family** members and among friends. And most communication breaks down because people don't listen to each other. So, it's important to learn how to truly listen to what the message is and the person behind the message.

- Concentrate on what the other person is saying more than what you will say next.

- Be mentally quiet.

- Avoid making snap judgments before someone finishes speaking.

- Listen respectfully.

- Reflect back on what you think the person said and meant, and find out if you understood it correctly.

- Understand the person as well as the message.

- Give your undivided attention; if you can't at the time, explain.

- Be honest but not ruthless when you don't agree with what the person is saying.

No matter whether we end up being married, or religious, or single, or in the priesthood, we first learn to communicate within the family. As children, we see how parents, grandparents, siblings, and relatives interact with one another: the things they say, the tone they use when they say things, their body language. We see the impact of their communication styles, but most of us are not consciously aware that we are being formed by all of this. It's usually only in reflecting on this as we mature that we can see the influence of others on our own communication styles. You've actually been reflecting on different aspects of these family influences throughout this book. You are on your way to consciously choosing to continue what is effective and loving in the way your family communicates and to avoid what is not.

How do family members speak with one another? How do they listen? These two skills have a huge impact on the experience of family life. But before people consider "how" they do either, they simply need to talk to one another—about their day, their team practice, their frustrating lab test, their friends, their goals as a family, their upcoming week, how they're feeling and what they're thinking. Recent campaigns to prevent smoking, drinking, and drug use among adolescents target parents and guardians, telling them "Talk to your kids," and "Listen to your kids." Honest communication, especially about difficult life issues, is essential to navigating all the changes that families go through when children grow into adolescents. Change is not easy; everyone has to learn new ways of being parents and children, to adjust to new responsibilities and roles, and to trust that even the most difficult situations can be faced together; it's never to late to start trying to communicate.

FAITH ACTIVITY

Understanding Family Needs In groups of five or six, role-play a typical family situation where different people have different wants and needs. Make sure the family in your skit has at least three different age groups interacting.

GROUP TALK

1 What do you think usually causes people's failure to understand each other? Explain.

2 How can you tell whether someone really is—or isn't—listening to you?

3 How do you feel when someone really listens to you as well as your words? When someone doesn't?

A Diverse Reality

As society becomes more and more complex, the experience of family becomes more diverse. Because of countless reasons, the structure of families has broadened, and the way a family functions has had to address societal and cultural changes, and the practical impact of those changes in the home.

Family life has changed throughout human history, and especially within the past hundred years. There is no room here for an adequate presentation on the development of family as institution over the centuries, but it's important to know that the way families live and function has changed in order to address the way our society lives and functions. Some of these changes are good, while others are not.

On the positive side, husbands and wives share life's tasks and obligations more as equals and children's opinions are valued more than in times past. The positive, healthy changes in family life have helped families grow. Although dramatic, upsetting social changes have affected family life, the family has been strong and flexible enough to adjust. Family means not only spouses and their children—there are many other kinds of families, including the growing number of households that have spouses raising relatives who are not their own children, of grandparents raising grandchildren, aunts and uncles raising nieces and nephews. Although its structure has changed, the family is still society's basic unit. The stability of the family is especially important in our rapidly changing world.

Family Varieties	
Type	**Description**
Nuclear family	A household of parents and their dependent children, biological or adopted
Stepfamily	A household that includes relatives by a parent's remarriage
Blended family	Includes both parents' children by their previous marriages
Single-parent family	Includes only one parent living in the household
Extended family	A group of relatives, which may include a nuclear family, who live in the same household or near one another

It is essential to acknowledge the reality of what families face today. Our consideration of family life needs to be grounded in what we, our friends, coworkers, acquaintances, and society at-large experience *and* what we are called to be as a Christian family. God's love is not limited to the "perfect" or "ideal" family, of which there are none. His grace is strong enough to lead all of us to love in the circumstances we face.

Quick Check

1. What does communication entail?

2. How can we listen to people's message conveyed by words and actions?

3. What are the different family structures in today's world?

4. What are some positive changes that have taken place in the way families function?

GROUP TALK

1. How do you think the way you think and feel about family life will affect your future decisions regarding marriage and children?

2. With which family structure are you most familiar? Which do you have questions about?

3. How important do you think the family is for our society? Explain.

A Path Toward God

The family, at its simplest, is this: the place where a person's life and journey toward God begins. The U.S. Bishops describe the family as: "an intimate community of persons bound together by blood, marriage, or adoption, for the whole of life . . . [it] proceeds from marriage—an intimate, exclusive, permanent, and faithful partnership of husband and wife." (*A Family Perspective on Church and Society*, USCCB, p. 17)

A man and a woman become "one flesh" in the Sacrament of Marriage. As soon as they pronounce their vows, they also become a new family. The bride and groom bring their separate family histories with them into the new relationship, now joined as a new family.

They also each bring with them a whole lifetime of learning from their respective families. Now, they are the center where a new family will learn about God, love, and life.

Blessed Pope John Paul II often wrote and spoke about families. In 1994, he wrote a Letter to Families in which he said:

> Among these many paths, *the family is the first and the most important*. It is a path common to all, yet one which is particular, unique and unrepeatable, just as every individual is unrepeatable; it is a path from which man cannot withdraw.

Gratissimam Sane, 2

FAITH ACTIVITY

Your Family Reflect on Pope John Paul II's statement that each family is "particular, unique and unrepeatable," using your own experience of family—yours and families of your friends. How can you depict the uniqueness of your own family? Write, draw, or in some other creative way, express your ideas about your family.

Awesome Responsibility At Catholic weddings the couple is asked if they will accept children lovingly from God. In fact, as we saw in the last chapter, being willing to have children is one of the criteria for a valid marriage. The couple says "yes" not really knowing how their lives will change if they are blessed with children. They have their own experience of being in a family, with all the good and the bad that comes with being in a family. But each family is unique, and what their family will grow to be is not yet known.

Most first-time parents go through a whole range of emotions and reactions when their child is born and as he or she starts to grow: sheer gratitude for the miracle of life, amazement, concern for the baby's health, fear, responsibility that they have never felt before, protectiveness, hope, exhaustion, and love beyond any they have felt before. Families need to realize that God is with them, and that love for their child and the support of the community will help see them through. Together they will learn about being new parents and providing for their child's physical and emotional needs.

Children have spiritual needs, too, which are first met through the words of comfort babies hear, the prayers prayed while rocking or feeding them, and the very virtues parents use to care for their children. It is in those moments that the faith formation of children has begun. As children grow, parents and extended family will teach them about Jesus and the faith of the Church, provide prayer experiences, and model and instill Christian virtues.

Just as parents gave their children life, parents have the amazing gift of beginning their children's life of faith. Creating a household of faith shouldn't be thought of as a separate responsibility, for it connects directly with nurturing the physical and emotional well-being of the entire family.

The Domestic Church

The earliest Christian churches often were in people's homes. When early Christians used the word "Church," the first image that came to mind was not of a building. Church was a gathering of the faithful. For them, as for us today, Church is a community of believers. The Church had a more familial or domestic flavor. In 1964, the Second Vatican Council reintroduced the term "domestic Church," referring to the family as a Church of the home:

> The family is, so to speak, the domestic church. In it parents should, by their word and example, be the first preachers of the faith to their children . . .
>
> *Dogmatic Constitution on the Church*, #11

> The Christian home is the place where children receive their first proclamation of the faith. For this reason the family home is rightly called "the domestic church," a community of grace and prayer, a school of human virtues and of Christian charity.
>
> *Catechism of the Catholic Church*, 1666

Calling the Christian home a domestic Church recognizes the family's dignity, sacred power, and fundamental importance as the place where every person's faith begins. Just by being a Christian family, a household is a domestic Church of some sort—it is the first experience of the Christian faith that a child or spouse knows. The perfect domestic Church does not exist, just as the perfect family does not exist. A family's holiness comes not from being perfect but because God's grace is working in and through it. God's grace helps family members to see every day as a new day, an opportunity to renew themselves, to love others, to make better choices, to seek reconciliation, to give forgiveness, to celebrate what is good in their relationships and to have the strength to admit what is not. A family is holy because Christ has promised to be faithful to his people, and he is present in all of the ups and down, joys and sorrows, changes and new stages each and every family live through.

As a domestic church, families continue the work of Christ and carry out his mission. How do they do this? Through the ordinary events of life.

- The spouses **have faith** in God and believe he cares about them. They give him thanks when things are going well, and they turn to him when things are difficult.

- They **love those around them** and continue to believe in their value. In this way they model God's love.

- They **foster intimacy**, from their own physical and spiritual union to the appropriate affection among all members. Sharing who they are—the good and the bad qualities—and still being accepted is irreplaceable in forming a close relationship with Christ.

- They **spread the message** of Christ's good news by talking about God, acting based on Gospel values, and setting an example for children who will help them recognize God's presence—often in surprising ways.

- They **educate** through teaching and example, helping children learn and practice values necessary for Christian living.

- They **pray** together, thankful for blessings, yearning for strength, needing guidance; toddlers, teenagers, and adults gather together, trusting and searching in their own ways.

- They **serve one another**, sacrificing their own wants for the good of others, sometimes struggling to do so with love.

- They **forgive and seek reconciliation**, letting go of hurts to make peace. By doing so family members come to believe that parents and God still love them no matter what.

- They **celebrate life**—birthdays, anniversaries, a first day of school or graduation, new jobs, old friends, holy days and holidays, when something tragic occurs, and in the joyful celebration of the sacraments. These celebrations typically involve gathering around a meal, and as

FAITH ACTIVITY

The Holy in the Ordinary Reflect on and write about these questions:

- What are some times your family has celebrated and affirmed life? What did you like most about these times?

- In what ways does your family—parents, siblings, grandparents, relatives—share faith and welcome others? How can you lead other family members to be more welcoming and to share beliefs?

- How can you help your family see God's grace in the ordinary experiences of life?

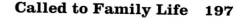

they share food and stories, they grow as the community of love Jesus calls us to be.

- They **welcome others** into their homes, caring for the needs of others.

- They **act with justice** by treating people in the community with respect, speaking out against discrimination, and working to end hunger, poverty, homelessness.

- They **affirm life** as God's precious gift to us, going against what destroys or harms life; within their families they discourage violent words and actions and strive for peaceful ways to resolve conflict; in this way the peacemakers of the next generation are formed.

- They **honor vocations** to the priesthood and the consecrated life by encouraging their children to be open to God's call, to listen for him and to respond to his grace; their encouragement comes through family prayer, involvement in parish life, and respectfully speaking of priests, sisters, brothers, and permanent deacons.

(See Pope John Paul II's 1994 *Letter to Families*)

A Community of Grace and Prayer Catholics turn to their parish community as a source of grace and a center for worship. We go there to celebrate the Eucharistic Liturgy and the other sacraments, to worship with an assembly of believers, to learn about our faith, and to unite with others in acts of charity and justice.

The parish is the place where each domestic Church can connect to the wider Church community. Prayer, catechesis, and faith formation in the parish cannot take the place of faith sharing and growth in the family. Home and parish, domestic Church and parish community, work in partnership with each other.

"The family and the Church–in practice, parishes and other forms of Ecclesial Community–are called to collaborate more closely in the fundamental task that consists, inseparably, in the formation of the person and the transmission of the faith."

Pope Benedict XVI, Address to the Participants in the Ecclesial Diocesan Convention of Rome, June 6, 2005

GROUP TALK

Discuss with classmates: Give some examples of times when your own parish and family have worked as partners in the education of young people.

Prayer and Blessings We turn to our parish to lead us in prayer. As we experience prayer and learn more about the different varieties of prayer, we see a prayer life that we can model at home. Parents and children can pray together in their homes, bringing from Mass the grace and inspiration for a life of prayer and good works all week long. The Catholic family should be the first place children learn to pray—at night, at mealtimes, in the morning, on special occasions, for those we know, for those we don't know, in thanks for what we have, and with requests for what we need. If they are taught how to pray from their earliest years, children learn that prayer is important.

We are blessed in all of the sacraments, and we bless ourselves with holy water as we enter and leave the church as a reminder of our Baptism. We can bless each other because God first blesses us; it's part of our sharing in Jesus' mission as priest, prophet, and king. Most of us might not even realize that we have the right, indeed the gift, to bless each other. We can bless each other in the morning and in the evening, as children leave for school, as we prepare for important events, and by honoring birthdays and anniversaries.

There are other types of prayer (sometimes called popular devotions or piety), which nourish our Christian life— prayers, practices such as the Rosary, Stations of the Cross, novenas, and devotion to saints. Many of these are rooted in different cultures, and here in the diversity of our nation we see a great variety of ethnic popular devotions. Some of them take place publicly in parishes; more of them take place privately in Catholic homes, that is, domestic churches. The Catholic Church encourages these popular prayers and devotions, not to replace the Mass and the other sacraments, but to enhance and enrich them. Such devotions in homes can evangelize other homes, express human wisdom, and enrich Catholic life.

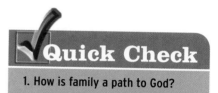

FAITH ACTIVITY

Family Devotions In small groups, discuss any traditional popular devotions your families like to pray. What prayers to Mary do you have? What saints do you pray to? Do you have any prayers for special occasions such as weddings, birthdays, or Christmas?

✓ Quick Check

1. How is family a path to God?

2. What needs do children have and how can families address them?

3. Why is the family called the domestic Church?

4. How is the family called to be a community of grace and prayer?

The Christian Family Movement

The Christian Family Movement (CFM) is a national network of small parish/neighborhood groups of families who meet regularly in one another's homes to reinforce Christian values, strengthen marriages, and help members grow in faith and community involvement. The group was founded in 1948 by two Catholic couples, Burnie and Helene Bauer of South Bend, Indiana, and Pat and Patty Crowley of Chicago, Illinois. The CFM continues it's tradition in Catholic parishes all over the United States and throughout the world. From its national headquarters in Evansville, Indiana, CFM provides print material for local groups to use for meetings and a newsletter called ACT that is published eight to ten times a year. CFM holds a national convention every three years.

The Christian Family Movement's mission is to promote Christ-centered marriage and family life, to help individuals and their families live the Christian faith in everyday life, and to improve society through actions of love, service, education, and example. The official prayer of the CFM reflects their sense of vocation:

"Holy Trinity, you are a family.

We believe you wish our families to reflect your heavenly community.

Jesus has called us to family ministry, and asked his heavenly Father

not to take us from the world, but to deliver us from evil.

And so we pray for the Christian Family Movement,

that present members may grow in grace and that new

families may join us.

Through good example and prayer, may our homes become

that which you desire them to be: true domestic churches,

temples of your glory, and schools of humanity, ushering

in the reign of God.

Amen."

FAITH ACTIVITY

The CFM and Your Parish Find a CFM group in or near your parish, or read some issues of ACT. What topics have been covered? How do the topics support the mission and goals of CFM? From your research, do you think CFM is relevant to today's Catholic families?

A Community of Virtue

As the domestic church, the family is "a school of virtue and charity." By this time in your formal education, you are probably familiar with the term *virtue*. In order to see how the family is a place where children learn virtue and all members grow in virtue, it might be helpful to revisit the meaning of virtue.

Once we know what we are supposed to do, we can get into the habit of doing what is right so that it becomes almost second nature to us. In the spiritual life, that permanent habit or disposition of doing good is called **virtue**. Virtuous living is the ultimate use of our human gifts of intellect and free will. Virtues are such habits of doing good that they govern our actions, guide our choices, and keep our lives ordered so that we are disposed to do what is right and good.

No doubt you already have some virtues that are well developed in your life. Probably you have others that need to grow. Which virtues grow in you, and how much they grow, is entirely up to you.

There are many human virtues, but they all can be grouped around four that the Church calls the *cardinal virtues*. The word "cardinal" comes from a Latin word that means, "hinge." Notice how these four virtues are like hinges to which all other virtues connect in some way.

The Cardinal Virtues	
Prudence	Prudence disposes us to see what is good and to find the right means to achieve the good. It is a natural guide for our conscience. It helps us apply moral principles to each situation in order to correctly choose what is right.
Justice	Justice is the constant and firm resolution to give God and others what is due to them. Justice toward other people leads us to respect others' rights, and to promote equity and the common good.
Fortitude	Fortitude strengthens our determination to do good, resist temptation, and to overcome obstacles in the moral life. With fortitude we can remain constant in doing good and we can overcome all fear, even fear of persecution, which might be the consequence of defending what is right and just.
Temperance	Temperance moderates our attraction to pleasure and gives balance to how we use material things. It helps us master our appetites and instincts rather than over-indulging in them.

GROUP TALK

To which of the four cardinal virtues would you connect the following human virtues:

honesty	generosity
modesty	serenity

What other virtues can you think of, and to which cardinal virtues would you connect them?

Virtues in Practice In the domestic Church, children learn the basics of faith, hope, love, prudence, justice, fortitude, temperance, and all the other virtues—not as lessons in a book to be memorized but as life lessons to be lived. Parents and guardians teach about virtue when they praise a child for sharing, when they listen to and take their adolescent's sound advice, when they talk about self-esteem issues, and when they build a child's confidence by expressing pride in his or her action.

Adult members of the family teach about virtue when they deal with problems such as childhood lying or stealing, fights between siblings or with neighborhood children, tantrums intended to get one's own way, and with preoccupations with the trendiest clothes or technology. Parents also teach about virtue when their children observe how they treat neighbors, speak about people at work, and show patience and respect toward family members. These lessons are so powerful that they form a child's earliest understanding and experience of right and wrong.

When you were younger, your family and faith community were charged with the responsibility of educating and guiding you to grow in virtue. While they are still involved, you are becoming more and more responsible for how much more you are willing to learn, and how well you are willing to live.

The family is a school to learn charity. Children learn to love by observing how family members love and treat each other. From their home, love radiates out to influence the people each family member meets in a given day. The power to love others is very evident in a Catholic family. Such love reaches out beyond the walls of the home to embrace neighbors, classmates, co-workers, and ultimately, strangers in need.

FAITH ACTIVITY

Virtuous Family Living Write a list of the virtues that you think should be present in a home and the values that the family should live by. Next to each virtue and value, indicate how you practice that virtue and cherish that value. Mark any virtues and values you especially want to develop in yourself. How could a family go about acquiring these virtues and values?

The Commandment with a Promise

The complex grouping we call "family" has been the most basic unit of society since the beginning of recorded history. So it is fitting that while all the commandments apply to individuals and families, one of them is specifically dedicated to the family—the Fourth Commandment, "Honor your father and your mother."

It was Saint Paul who pointed out that when the Fourth Commandment is listed in the Book of Exodus 20:12, it is the first commandment to have a promise attached to it.

Children, obey your parents in the Lord, for this is right. "Honor your father and mother"—this is the first commandment with a promise: "so that it may be well with you and you may live long on the earth."

And, fathers, do not provoke your children to anger, but bring them up in the discipline and instruction of the Lord.

✝ Ephesians 6:1–4

We are promised that if we keep this commandment, we will be prosperous and will live a long life. And isn't it interesting that when Paul wrote about this he immediately added the instruction to fathers not to provoke their children to anger? Paul lived with the paradox we all live with—sometimes we are both children and parents at some point in our lives.

The Fourth Commandment is the first of the seven commandments that deals with how we are to love our neighbor. The Old Testament teaching on the Fourth Commandment, teaching in the New Testament, and contemporary teaching in the *Catechism of the Catholic Church*, all agree that this commandment refers to our obedience to all lawful human authority, and that it tells us how to relate to our parents, not only as children, but also as adults.

The honor in this commandment must be given in both directions between parent and child. We owe our parents respect, gratitude, obedience, and assistance. Small children can only learn to give these things by receiving respect from their parents and by seeing their parents give this kind of honor to each other and to their own parents. As they are taught to honor their parents as children, family life can be more harmonious and joyful. Or as the promise given with the commandment says, "it may be well with you and you may live long on the earth."

Human History From the beginning of time, parents and children have found it difficult to get along at times. Often it is in our adolescent years that we find our parents most "provoking," and they find us the same. Adolescents are starting to "leave home" in some ways—becoming more independent, connecting with other groups outside the family. The pull between wanting to stay home and wanting to leave can cause emotional stress for a teen. In the meantime, the readjustments parents need to make as their children grow and change can cause them stress.

Honoring and respecting each other will go a long way to reduce tension and promote communication. As adolescents look to the future, to the time when they will leave home, they need their parents respect and encouragement. As their teenaged children ask, "What will my vocation be?," parents need to be guides. They must remember and teach that their teen's first calling as a Christian is to follow Jesus, and they must help their teen discern how to do that.

Healing The two-way direction of the Fourth Commandment also provides opportunities for parents to teach their children important lessons about forgiveness. Not only do they need to be taught to say "I'm sorry" to someone they have hurt, they need to hear their parents and older family members apologize to them and to each other when it is warranted. They need to see forgiveness granted and the peace that comes from reconciliation after a painful family experience. Most of all, parents need to link the healings and forgiveness necessary in families to the sacraments. Both the Eucharist and the Sacrament of Reconciliation are bountiful sources of grace and forgiveness.

Participating together each week in the Mass builds a bond between family members. The bond is above all a union with Christ, for each time we receive his Body and Blood we get closer to our Lord. Our family unity and the unity of the Mystical Body of Christ are reinforced in the Eucharist. Families are also strengthened through reception of the Sacrament of Penance and Reconciliation. We are all called to conversion and repentance, the movement of return to God, and to reconciliation with those whom we have hurt or who have hurt us. In the Sacrament of Reconciliation—with our statement of sorrow, remorse for sins committed, and a firm resolve to sin no more—we have the model for our returns to each other when we become alienated from those we love.

Quick Check

1. What are the four cardinal virtues?

2. How is the family called to be a school of virtue and charity?

3. How does the Fourth Commandment direct family life?

4. How do the sacraments guide family life?

Family Life Ministry

It's interesting how different Church offices and ministries have evolved. We saw in the Christian Family Movement a grassroots success story of couple-to-couple outreach and ministry that exists in parishes, but is not part of the parish and diocesan structure.

As CFM was growing, a parallel idea was growing. The ministry in parishes that had for many years been done by priests and sisters was becoming more complex and diversified. As Church members came to recognize the Vatican II teaching on the call of the laity to share in the Church's mission as priests, prophets, and kings, some new ministry offices started to appear in some dioceses and even a few parishes.

In the twenty-first century virtually every Catholic diocese in the United States has a Family Life Office. They are all linked to the United States Conference of Catholic Bishops through the Committee on Marriage and the Family.

Many diocesan Family Life Offices include in their ministry promoting the Church's teaching against abortion. While there are still strong elements of pro-life activities and themes in diocesan Family Life Offices, diocesan leaders have come to recognize how more is needed in order to assist Catholic married couples to live their vocations. Diocesan Family Life Offices, while continuing to provide education about, and sponsor events for, the Right to Life efforts, also offer education on Natural Family Planning, adoption, child-raising, and end-of-life issues. You will find diocesan Family Life Offices sponsoring programs for engaged couples, events to promote religious vocations, retreats for parents and children, along with many other offerings.

This kind of ministry has always been present in parishes—often done by the pastor, or by some couples in the parish. Ministry to families might also be part of the work of an associate pastor, a lay pastoral associate, or even a director of religious education. Over the past ten years, some parishes have established a Family Life Office with a paid director on the staff either part-time or full-time. Very large parishes with several thousand families were among the first to establish this office and staff position.

At the parish level, a Family Life Office often serves as a liaison with the diocesan Family Life Office, informing parishioners of programs and special events coming up in the diocese for parents and families. The parish office also serves to connect parish family members with each other. A parish will typically sponsor two or three family-education or couple-education programs each year. Day-to-day, most Family Life Offices provide formal and informal support groups centered around issues in families, while maintaining a library of educational and inspirational reading and film materials.

FAITH ACTIVITY

Your Family Life Office Research the Family Life Office in your diocese and in your own or any nearby parishes. Look for information that explains the office's mission and tell about upcoming events. Find out if their ministry includes anything concerning adolescents—information, opportunities to discern one's vocation, social events.

Intentional Living

As individuals and families, we cannot predict the future and see the sudden accidents, new arrivals, or sharp turns that will change outcomes for us. We can, however, pay attention to what is really happening around us, and quite possibly see signs of an impending disaster in time to steer away from it or better prepare to recognize the good that someone has accomplished. If we're honest with ourselves, most of the time we have enough information available to make informed decisions and to choose positive consequences.

We can take past experiences and apply things we've learned from them to events happening now. We can understand what possible consequences are ahead if we follow a certain path by looking back to what happened to us at an earlier time in similar circumstances. Even better, we can look back to what happened to *other people* in previous situations and use that information to help us make good, moral decisions.

In this way, we can live intentionally and make informed decisions. Yet, all too often, people ignore lessons from their past, or examples from other peoples' lives. They even miss the huge storehouse of wisdom available to us in the Church—the Scriptures, doctrines, traditions, elders, family members, catechetical classes, sacramental instructions, teachings of the Pope and bishops, and testimonies of holy, Catholic people.

GROUP TALK

Discuss with a group of classmates:

- Discuss whether you think it's possible to "live intentionally," or if there are too many unexpected events that throw us off our path.

- Why do you think many people miss or ignore the signs and information that are available to help them make good, moral decisions?

- What examples can you recall of situations where you or someone close to you made an informed decision based on past experience.

Living the Sacrament

Those who have a vocation to the married life and who marry in the Catholic Church do not have to be bewildered, doubtful, or unaware of what their marriages mean. The Sacrament of Marriage is an *intentional* sacrament. If you choose to make marriage vows, you will learn that the choice is a *daily* one. Saying "I do" on your wedding day is only the beginning of a lifetime of "I do's."

The couple states this during the wedding ceremony. Specific words may vary, but their vows look to the future and include the intention that they are not just for that day but forever. When asked if he will take his bride, usually radiant in her wedding gown, as his wife, the groom joyfully says, "I do." He continues to say, "I do" in all the days ahead. He does this for his wife when she is beautiful and when she's not, when she's healthy and when she's not, and so on.

His wife continues to say "I do" as she did the day she married her handsomely dressed groom. She does this for her husband when he's handsome and when he's not, when he's healthy and when he's not, and so on. Thus, a couple gives each other the Sacrament of Marriage daily. The more intentional they are about this, the stronger and deeper their marriage bond will be.

Intentional Planning Many couples consider when to have a baby, as when to "start a family." In reality, on their wedding day, a couple officially *starts a family*. The two of them, often introduced to the assembly at the end of the ceremony as "Mr. and Mrs____ " are a family. Just a few moments before they are introduced, they publicly agree to accept any children God will send them. So, on their wedding day they say they *are* to be a family, and they *intend* to have children.

Perhaps they intend to delay having their first child, or want space between children. As we have seen, the Church encourages this kind of responsible family planning, as long as the means to achieve it are natural and there are just and serious reasons, not selfish ones, appropriate to responsible parenthood. (See *CCC*, 2368). Ultimately, however, the conception of a child is God's decision. By virtue of being married, a couple intends to have children but is not completely in charge of when, how many, or even if this will happen. Children are a gift from God.

Every human life—from the moment of conception until death—is sacred. Each human has been brought into being in the image and likeness of God. Married couples participate in God's creative act, but cannot control it. Because of this, the Church teaches very clearly about both **artificial birth control** and artificial means of conception.

As we saw in Chapter 6, natural methods of spacing births are allowed and even promoted by the Church. There can be good reasons why a couple would want to prevent a pregnancy at a certain time, but the Church is very clear that a good intention does not give the couple the right to use morally unacceptable birth control methods.

The Church certainly recognizes the anguish some couples experience because they are unable to conceive a child, and even commends research aimed at reducing human sterility. But it places this condition on such research: It needs to be placed "at the service of the human person, of his inalienable rights, and his true and integral good according to the design and will of God"[1] (*CCC*, 2375). Therefore, methods such as artificial insemination, in vitro fertilization, and surrogate pregnancy are all morally unacceptable. They separate the conjugal act of love between husband and wife from the procreative act of bringing human life into the world.

Many couples who want but cannot conceive children place their hope for having a family in adoption. The adoption process can be a lengthy one, both in getting approved to adopt, which is for the welfare of the child, and in waiting for a child. However, adoption can be a beautiful, loving, and even life-giving choice.

GROUP TALK

1 Before deciding to have or adopt a child, how should couples prepare themselves for the inevitable adjustments and changes in lifestyle?

2 What qualities do you think would help someone be a good parent?

3 What qualities do you think would make it difficult for someone to be a good parent?

Intentional Parenting When a couple promises at their wedding to accept children, more is said in detail about how they are to bring them up after birth. That instruction from the Church is mentioned in the instruction the couple receives before marriage, and is echoed during the baptismal liturgy:

> You have asked to have your child baptized. In doing so you are accepting the responsibility of training him (her) in the practice of the faith. It will be your duty to bring him (her) up to keep God's commandments as Christ taught us, by loving God and our neighbor. Do you clearly understand what you are undertaking?
>
> *The Rite of Baptism, 77*

The Baptism liturgy implies that parents are to practice intentional parenting, to build a community of love and virtue, grace and prayer. Parents and adult family members can teach and model values that will help their children become responsible, faithful, caring, and disciplined. By identifying values such as honesty, generosity, compassion, kindness, chastity, tolerance, justice, respect for life, and peacemaking as Gospel values, parents give witness to Jesus' message and the importance of that message to them and their families.

Love is shown through addressing the material, emotional, and spiritual need of children. This takes place when parents spend time with their children, when they give them guidance and discipline them, when they shower them with affection, and when they teach their children how to pray and grow in faith. (See *Putting Children and Families First: A Challenge for our Church, Nation, and World,* United States Catholic Conference.)

The Unexpected

The truly amazing thing is that, in spite of all the challenges families face, spouses continue to share love, welcome the gift of life, and want to give their children the best they can by creating a happy, safe home. Of course, every family will falter at times, will experience difficulty, and will doubt themselves. No family is perfect, and most of them have growing pains as children and parents enter different stages and times in their lives. As children grow, parents need to acknowledge the amazing pressures adolescents face—to drink alcohol or smoke cigarettes, do drugs, have premarital sex, harm their bodies, disrespect authority, or damage other people's property. Parents have to talk to their adolescents about these things, give them the right set of values with which to respond, and make sure they are not put in any situation that requires them to make an adult decision.

Some families face problems so serious that they need to reach out for help. We all know families who have or are living through these challenges; it may even be our own families. It probably seems impossible to consider asking for outside help and support, for so many reasons. However, this is a vital necessity for the healing and perhaps safety of the family. Children and teenagers need to know they matter, they are important and have worth, they are capable of being loved and loving, and they should reach out to someone to get help. Talking to a school counselors, a peer counselor in or out of school, a trusted teacher or coach, someone on an anonymous crisis hotline, a friend who may have experienced the same thing are all first steps that can lead to naming and addressing what is hurting a family. Solutions can be found if the first step of asking for it is taken.

FAITH ACTIVITY

Outreach in Your Community Read your parish bulletin and check bulletin boards or other reading material advertising the various support and outreach groups available to parishioners. Does more information need to be made available so parishioners, particularly newcomers, or anyone in a particular crisis will know where to turn? How could you help? Contact the chairperson of any particular group in which you are interested and ask how you or your friends might be able to help—perhaps with advertising, driving, childcare, etc.

Strains on the Family Serious illnesses and chronic conditions can stretch a family, or they can strengthen the bonds of love. A child with a physical disability, a heart condition, cancer, or some other serious illness that will take months to cure or can never be cured is one of the most difficult mysteries of human life. We ask, "How can God let innocent children suffer?"

A strong adult in a family who is suddenly struck down by an illness or rendered disabled by an accident is also part of the mystery of suffering. The adult is seriously ill or injured, and his family and friends, can cry out, "Why?" Other examples include, an elderly family member who is suddenly unable to care for himself, who loses his memory, or who becomes incontinent or bedridden. These are each parts of the mystery of suffering and cause many to ask, "Why?"

For the family dealing with these things the question is not usually, "Why?" Instead they find themselves asking "How?" "How are we going to deal with this? How can we still be our family? How can we rely on others to help during this time?"

Support and guidance from the Church through the local parish should be available for all Catholic families experiencing crises. Besides health problems, families may have unemployment, underemployment, a member with a substance abuse, a member overseas in the military, someone in prison, or other serious challenges. What can their parish do for them? Sometimes financial support can be given for a time. Always prayer support should be given. And more and more parishes have support groups made up of people who have been through the same situation in their marriages.

FAITH ACTIVITY

Family of Origin Throughout this chapter, you've looked at what the Christian family strives to be and the reality of what families face today. Spend some time privately thinking about your family patterns—how it functions, its priorities and values, family members ability to show love and forgiveness, its traditions and customs, its weaknesses and unique challenges. What do you want to intentionally pass on to the next generation in your family? Why? What do you want to intentionally change? Why? How do you think you can go about preserving what you want to keep and changing what you wouldn't want to leave behind?

"An Interplay of Light and Darkness"

In his Apostolic Exhortation to families, Blessed Pope John Paul wrote his reflections on the situations for families in today's worlds. After listing many positive and negative influences, he wrote, "The historical situation in which the family lives therefore appears as an interplay of light and darkness." (*On the Family*, #6)

GROUP TALK

Without referring to the list below, work with two or three classmates to generate a list of elements of "light" which promote goodness in families today. Then compare your list to that of Pope John Paul II below.

Here are the elements of light for today's families that Pope John Paul identified:

- A more lively awareness of personal freedom

- Greater attention to the quality of interpersonal relationships within marriage

- Greater attention to the dignity of women

- Greater attention to responsible procreation

- More concern about the religious education of children

- Awareness of the need to develop interfamily relationships for the sharing of spiritual and material assistance

- Rediscovery of the family's important place in the Church as a responsible agent for the building of a more just society.

(See *On the Family*, #6.)

It's quite probable that the lists you and your friends made differ from Pope John Paul's list. However, it is likely that you mentioned some of the same concepts he did, perhaps in different words. It's also probable that the Pope would add new things to his list if he could rewrite it today.

Christian Foundation for Children and the Aging (CFCA)

It's quite possible that you have heard a speaker for the Christian Foundation for Children and the Aging at your parish, and have seen the photos of children and elderly people who need a sponsor. The CFCA speakers are lay people and priests—diocesan or members of religious orders—from the U.S., inviting U.S. Catholics to reach out to someone from another country.

CFCA is a not a religious order. It is a lay Catholic organization committed to creating relationships between sponsors in the U.S. and children and aging persons in twenty-five developing nations around the world.

In 1981, Jim, Bud, and Bob Hentzen; their sister, Nadine Pearce; and their friend Jerry Tolle had a dream of helping people in Third-World Countries—where Bob and Jerry had both been lay missionaries—by getting people in the U.S. to sponsor them. They felt the one-to-one connection would not only allow people in the U.S. to provide ongoing help for the poor, but would allow the poor to share their gifts with U.S. Catholics as well. The foundation still emphasizes the "two-way street" that preserves the dignity of the sponsored person and depends on personal outreach from sponsors.

CFCA's stated purpose is "to create a worldwide community of compassion through personal outreach." The foundation names four core values that guide everything they do as an organization:

- The Gospel call to serve the poor.

- Honesty and transparency of operations.

- Recognizing the God-given dignity of each person.

- Mutual respect between sponsor and sponsored person.

From that dream and with those core values, the CFCA worldwide community reaches out from the U.S. to twenty-five countries. More than 275,000 Catholics are sponsors to more than 310,000 children and aging friends. Staff members and volunteers are present at CFCA sites in each country to see that each elderly person and child is helped in such a way that they can stay within their families and/or communities and lead productive lives.

CFCA sponsors make a commitment to send a monthly monetary donation and to pray for their sponsored friends. They are also encouraged to send letters and photos to their sponsored friends who also send cards, letters, and photos regularly.

CFCA staff and volunteers provide education, medical care, financial aid, and spiritual support at each CFCA site. They work to get the families of sponsored children involved in their education and in outreach to those who are not yet sponsored. CFCA-sponsored "mothers' programs" gather thousands of mothers in one region for a chance to meet and speak on behalf of their families and villages.

In Rockford, Illinois we visited a nice house that doesn't look big enough to hold twenty children and two parents, and we met Rose and Alan Malivolti. At the moment there are only fifteen children living there, but there have been twenty there at one point. No one knows if or when there might be more. After all, when Rose married Al thirty-three years ago, she told him she intended to have twenty-one children!

ROSE: I don't know where I got that number, but I know I said it all the time, ever since fourth grade.

AL: It sounded good to me, and somewhere along the way we just got too busy to keep counting. So somehow we ended up one short.

INTERVIEWER: Some of the twenty are foster children, right? They aren't all yours?

R: We've had foster children, too, but the twenty are all ours. Four of them are our biological children, and sixteen are our legally adopted children. The "original four" are all on their own now–two are married; one is single; and the youngest boy is in the seminary. Our oldest adopted child is also married.

A: We are actually grandparents now, but that hasn't stopped us from adopting! Our youngest son is six. He and his three siblings came to us from Haiti.

I: Your first eight adopted children came from South Texas, right? All siblings?

A: Their mother was dying of cancer, and she wanted someone to promise to keep her children together. No one in any agency or church in Texas could promise her that. They didn't have the system set up that way. Someone offered to take five of them, but no one wanted all eight.

R: And that just wasn't acceptable to Blanca. When I heard about her, I contacted a friend of hers and said, "We'll take them!" I didn't even call Al first.

A: Rose didn't need to call me. She knew I wanted to adopt kids as much as she did. She knew I'd agree there was nothing more important than keeping a family together and giving them all a home.

R: From the moment Al and I got married, I knew God had been preparing us just for this. When I was in fourth grade, my teacher told us that she had been a child in an orphanage, but no one had ever adopted her. She had never lived in a family, in a regular home. I was nine years old, but that very minute, I was so thunderstruck at the idea of a little girl never living in a family that I just knew I had to do something to keep that from happening to some other little girls.

I: So you contacted the people in Texas and went down to get eight kids?

R: There were tons of red tape and hours of arguing, but we also had wonderful quiet times with Blanca and the children when we could make the promise she asked of us. All she kept saying was, "Will you love my children?"

I: And it looks like you have! But now, why eight more from Haiti?

A: When we were down there in the orphanage there were sixty kids crowded into one big room, and I asked Rose, "Can we take them all?" That's how badly I wanted to give every one of those kids a real home, real love, and a real chance at life.

R: But we only took four and that was hard enough! Red tape and politics like you wouldn't believe.

A: We got four more just a couple of years ago–in fact we have two more adoptions to be finalized. Two of these last four are physically disabled and very ill.

I: So, why have you done all this?

A: It's what we promised each other when we got married–to be good parents to children who needed a good home.

R: It all comes down to this: "Seek God's will and then do it." I'll tell you, if we weren't Catholic we would not have been able to do this. It's all come about by prayer–our prayer, the prayers of our children, parishioners, priests. The Poor Clare Nuns have prayed all night for us on occasion–and we've had miracles. Every single adoption has had a miracle connected to it.

I: So what would you say raising twenty children has done for your marriage?

R: Being the parents of these children has defined our marriage.

who will you become?

Your analysis of your communication style on Page 190 gave you a picture of where you seem to fall on a spectrum between introspective and outgoing attitudes. Both extremes have advantages and drawbacks.

Now, evaluate your communication skills as they relate to a family.

Choose the place on the scale where your opinion about each statement falls.

1. Talking about money will be

a source of a lot of tension. ———————————————— easy because we love each other so much.

2. We should keep our money

in a joint account. ———————————————— in separate accounts.

3. When it comes to telephones,

I'm going to need my own line. ———————————————— I wish we could live without one.

4. When it comes to television,

I hardly ever watch it. ———————————————— I watch two or more hours a day.

5. I like to eat dinner

in front of the TV. ———————————————— in the dining room

6. When my in-laws come to visit,

I'll do my best to enjoy their company. ———————————————— I'll endure them.

7. I hope we have neighbors

who'll be close friends. ———————————————— who'll leave us alone.

8. When it comes to raising children,

we'll talk everything over. ———————————————— I'll let my spouse be in charge.

How do you think you would do communicating with a spouse and children? What skills do you think you should start working on now before you even decide to get married?

Prayer

Leader: We call on the Holy Trinity to bless us all as we pray:

All: In the Name of the Father and of the Son and of the Holy Spirit. Amen.

Reader: A reading from Saint Paul's Letter to the Ephesians:

"I bow my knees before the Father, from whom every family in heaven and on earth takes its name. I pray that, according to the riches of his glory, he may grant that you may be strengthened in your inner being with power through his Spirit, and that Christ may dwell in your hearts through faith, as you are being rooted and grounded in love" (*Ephesians 3:14–17*).

The word of the Lord.

All: Thanks be to God.

Leader: Let's each raise up a prayer for families now. We will go around the classroom, and when it's your turn, simply read the prayer line and fill in the blank in any way you feel called to pray. After each individual petition we will all pray the response.

[Leader and reader begin and then leader indicates when each student should pray in turn.]

Individual Prayer: Heavenly Father, please help our families to ——————————— .

All: May Christ dwell in our hearts through faith, as we are being rooted and grounded in love.

[After all have prayed individually, leader continues.]

Leader: We gather all our individual prayers together now, and pray together the words that Jesus our Brother taught us to pray.

All: Our Father, who art in heaven . . .

Leader: May God bless us as we go to be with our families and friends this day.

ALL: In the name of the Father and of the Son and of the Holy Spirit. Amen.

Study Guide

▶Check Understanding

1. Explain what communication requires.

2. Recall some of the ways we can listen to what is being said and who is saying it.

3. List and describe the different family structures in today's world.

4. Name some positive changes that have taken place in the way families function.

5. Describe how the family is a path to God.

6. Explain why the family is called the domestic Church.

7. Give examples of the types of needs children have and how families can address them.

8. Point out some ways the family is called to be a community of grace and prayer.

9. Define the four cardinal virtues.

10. Summarize how the family is called to be a school of Christian virtue.

11. Identify how the Fourth Commandment directs family life.

12. Explain how the sacraments guide family life.

13. Express in your own words what intentional living means.

14. State the Church's teachings on artificial birth control and means of conception as well as the rationale for these teachings.

15. Describe what is meant by intentional parenting.

16. Point out some positive influences on family life today.

▶Apply and Develop

17. Examine the various family structures described in this chapter and show how each can be a graced community.

18. Prepare a chart of the different ways families continue the work of the Church in the home.

19. Compare and contrast the ways that children and parents are called to live out the Fourth Commandment.

20. Propose a plan for helping families be beacons of light in today's world, with specific mention of Pope John Paul II's "interplay of light and darkness."

▶Key Words

See pages noted for contextual explanations of these important faith terms.

artificial birth control (p. 208)

domestic Church (p. 196)

family (p. 192)

virtue (p. 201)

CALLED TO DISCIPLESHIP

CHAPTER 8

CHAPTER GOALS

In this chapter you will:

★ consider the uniqueness of each person and how we are all called to use our gifts, and the implications of both for us and for the Church.

★ recognize how Christian vocation leads to true inner peace, joy, and commitment.

★ learn how living the Beatitudes is a realization of our need for God in our lives and our call to act on behalf of others.

★ discover how the images of salt and light apply to disciples of Christ.

★ meet a religious sister who has stood up to the sin of racism both personally and systemically.

WHO ARE YOU?

Rate each statement below. Put an "x" below one of the three headers and above the line next to each statement to indicate how you rate its importance.

	Absolutely necessary to a person's success	Nice, but a person can be successful without it	Not part of how I measure success

1. A job I like _____
2. A job that pays well _____
3. A salary that allows for luxuries _____
4. Own my own home _____
5. Own more than one car _____
6. A college education _____
7. Good friends _____
8. Good health _____
9. A good reputation _____
10. Active membership in a specific parish _____
11. Membership in a civic organization _____
12. Membership in a faith community _____
13. Political involvement _____
14. Participate in local politics _____
15. Participate in the sacraments _____
16. Married with children _____
17. Married without children _____
18. Single _____
19. Able to negotiate and compromise _____
20. Willing to work hard _____
21. Work overtime frequently _____
22. Save a fixed amount of money _____
23. Provide monetary support to the Church _____
24. Serve those in need _____
25. Take a vacation _____
26. Travel _____
27. Create and/or follow family traditions _____
28. Have personal integrity _____
29. Live by a set of principles _____
30. Stay out of debt _____

Called and Gifted

The desire to succeed is one that most people share. Who wouldn't want to be successful in school, sports, music, performance of any sort, clubs, work, careers, relationships, and life? But how do we measure success? It's a very subjective thing, in several different ways. What criteria does a person use to determine success? From completing the exercise at the beginning of this chapter, you probably found as many criteria sets as students in your class. And how much of any one criterion merits success? Again, this varies by each individual, and society even weighs in on what is needed to be successful. With all of these perceptions, and sometimes misconceptions, perhaps we should be asking a slightly different question—one about meaning. What makes your life meaningful? What brings meaning to your life? How do you measure meaning in your life?

Throughout this course, you have spent time getting to know yourself better. You've thought seriously about who you are. You have considered your talents, skills, and abilities; you've looked at your perspective on the impact faith has on life as well as your values and priorities. You have reflected on the role of prayer in your life and your attitude toward and commitment to serving others. You've surveyed how you relate to others and how you communicate in those relationships. In different ways, each of these aspects of who you are brings meaning to your life.

You have also spent time making connections and looking for patterns in your life—to get a sense of who you want to become, to see how God is acting in your life now and how he might be calling you live in the future. You've invested time and energy so that you can understand yourself more and thus better respond to God and others in your life. You've continued your search for meaning. In all of these ways you have made a commitment to accept and grow into the amazing person God created you to be.

Now there are varieties of gifts, but the same Spirit; and there are varieties of services, but the same Lord; and there are varieties of activities, but it is the same God who activates all of them in everyone. To each is given the manifestation of the Spirit for the common good.

✝ 1 Corinthians 12:4–7

Paul's words to the people of Corinth are as reassuring today as they must have been over two thousand years ago. Each and everyone one of us has a purpose, a gift to share, an ability to put to good use, and a talent through which God works and moves. Each and every one of us is a unique combination of talents, gifts, abilities, hopes, and dreams that make us who we are as God's children. We are called to use our uniqueness in unique ways, in ways that no one else could, for the good of others. And the same Spirit who gives us our gifts gives us the courage, perseverance, hope, and passion to share them with others.

Amongst all this uniqueness we have something fundamental in common: God's universal call to holiness. We are not only gifted by God, but we are also called by him to use our gifts. We develop our gifts by sharing them in our families and circle of friends, at school and at work, with our parish and wider communities. Sometimes it's not always easy to recognize a gift from God, and you might not see it as such until someone points it out to you. That's one of the benefits of sharing who we are with people around us, but that's not the only reason.

As you discern what God is calling you to be and do, you need to know your gifts and assets. You also need to know your limitations, and how all the different facets of your personality work together for you. You need to think about what kinds of people will work best with you and what type of husband or wife would be good for you, if you are being called to the married life.

Meaningfulness We create meaning in our lives when we develop and bring to others the God-given abilities and talents that fill us and make us whole. To have a meaningful life, consider the following:

Enjoy what you do. Your daily attitude will have a huge impact on the happiness you and others experience—and to your productivity.

Let God into your life. Your relationship with God influences everything about who you are and how you live. Allow the Spirit to open your heart so that you can hear the Father's call and follow the Son's path. The relationship of love that is God's can guide you, direct you, sustain you. Trust and believe. Pray and worship.

FAITH ACTIVITY

See Your Gifts How aware are you of your gifts? In groups of five or six, try this: Have each person in the group write down a personal non-material gift they see that each other person has. Give the lists to each other. Did everyone write things you expected? Did any write things that you hadn't thought of about yourself? Did any write things you disagree with?

Remember that who you are is as important as what you do. The kind of person you are directs and shapes your actions. The world's greatest persons are known for their characters as much as their achievements. First and foremost you are a child of God who can love, care, and share his message of hope. Be a good person. Then you can become a great one.

Establish and adhere to your priorities. God and people should come first, so put them first. Don't dedicate so much time or energy to your work or hobbies that your personal and spiritual life and relationships suffer.

If our meaning and purpose are bound up in following God's call, what does that mean for those of us—all of us—who at some point in our lives just don't know if we are where we are meant to be? This is a natural part of life. We won't always know where we are going, or if we are even on the right path. And sometimes we might not know where the path is taking us, and we might feel lost or confused or think our efforts are taking us nowhere. Especially at those times, don't lose sight of the overall purpose we all share: to know, to love, and to serve God. Take things one step at a time and realize that whatever path you walk in response to God's call, he and the Church community will always be walking with you.

GROUP TALK

1 Who has walked on the path of discovery with you? How have these people made a difference in your life? Have you told them how much they mean to you?

2 Think of a time you supported someone when he or she felt lost or confused. How did you help them?

3 What has meaning in your life? Who brings meaning to your life?

4 What do you think living a meaningful life feels and looks like?

The Community's Gifts

The Church is also called and gifted, but sometimes some of her members don't always recognize and use their gifts. This happens when we, the People of God, fail to see the gift that *each other member* is for the whole Church. When any person or group of people is ignored or passed over as of no importance, great gifts are lost.

If an ethnic group is pushed to the back or ignored, the Church is deprived of the gifts of that group's culture and history, gifts meant to be part of the Church. If people are judged to be too old, gifts from their younger years might still be celebrated. But even more precious gifts of wisdom, age, and grace are often ignored or pushed aside. If people who have disabilities are only seen as people to be helped, gifts that they could offer that would help enrich the Church will be missed or dismissed.

Perhaps, in some cases, it is you and your peers who are ignored and passed over by the Church. The ideas of people your age at times may be dismissed as "impractical." Many times the innovators are told to curb their enthusiasm, when in reality the fresh ideas and energetic enthusiasm of youth are often just what the Church needs.

> " Yes, now is the time for mission! In your Dioceses and parishes, in your movements, associations and communities, Christ is calling you. The Church welcomes you and wishes to be your home and your school of communion and prayer. Study the Word of God and let it enlighten your minds and hearts. Draw strength from the sacramental grace of Reconciliation and the Eucharist. Visit the Lord in that "heart to heart" contact that is Eucharistic Adoration. Day after day, you will receive new energy to help you to bring comfort to the suffering and peace to the world. Many people are wounded by life: they are excluded from economic progress, and are without a home, a family, a job; there are people who are lost in a world of false illusions, or have abandoned all hope. By contemplating the light radiant on the face of the Risen Christ, you will learn to live as 'children of the light and children of the day' (1 Thess. 5:5), and in this way you will show that 'the fruit of light is found in all that is good and right and true' (Eph. 5:9). "
>
> **Message of Pope John Paul to Youth, July 2002**

Have an open discussion about the following:

- Who are some of the individuals or groups in your parish whose gifts are being recognized and used? What difference does that make for your parish? Are there other gifts that need to be acknowledged and encouraged? From whom?

- Who are some students, teachers, or others at your school whose gifts are being recognized and used? What difference does that make for your school? Are there other gifts that need to be acknowledged and encouraged? From whom?

- What might your school be missing as a result?

- How does or can your parish or school use your gifts and talents? Which ones?

FAITH ACTIVITY

The Four Calls With a small group, take one of the four calls identified in the Bishops' statement. Write the call in the middle of a large piece of poster board, and around it write ways that people your age and families can respond to that call. Use what you've learned in this course and any of your own experiences to complete this activity.

In 1995, the United States Bishops released a statement entitled *Called and Gifted for the Third Millennium*, an updated version of a statement released fifteen years prior. Both the revised and original statement focused on four calls that the whole Church shares: the call to holiness, the call to community, the call to mission and ministry, and the call to adulthood/Christian maturity. These four calls have been the foundation for our consideration of vocation and discernment. The prayer that introduced this Bishops' statement is a very appropriate reflection as we are finishing this course.

Quick Check

1. How are a successful life and a meaningful life alike and different?

2. What does Saint Paul say about gifts in 1 Corinthians?

3. What are some suggestions for achieving a meaningful life?

4. What are the four calls highlighted in the Bishops' statement *Called and Gifted*?

> GOD of love and mercy, you call us to be your people,
> you gift us with your abundant grace.
> Make us a holy people, radiating the fullness of your love.
> Form us into a community, a people who care,
> expressing your compassion.
> Remind us day after day of our baptismal call to serve,
> with joy and courage.
> Teach us how to grow in wisdom and grace and joy
> in your presence.
> Through Jesus and in your Spirit, we make this prayer.
> —*Called and Gifted for the Third Millennium*

Joy and Commitment

At the Last Supper, the night before he died, Jesus said to his apostles:

"As the Father has loved me, so I have loved you;
abide in my love.
If you keep my commandments, you will abide in my love,
just as I have kept my Father's commandments and abide
in his love.
I have said these things to you so that my joy may be in you,
and that your joy may be complete."

✝ John 15:9–11

There's no doubt about it—Jesus knew that following him would bring us joy.

Christians who faithfully live their vocations *will have joy*, no matter what else they find or lose, achieve, abandon, or earn in their lifetimes. It is our destiny—as humans made in God's image and capable of freely thinking, choosing, and loving—to reach eternal union with God. By eternal union we mean joining God completely, being reunited to him in friendship for all of time. From the moment we were conceived, we were called and made for joy.

For such a short word, *joy* carries a lot of weight. Though sometimes interchanged with *happiness* or *gladness*, joy has an extra dimension to it. Joy is a feeling of well-being like the other two words imply, but the feeling stems from the realization of a goal or the meaningful fulfillment of a destiny. Joy is very deep and very satisfying, partly because before we feel it we often feel that something is missing or unfinished. It is written: "Weeping may linger for the night, but joy comes with the morning" (*Psalm 30:4–5*).

Mysteriously, we can feel great joy while not feeling very happy, or well, or safe. Deep joy comes with the knowledge that we are loved, that we are in the place we ought to be, that we have achieved true meaning in our lives, that we are fulfilling our destiny. We can feel joy and sorrow at the same time. There is a beautiful passage in the Book of Ezra that illustrates this. The Hebrew people had returned home after years of exile. Jerusalem, including the Temple, had been destroyed; but now a new Temple had been built. At the dedication of the new Temple, "old people who had seen the first house on its foundations, wept with a loud voice when they saw this house, though many shouted aloud for joy, so that the people could not distinguish the sound of the joyful shout from the sound of the people's weeping" (*Ezra 3:12–13*).

Our Vocation to Beatitude

In Chapter Two we briefly discussed the Beatitudes and the values we get from these teachings of Jesus. And we will discuss how the Beatitudes guide our lives as disciples of Christ. But it is important to first look at the word *beatitude*. This is the word the *Catechism* uses to discuss our true vocation. Usually a writer will mention the word as a synonym for *blessing*, and then stop using it. It's very telling that the *Catechism* uses the word **beatitude** in all discussion of our salvation and vocation, instead of any other word like *blessing*, *happiness*, or even *joy*

We have a "vocation to beatitude;" that is, we are called to *total union with God*. The *Catechism* explains:

> Beatitude makes us 'partakers of the divine nature' and of eternal life.[1] With beatitude, man enters into the glory of Christ[2] and into the joy of the Trinitarian life. Such beatitude surpasses the understanding and powers of man. It comes from an entirely free gift of God.
>
> *Catechism of the Catholic Church*, 1721-1722

This is quite a statement about who we are and who we are made to become. We know that grace is a sharing in God's own life, but phrases like "partakers of the divine nature" bring a new depth of understanding to sharing in God's love. The Son of God took on our human nature while completely and wholly maintaining his divine nature, so that we could share in his divine nature, becoming more like him. We are made in the light of Christ and for Christ, called to live out our being made in the image of God as he intended. We are connected to and enter into Jesus' glory, and the joy of his relationship with the Father and the Holy Spirit. We enter into the community of love that is the Trinity. This sharing commits us to God's Kingdom and its values.

FAITH ACTIVITY

Mixed Feelings Recall a time when you laughed and cried at the same time, or you cried "tears of joy." What was the occasion or event when this happened? What different emotions converged to cause that to happen? Reflect on this experience and express your thoughts in a prayer, poem, song, or piece of art.

Christ's redemption through his death and Resurrection, and our participation in that mystery through the grace first received at Baptism, makes this total union with God possible. However, we have to respond to that call daily, we have to choose to love and make decisions based on Christian values and Church teachings. This call commits us to God's Kingdom and the values and vision that he has for all his people. That's where the Beatitudes give us some direction.

> *Blessed are the poor in spirit,*
> *for theirs is the kingdom of heaven.*
>
> *Blessed are those who mourn,*
> *for they will be comforted.*
>
> *Blessed are the meek,*
> *for they will inherit the earth.*
>
> *Blessed are those who hunger and thirst for righteousness,*
> *for they will be filled.*
>
> *Blessed are the merciful,*
> *for they will receive mercy.*
>
> *Blessed are the pure in heart,*
> *for they will see God.*
>
> *Blessed are the peacemakers,*
> *for they will be called children of God.*
>
> *Blessed are they who are persecuted for the righteousness sake,*
> *for theirs is the kingdom of heaven.*

> *Blessed are you when people revile you and persecute you and utter all kinds of evil against you falsely on my account. Rejoice and be glad, for your reward is great in heaven, for in the same way they persecuted the prophets who were before you.*

✝ Matthew 5:3–12

FAITH ACTIVITY

Sermon on the Plain Look up Luke 6:7–26, Luke's version of the Beatitudes is sometimes described as the "Sermon on the Plain," because Jesus spoke it on level ground. Compare and contrast this version of the Beatitudes to Matthew's version.

This list of blessings spoken by Jesus must have shocked the group he was speaking to. It's hard for us to imagine the impact of his words. We've heard them often, but not only were they new to the disciples and those gathered that day, they were a radical departure from what they were used to hearing about how to live a good life.

The Beatitudes, spoken by Jesus in his Sermon on the Mount, fulfill God's promises in the Old Testament by showing us that the promises do not lead to an earthly kingdom, but to the Kingdom of Heaven. God has placed a desire for happiness deep in each human heart, and the Beatitudes respond to that desire. They teach us what we must do to reach the final end to which God calls us: beatitude, rest with him in his kingdom.

While the Beatitudes focus on future fulfillment, they also guide us to living in a way that leads to fulfillment in the present. In the Beatitudes we aren't reflecting on eight different groups of people, but on the character that each disciple is called to form and live by. In that way, the Beatitudes can be considered signposts and direction markers on our path to responding to God's call to know, love, and serve him. We will now take a closer look at each of the Beatitudes.

GROUP TALK

As you read the Beatitudes, think about Christians you know or have read about. Which Beatitudes have you seen in action—lived by someone choosing to consciously carry them out in some concrete way?

▲ Redemptorist priest leads Stations of the Cross on Good Friday at a retreat center in New York.

Poor in Spirit, Open to God The first beatitude, blessed are the poor in spirit, requires emptying ourselves, setting aside our spirit of self-concern, so that the Holy Spirit who dwells within us can have room to breathe. This is one of the great effects of participating in the Sunday Mass. It helps us be less self-absorbed and to think about the bigger world picture, the larger community to which we belong. Jesus exemplifies what it means to be "poor in spirit" as he gave of himself totally and completely upon the cross.

Being poor in spirit means trusting in God. If we think we can make a difference in the world by ourselves, we will soon be disillusioned. However, if we realize that God works through us, then we trust that our actions are not isolated acts but are part of a whole. Acting in communion with Christ and his Church, therefore, magnifies our good works many fold.

For many years now, Catholic colleges and high schools have encouraged their students to participate in outreach projects. Some students spend their spring break or their summer vacation in Latin America working with homeless people to build homes, or helping other people in need. One of the great benefits of programs such as these is that students are able to put a name and a face on people who are poor. Therefore, the students are making room within themselves for people and structures they might otherwise have locked out of their consciousness and concern. Through such service activities, young people learn to be poor in spirit.

FAITH ACTIVITY

Look Inside Are you:
Self-absorbed or self-emptying?
Self-centered or other-centered?
Aware of God or unaware of God?
An active participant or a bystander?
Involved in service or uninvolved in service? Informed about problems in the world or uninformed? Passionate about contributing to life or dispassionate?

Give examples to support your answers. Choose one of the pairs and explain why you would want to be one way or the other.

Those Who Mourn–Sharing the Gift of Tears "Jesus began to weep" (*John 11:35*). These words make up a very short verse in the Bible, but they tell us a great deal about Jesus and about what it means to live the Christian life. They record the response that Jesus made upon hearing that his friend Lazarus had died. We may feel uncomfortable attending a funeral or visiting someone who is sick in a hospital.

Part of our discomfort is that we don't know what to say, and part of it is we would like to make things better when we can't. The best gift we can give to others at such times is to mourn with them, as Jesus did with the sisters of Lazarus.

Certainly our world is not all what we would like it to be; we ourselves are not all that we want to be. The first step on the way to facing life's problems and working toward change is to cry, to be upset, to mourn. Crying reveals our humanness. Unless we're experienced actors, it happens uncontrollably; we cry because we have been deeply touched by another's pain or our own. For example, we may come to see our own failures and shortcomings. They may cause us to mourn and suffer deep within ourselves where no one else can see the pain. But, by the grace of God, we can begin to take our suffering and transform it into something beautiful for God. To mourn is not a passive Beatitude. When we mourn, we are touched and we are changed. As we change, we may be moved to action. Jesus assures us that in the end, through our mourning, we will be comforted.

Quick Check

1. How does the meaning of the word joy differ from happiness or gladness?

2. What is *beatitude*?

3. What are the Beatitudes?

4. What does it mean to be poor in spirit and mournful?

Catholic Relief Services

Headquartered in Baltimore, Maryland, with field offices on five continents, Catholic Relief Services provides developmental assistance and humanitarian relief for disadvantaged and vulnerable people in nearly 100 countries and territories around the world.

Drawing upon Catholic social teaching with its emphasis on justice and the dignity of each individual person, CRS has a broad range of outreach programs. It supports international efforts aiding agriculture, community health and nutrition, education, emergency response, HIV/AIDS prevention, building peace, safety-net programming, and even microfinance, which teaches business practices and consumer education. Some of its many domestic efforts include advocacy, farmer-to-farmer support, parish outreaches, and various youth outreaches. It is committed to fighting the injustices of poverty, exclusion, intolerance, and discrimination everywhere.

CRS provides programs for high school students, young adults, and people of all ages to raise awareness and put their faith into action. Here are some examples you may participate in:

▼ Two students in the Deheisha Refugee Camp in the West Bank access the CRS Web site.

- Each Lent through Operation Rice Bowl parishes and schools pray, fast, and give alms as a way to be in solidarity with those around the world who face hunger and poverty.

- Young people across the United States fast, pray, serve, and learn through Food Fast, an annual, 24-hour hunger awareness retreat.

- Parishes participate in Fair Trade programs, involving otherwise under-priced products such as coffee and chocolate, so that farmers overseas receive a fair and just price so they can provide a more adequate standard of living for their families.

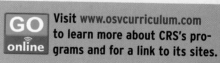

GO online Visit www.osvcurriculum.com to learn more about CRS's programs and for a link to its sites.

Global Solidarity Schools Initiative (GSSI) is one of the newest such programs.

Dependence on God and Action for Others

As we discussed in the previous section, the Beatitudes present Gospel values to live by. They give us the hope of a future life of fulfillment in God if we acknowledge our need and dependence upon him. When we realize our need for God, we grow to trust in him and hope in his ways.

The Meek: Finding God in Our Littleness

As we can see from Jesus' life, meekness does not mean weakness or being timid. Rather it means a compassionate use of one's strengths for the good of others. To be meek means to be open to conversion. When Jesus said to the people of his day, "repent, and believe in the good news" (*Mark 1:15*), he was encouraging people to be meek. For instance, treating "outsiders" at school with disdain in order to be part of a popular clique, not being open to others, violates a spirit of meekness. Meekness suggests that unless we find joy in God and ourselves, we will never truly be happy.

▲ Sister of Saint Joseph of Carondelet, Los Angeles province, teaches a second grader at St. John Chrysostom School in California.

GROUP TALK

1. What teacher, coach, or other person has shown you a lot about attitudes and character?

2. Who in your family or network of close friends possess strength of character and compassion?

3. What are some situations that people can act with a spirit of meekness to help others?

4. How can an active prayer life help people find God in their littleness?

Hunger and Thirst for Righteousness: Aligning Our Lives to God This particular beatitude is about the Christian's deep-seated, intense longing for knowing and living in God's light and love and law. We are to focus on God's will in every aspect of our lives, so that in our relationships and in the world, we refect on God to others.

And there is another way to look at this beatitude. As children of God and followers of Christ, we are challenged to see and get beyond what seems to limit us (ourselves, a bad relationship, a difficult family situation, an oppressive institution or structure).

We are challenged to learn from our experience and be motivated to take positive action that can lead to conversion and a newness in life. When we can see beyond our own inadequacies and experience, the transforming grace of God, we ourselves can become agents of transformation. A fundamental characteristic of what it means to be Catholic is working for justice. Indeed, the wording of this beatitude indicates that working for justice is as essential for the Christian life as food and drink are.

The Merciful: Finding God in Others Mercy implies caring for those whom most other people overlook and caring for people despite their failings and faults. It also means forgiving and acting out of kindness. Mercy gives freely to those to whom one is not expected to give at all; it forgives those who have harmed us. Mercy requires that people bring kindness, gentleness, and concern into their everyday relationships. Jesus gives us the simple but profound message that, in the end, those who show mercy will receive mercy.

GROUP TALK

Before discussing these questions in small groups, silently reflect on some experiences of forgiveness and mercy in your own life.

1 What is a situation today in which people can act with mercy? What would happen if the parties involved acted with mercy?

2 What are some times that forgiving someone else can be difficult? What happens when forgiveness is withheld? When forgiveness is given?

3 What are some examples in the Gospels of Jesus being merciful and forgiving? What can we learn from his actions?

FAITH ACTIVITY

Looking More Deeply In small groups, choose one situation that your school or local community faces right now. Describe how looking at it more deeply could help you and others understand it better and get involved to make a difference. Share your findings with the class.

Pure in Heart: Looking More Deeply In the Bible, the *heart* refers to the whole person, including intellect, freewill, emotions, and actions. This beatitude calls us to focus every aspect of our entire being in pursuit of living and doing as Christ is. It puts before us the goal of modesty, which is characterized by being patient, discreet, and decent.

Not only will the pure of heart see God, but they will see things as God sees them. We encounter many forces that attempt to direct our gaze—just think of the many commercials that we see on television and in popular magazines. Ads can and do attract our attention. Purity of heart, however, means seeing instead from the depth of our being, symbolized by the word *heart*. From this place, the core of our being, our gaze is on God and is God–like.

Peacemakers: Clinging to the Dream This beatitude advocates peacemaking, not peace. It calls for an active involvement in bringing about reconciliation between those in conflict, whether on a personal level or in society. Peacemakers sometimes struggle, meet with people they may not like, and challenge themselves and others. Peacemaking requires honest, heart-to-heart dialog, and working to eliminate the causes of alienation, fear, and tension that bring about conflict and hostility. Jesus himself, known as the Prince of Peace, often seemed to disturb the peace rather than uphold a false sense of it. Jesus knew that there exists an important difference between avoiding conflict and true peace.

Persecuted: Taking on the Challenge Many of us would like to live in a world where goodness is rewarded and wrongdoers get what they deserve. The last Beatitude points to a different experience of the world. During the early centuries of the Church, being persecuted became one of the hallmarks of the Christian life. Since people are still hurting in our world—often because of some form of injustice—anyone who attempts to alleviate suffering or stands up to injustice may encounter persecution.

Blessed Are You

The *Catechism* describes a blessing as "an encounter between God and man" (*CCC*, 2626). In a blessing, there is a dialogue between God's gift to us and our acceptance of it. This is why, while we often pray, "God bless you," we also pray, "Blessed be God." Because God blesses us, we in return can bless God, who is the source of every blessing.

The Beatitudes are the same for everyone. Whether you join a religious order, get married, become a diocesan priest, spend your life in a monastery, are an ecclesial Church minister, work in a factory or a bank, or dedicate yourself to your family as a stay-at-home parent, the Beatitudes are *your* blessings. God is calling you to a vocation that will shower you with blessings and fill you with joy.

Quick Check

1. What do the Beatitudes have to do with dependence on God?

2. What do the Beautitudes teach us about being meek and thirsting for justice?

3. What do the Beautitudes teach us about being merciful and pure in heart?

4. What do the Beautitudes teach us about being peacemakers and being persecuted?

Glenmary Home Missioners

Glenmary Home Missioners is a society of Catholic priests and brothers committed to serving rural America. It was founded in 1939 in Cincinnati, Ohio, by Father William Howard Bishop, a rural pastor from the Archdiocese of Baltimore. The purpose of the society is to establish the Catholic Church in rural regions of the United States, nurturing the Catholic minority, and reaching out to those who are not active in their faith, the unchurched, and to those who are poor. Ecumenical cooperation is a hallmark of Glenmary's style of home mission ministry. Lay men and women partner in many ways with Glenmary members to carry out Glenmary's mission to rural America. Father Bishop also founded a group of religious women, the Glenmary Home Mission Sisters.

Glenmary currently staffs over fifty missions and ministries in the small towns and rural areas of Appalachia, the South, and the Southwest. They minister to the spiritual and material needs of people in the dioceses of Birmingham, Cincinnati, Covington, Jackson, Lexington, Little Rock, Nashville, Owensboro, Raleigh, Richmond, Savannah, Tulsa, and Wheeling-Charleston.

- Nearly 1.5 million people live within Glenmary's mission territory. Of these, just under 11,000, or 0.7 percent, are Catholic.

- A significant percentage of the total population is unchurched (that is, does not attend any church on a regular basis).

- The poverty level within Glenmary mission areas is almost twice the national average.

- In the southern United States, about 173 counties have no Catholic congregation. Approximately 196 others have a Catholic congregation, but no resident pastoral minister.

Glenmary's mission statement is: "Alive with the fire of the Holy Spirit, [the Glenmary Home Missioners] go to rural and small-town U.S.A., where the Catholic Church is not yet effectively present, proclaiming and witnessing the Good News of Jesus Christ and the power of God's love, mercy and justice transforming the world."

(Glenmary Home Missioners
Mission Statement, 1995).

Harpers Ferry National Historic Park,
Harpers Ferry, West Virginia ▼

Salt and Light

"You are the salt of the earth; but if salt has lost its taste, how can its saltiness be restored? It is no longer good for anything, but is thrown out and trampled under foot.

"You are the light of the world. A city built on a hill cannot be hid. No one after lighting a lamp puts it under the bushel basket, but on the lamptstand, and it gives light to all in the house. In the same way, let your light shine before others, so that they may see your good works and give glory to your Father in heaven."

Matthew 5:13–16

You no doubt are familiar with this teaching of Jesus, which is part of his Sermon on the Mount. The message is a very powerful one for us today. We are to be like salt—which preserves and flavors—and light—which gives illumination and insight—to a world that does not always understand or agree with us. Christianity is not an escape or retreat from the realities of life. It is a call to live by the Beatitudes and bring the values of God's Kingdom into all aspects of life.

In the ancient world and at the time of Jesus, salt was used to season and preserve food. Salt was a basic commodity, something that occurred naturally. There was no refrigeration during this time, and meat could spoil quickly unless it was properly salted and cured. The analogy for us is that, as children of God, we are to flavor the world around us with kingdom values, thus helping protect the people of the world from the negative influences that pull them away from what is right and just. And, if, as Jesus' followers, we were to lose our distinctive character, and fail to live by the values Jesus set out, we would lose our impact in the world.

If you have spent some time in the kitchen or watched a cooking show on television, you might know that salt brings out the robustness of other flavors. Salt enhances the taste of something else. Salt is seldom eaten by itself. To compare that to the life of discipleship, we don't follow Christ alone but within our various communities: families, school, parish, diocese, and even the universal Church. The talents and gifts of others in our community enhance our individual gifts and talents, and vice versa. Our unique flavors contribute to preserving the message of God's love in the world today. By our Baptism we are called to be Christ to one another, so together we can be Christ to the world.

Light is another basic element of life. Light serves to illuminate and penetrate the darkness. The Scripture writers used it often to describe God, the Messiah, and the people of Israel. Jesus used it to describe himself. In this passage Jesus uses it to describe the effect of the world by those who embrace the Beatitudes and live the Gospel message. Such people will illuminate the world's darkness, bringing it light and life.

The Church is to be a community whose way of life draws others to God. The very purpose of light is taken away if it is hidden. It seems so obvious, but light is meant to shine, to radiate energy, to be seen, to be felt, to be shared. Our light is what we say and do. And we are called not to hide our discipleship but to live it openly so that others can see who and what we are. In this way others might see some of God's image in us and come to have faith themselves.

As has been taught throughout this course, we are relational by nature. God created us to be in community, and we need to trust in the communities that are life-giving in our lives. Our parish community has so much to offer us as we discern how to best let our light shine.

> Today, more than ever, our parishes are called to be communities of 'salt' and 'light'; to help believers live their faith in their families, communities, work, and world. We need parishes that will not 'lose their flavor' nor put their 'light under a basket.' We seek to build evangelizing communities of faith, justice, and solidarity, where all believers are challenged to bring God's love, justice, and peace to a world in desperate need of the seasoning of the gospel and the light of Catholic teaching.

> *Communities of Salt and Light: Reflections on the Social Mission of the Parish, Volume VI, page 549*

The Catholic Church is light for the world when she shares Jesus' Good News of hope and salvation and invites people to learn more about Christ. She is light for the world when she celebrates Christ's presence in the sacraments. She is light through her moral teachings and the guidance she gives for identifying what it means to live as a Catholic in today's world. She is light when she takes stands on political, social, and economic issues that affect people's lives. She is light for the world when she advocates for the respect and protection of the human dignity that all people share because we are made in God's image and likeness.

FAITH ACTIVITY

What Flavor Are You? If you had to describe yourself and the unique contribution you bring to your family, school, and neighborhood, what flavors or spices would you be? How does your interaction in each of these communities affect the community and its members? What do you gain from being part of each of these communities?

GROUP TALK

1 How would you describe your light?

2 In what ways can your light make a difference in bringing God's love, justice, and peace to those around you? to the world?

3 How does your parish accomplish the tasks described above? Who contributes to that happening?

4 What are some other things your parish can do to build a community of faith, justice, and solidarity?

Evangelization

We've already seen, the Church's missionary mandate to preach the Good News of salvation to all has been a compelling force in history. It continues to be such a force today. The Church is universal; therefore she is called to reach out to embrace people everywhere. She does this through each Church member faithfully living his or her Christian vocation.

Like the founders of religious orders and their followers in religious life, every baptized Christian is led forward in their mission by the love of Christ and urged on to contribute in some way to the building of God's Kingdom. We are each called to contribute to the effort of **evangelization**, to bring the Gospel to the world. As each of us responds to the urging of the Holy Spirit, we are cooperating with the Church's mandate to proclaim Christ's Gospel to all nations. By our efforts, others are meeting Christ—hopefully identifying how they can turn their lives toward God in a process of conversion, and ultimately having faith.

The work of evangelization isn't something that happens across oceans and in other continents. Evangelization isn't just about bringing the Good News to people who have never heard it before. It also involves bringing again the Good News to people who may have heard the Gospel message proclaimed, but for whatever reason could not respond to it at that time in their lives. It's about sharing the Word of God with people who once believed but no longer practice their faith. And, evangelization isn't focused on individuals alone, but on society and culture. Evangelization promotes life and hope and Gospel values to counter and to transform the aspects of culture that take away from the dignity of the person.

But how do we go about evangelizing? What does evangelization look like? It looks a lot like what we've been reading about and contemplating in this course. It looks like people, in all states and walks of life, sharing the Gospel values by the way they live and the things they say.

The *National Directory for Catechesis* describes the work of evangelization this way:

> "The Church's evangelizing activity consists of several essential elements: proclaiming Christ, preaching Christ, bearing witness to Christ, teaching Christ, and celebrating Christ's sacraments [Cf: On Evangelization in the Modern World][3]
>
> *National Directory for Catechesis*, 17C

As you can see from the above elements of evangelization, it requires the work of all baptized Christians using their unique gifts to benefit others. We are called to read the Scriptures, to meet the person Jesus in the Gospels and grow closer to him. We are called to tell others about him and his message, to give an example of Christian discipleship by the choices we make, the things we say and do; to bring ourselves and others to a better understanding of Christ and his Church's teachings; to participate in the celebration of the sacraments with our community of faith.

What role you play in this work will vary depending upon your talents and abilities, your state in life, and how you choose to respond to God's call.

Getting the Word Out It took a team of medieval monks forty years to produce one copy of the Bible, writing in ink with quill pens on parchment paper. Now, the Bible is available on CD-ROM and on the Internet—allowing users fast access to dozens of different Scripture translations online.

The Pony Express teamed multiple horses and riders out West to deliver mail and supplies to homesteaders in nineteenth century America. A letter might have crossed the country in several weeks; a package might have taken months. When the telegraph was invented, it could send a message in an astoundingly short time. Today information travels even more quickly and easily via cell phones, e-mail, instant messaging, and web cams. Some governments used to be able to withhold much important information from their citizens. Now, some of those same citizens in isolated villages have cell phones, fax machines, the Internet, and televisions with satellite dishes. These grant access to information that is more difficult to deny.

Up until the end of the twentieth century, when breaking news occurred while a newspaper was being run off, editors often stopped the presses to insert a last-minute story. Typesetters would hurry to their positions to set up the new story letter-by-letter so the printing presses could run again. Today, word processing programs on computers allow stories to be inserted almost instantly, and printing to be done simultaneously at locations across the globe.

Multicultural Centers and Institutes

The Mexican American Cultural Center (MACC) is a Catholic institute located in San Antonio, Texas for multicultural pastoral training and language studies. MACC was founded in 1972 by a collaboration of PADRES–an organization of Mexican American priests; Las Hermanas–a group of Mexican American religious sisters; the Texas Catholic Conference of Bishops; and the Archdiocese of San Antonio. Millions of Spanish-speaking Catholics already lived in the United States, but no pastoral, liturgical, or educational materials were printed in Spanish for them. In addition, very few trained religious leaders were Latino or had a good understanding of Latino culture and the Spanish language. These organizations began discussing ways to get materials translated into Spanish, to teach Spanish to Church ministers, and to train ministers to be sensitive to Latino realities and appreciative of Mexican culture.

The Mexican American Cultural Center that was born over thirty years ago has grown to be a vibrant place of learning and cultural exchange, Spanish language immersion, preparation for ministry among Latinos, and preparation for participants to be agents of social change among migrant workers and immigrants. It has a beautiful, new campus with four dormitory buildings, a chapel, spacious grounds, classrooms, meeting rooms, and a cafeteria. It always seems busy.

People come from all over the world to attend week-long workshops, summer programs, or semester courses. People from all walks of life have come to MACC in San Antonio and to its adjunct campus in Guadalajara, Mexico, seeking preparation for ministry among Spanish-speaking people or looking for strategies to help bring about social change among Mexican migrants. They leave MACC to go all over the world as teachers, missionaries, chaplains, medical personnel, community organizers, and parish ministers.

MACC is not a college, but students can get credit for the courses they take in either of the semester-long formation programs: "Leadership for a Multicultural Church and Society," and "Leadership for Hispanic Ministry in the Third Millennium." Some people come to MACC solely to learn Spanish, where it is taught with an emphasis on pastoral language needed by ministers.

MACC also has mobile teams that take presentations to parishes and dioceses across the country and around the world. Presentation topics include: Principles of Hispanic Ministry, Home Visitation and Evangelization Among Hispanic People, Hispanic Expressions of Faith and Religiosity, Celebrating the Sacraments with Hispanic Communities, Welcoming New Immigrants, Understanding the Roots of Racism, and Challenges in Building Multicultural Communities.

The Mexican American Cultural Center's mission statement is: "to empower and educate leaders for service in a culturally diverse church and society." That's the one, holy, catholic, and apostolic Church in action!

The Institute for Black Catholic Studies is hosted by Xavier University in New Orleans, Louisiana. Founded by Saint Katharine Drexel and the Sisters of Blessed Sacrament in the 1920s, Xavier University is the only university in the world of its kind–both black and Catholic. Overall, it has 43 majors and 19 departments in its colleges of arts and sciences. The Institute for Black Catholic Studies began here in 1980, and is currently a member organization of The National Black Catholic Congress.

As part of The National Black Catholic Congress, The Institute for Black Catholic Studies works with other national Roman Catholic organizations that represent African-American Roman Catholics. The Institute for Black Catholic Studies educates Church ministers in the development of ministerial strategies for evangelizing African Americans within or outside of the Church, and also in the establishment of social justice within the Church and black Community as a whole. Thus, it works for the improvement of the spiritual, mental, and physical conditions of African Americans. Its interdisciplinary program features courses in theology, history, philosophy, social science, and the Bible– all taught in conjunction with ministry practicum. Ministry is the essential element of these studies and black leadership development is its goal. A Master's Degree program, a certificate program, and an enrichment program are all made available to train Church leaders in this area of ever-growing need in the United States and throughout the world.

In addition to theology and black Catholic Studies, Xavier University is also known for its college of pharmacy. Moreover, its men's and women's basketball teams frequently appear in the NCAA tournament. All of this fits within the rubric the university's overarching purpose: to promote a just and humane society celebrating diversity. Thus, Xavier is well-rounded and well-known.

For links to The Institute for Black Catholic Studies, Xavier University in New Orleans, Louisiana, and the National Black Catholic Conference visit www.osvcurriculum.com.

GO online

GROUP TALK

In 2000, the U.S. Catholic Bishops wrote a letter about ministry among immigrants called *Welcoming the Stranger Among Us: Unity in Diversity.* In that letter they encourage all ministers in the U.S. Church to learn a language other than English and to "acquire cultural knowledge relevant to their ministry" (37).

Discuss in small groups:

- Why do you think the U.S. Bishops are encouraging Church ministers to learn a second language?

- What knowledge about language and culture might ministers need that would be relevant to their ministry?

Today and into the Future How are you called to bring the Good News to others, now and in the future? How will you know what that vocation is? Listen carefully—to the word of God, to the Church, to yourself, to God speaking to you in prayer and solitude, and to the people around you. You will hear your call from those voices. Pay attention—what are your gifts? What are the needs in the world around you? You will find your call in these.

You *are* the salt of the earth, and so you will bring your own sanctified seasoning to the work you do to build up God's Kingdom. You *are* the light of the world, and so your light will be used for the kingdom if you let it shine.

In one of his World Youth Day messages, Blessed Pope John Paul II wrote:

> Dear young people, do not be content with anything less than the highest ideals! Do not let yourselves be dispirited by those who are disillusioned with life and have grown deaf to the deepest and most authentic desires of their heart. . . . 'You are the light of the world.' In this secularized age, when many of our contemporaries think and act as if God did not exist or are attracted to irrational forms of religion, it is you, dear young people, who must show that faith is a personal decision which involves your whole life. Let the Gospel be the measure and guide of life's decisions and plans! Then you will be missionaries in all that you say, and wherever you work and live you will be signs of God's love, credible witnesses to the loving presence of Jesus Christ. Never forget: 'No one lights a lamp and then puts it under a bushel' (*Matthew, 5:15*)!

Message of Pope John Paul II to Youth, July 2002

FAITH ACTIVITY

Message for Young People Write your personal response to this message from Pope John Paul II. What does he say here that applies to you? What questions do his words raise for you? What images of yourself in the future come to mind?

▼Pope John Paul II addressed young people at World Youth Day

Quick Check

1. What were the significance of salt and light in every day life during Jesus' time?

2. How are salt and light images for discipleship?

3. What is evangelization?

4. What are the elements of evangelization?

There is laughter coming from the office where we went to meet Sister/Doctor Jamie Phelps, O.P., Ph.D. The laughter is hers and her joy is genuine, sparkling from her eyes. Sister Jamie has been a member of the Dominican Sisters of Adrian, Michigan, for almost fifty years. Doctor Phelps has a Doctor of Philosophy degree in Systematic Theology, and is currently a Professor of Systemic Theology and the Director of the Institute for Black Catholic Studies at Xavier University, New Orleans. We catch up with her at Notre Dame University in South Bend, Indiana, where she is a visiting professor.

INTERVIEWER: Sister/Doctor is quite a title! Did you always want to be a theologian?

SISTER JAMIE: (Laughs) It's pretty heady stuff for a black girl who was born in Alabama and grew up in Chicago, I can tell you. No, I can't say I always wanted to be a theologian—I think in a way I always was one. I loved to study and I loved to think about God. But I can say that I have always wanted to be a religious sister, at least since I was five or six years old. Of course, at that time I told anyone who asked that I wanted to be "either a nun or a telephone operator!"

I: Where did you get the idea for those dreams?

SJ: Actually, the two both came from the same place. My parents taught all of us we were to help people. They told us we needed to develop our personal talents in order to help the community. At age five, I thought nurses were the most helpful people, but I knew I couldn't be a nurse—I couldn't stand blood! So I thought of a telephone operator, because they always asked, "How may I help you?" But then I got old enough to go to Catholic school and meet the sisters who taught us. I knew then there was no life that would be better for being helpful!

I: Did the desire to be a sister stay with you all through school?

SJ: It did. In fact, it got even stronger. I grew up in a very Catholic culture in a very ethnically mixed neighborhood in Chicago. My home was Catholic; my school was Catholic; my neighborhood was Catholic. When I made my First Communion I knew for sure God wanted me to be a sister, and that conviction never changed.

I: Back in those days, couldn't girls enter an aspirancy of a religious order for high school?

SJ: They could! But I couldn't. I wanted to. But the sisters felt that I needed more time before I joined them. Some of it had to do with me being black. They wanted me to experience more of the black-and-white world outside the convent before I joined. I was disappointed about having to wait, but I did as they asked. Then in 1959, I entered the convent.

I: Was being black a problem? Were there many black sisters?

SJ: The Adrian Dominicans welcomed me with open arms. Of course, there was racism in some people. There's always racism. But I was always blessed with superiors in my order who supported me and were advocates for me. There weren't any black sisters in my group then and there aren't many now—anywhere! I wish that wasn't true, but it is. We need more people to come forth for this vocation from the black community.

I: How do you think we can get them?

SJ: (Laughs) One person at a time, just like always. I think the call for young women today still needs to be a lot like my call. My call had to be something that would let me grow in wisdom, age, and grace, letting me contribute to the community as the best Christian I can be. That's the same for everyone of any color.

I: You've stayed close to the black community all your life, haven't you?

SJ: I've done a lot of work in the areas of black Catholic studies, the empowerment of black Catholics, the history of black Catholics, and lay ministry training for black Catholics. I'm a founding member of the National Black Catholic Sisters' Conference. We've been around since 1968, believe it or not!

I: If you had it to do over again?

SJ: I'd be a Dominican Sister. I love the Dominican ideals of searching for truth and putting contemplation into action. I love the shared prayer, the reflection, the habit of examining how your actions relate to your spirituality. I've grown spiritually in ways I wouldn't have grown in any other life. God's been good to me!

who will you become?

> Consider what a meaningful life means for you.

Look over the ratings you gave each item at the beginning of this chapter. Then, page back through the whole book and/or your notebook for this course to recall your opinions, ideas, and insights about earlier topics. Then create a personal message for a meaningful life.

Include your

- convictions about your faith
- hopes for the future
- values and priorities
- description of a good life
- requirements for relationships
- ideals for family
- areas for growth
- professional goals
- dreams for happiness
- thoughts about your vocation
- reflections on the importance of prayer and participation in the Mass and other sacraments

❯ Prayer

Leader: Let us bless the Lord, who has created all things and given us dominion over them.

All: Blessed be the name of the Lord! Blessed be God in all his creatures. In the Name of the Father and of the Son and of the Holy Spirit.

Reader: A reading from Saint Paul's Letter to the Romans (Reader reads Romans 8:22–28) The word of the LORD.

All: Thanks be to God. (Pause for silent reflection.)

Leader: Let us pray Psalm 8 together as a prayer to the Spirit, asking for help in our weakness, for direction in our decision making, for instruction in our prayer, and for patience as we wait for the future.

Right Side: O LORD, our Sovereign, how majestic is your name in all the earth! You have set your glory above the heavens.

Left Side: Out of the mouths of babes and infants you have founded a bulwark because of your foes, to silence the enemy and the avenger.

R: When I look at your heavens, the work of your fingers, the moon and the stars that you have established;

L: what are human beings that you are mindful of them, mortals that you care for them?

R: Yet you have made them a little lower than God, and crowned them with glory and honor. You have given them dominion over the works of your hands;

L: you have put all things under their feet, all sheep and oxen, and also the beasts of the field, the birds of the air, and the fish of the sea, whatever passes along the paths of the seas.

All: O LORD, our Sovereign, how majestic is your name in all the earth! Amen.

Study Guide

►Check Understanding

1. Expand upon how a successful life and a meaningful life are alike and different.

2. Summarize what Saint Paul says about gifts in 1 Corinthians.

3. Restate the suggestions presented in this chapter for achieving a meaningful life.

4. List the four calls highlighted in the Bishops' statement *Called and Gifted*.

5. Distinguish between the meaning of the words *joy*, *happiness*, and *gladness*.

6. Define *beatitude*.

7. Identify the purpose of the Beatitudes?

8. Describe what it means to be poor in spirit and mournful.

9. Explain what the Beatitudes have to do with dependence on God.

10. Express what it means to be meek and to thirst for justice.

11. Describe the Beatitude values of being merciful and pure in heart.

12. Tell what the Beatitudes teach about being peacemakers and being persecuted.

13. Explain the significance of salt and light in everyday life during Jesus' time.

14. Give examples of how salt and light are images for discipleship.

15. Define *evangelization*, and explain why it's important.

16. Summarize the elements of evangelization.

►Apply and Develop

17. If you were asked to present the meaning of "called and gifted" to a younger class, what would you say?

18. Choose one of the Beatitudes and hypothesize how communities—families, schools, neighborhoods, countries, and wider society—would be different if everyone lived by that Beatitude.

19. Select another Beatitude and describe how strengthening characteristics of Christian discipleship could positively influence your life over the next five years.

20. Illustrate how the elements of evangelization can be of assistance to young adults as they discern how God is calling to them to live out their Baptism.

►Key Words

See pages noted for contextual explanations of these important faith terms.

beatitude (p. 227)

evangelization (p. 239)

CATHOLIC SOURCE BOOK
Scripture

The Catholic Bible contains seventy-three books—forty-six in the Old Testament and twenty-seven in the New Testament.

The Old Testament

The Pentateuch

Genesis	Exodus	Leviticus	Numbers	Deuteronomy

The Historical Books

Joshua	1 Samuel	2 Kings	Ezra	Judith
Judges	2 Samuel	1 Chronicles	Nehemiah	Esther
Ruth	1 Kings	2 Chronicles	Tobit	1 Maccabees
				2 Maccabees

The Wisdom Books

Job	Proverbs	Song of Songs	Sirach (Ecclesiasticus)
Psalms	Ecclesiastes	Wisdom	

The Prophetic Books

Isaiah	Ezekiel	Amos	Nahum	Haggai
Jeremiah	Daniel	Obadiah	Habakkuk	Zechariah
Lamentations	Hosea	Jonah	Zephaniah	Malachi
Baruch	Joel	Micah		

The New Testament

The Gospels

Matthew	Mark	Luke	John

The Acts of the Apostles

The New Testament Letters

Romans	Ephesians	2 Thessalonians	Philemon	2 Peter
1 Corinthians	Philippians	1 Timothy	Hebrews	1 John
2 Corinthians	Colossians	2 Timothy	James	2 John
Galatians	1 Thessalonians	Titus	1 Peter	3 John
				Jude

Revelation

Creeds

Nicene Creed

I believe in one God,
the Father almighty,
maker of heaven and earth,
of all things visible and invisible.

I believe in one Lord Jesus Christ,
the Only Begotten Son of God,
born of the Father before all ages.
God from God, Light from Light,
true God from true God,
begotten, not made, consubstantial with
  the Father;
through him all things were made.
For us men and for our salvation
he came down from heaven,

At the words that follow up to and includ-
ing and became man, *all bow.*

and by the Holy Spirit was incarnate of
  the Virgin Mary,
and became man.
For our sake he was crucified under
  Pontius Pilate,
he suffered death and was buried,
and rose again on the third day
in accordance with the Scriptures.
He ascended into heaven
and is seated at the right hand of
  the Father.
He will come again in glory
to judge the living and the dead
and his kingdom will have no end.

I believe in the Holy Spirit, the Lord, the
  giver of life,
who proceeds from the Father and
  the Son,
who with the Father and the Son is
  adored and glorified,
who has spoken through the prophets.

I believe in one, holy, catholic and
  apostolic Church.
I confess one Baptism for the
  forgiveness of sins
and I look forward to the resurrection of
  the dead
and the life of the world to come. Amen.

Apostles' Creed

I believe in God,
the Father almighty,
Creator of heaven and earth,
and in Jesus Christ, his only Son,
  our Lord,

At the words that follow, up to and
including the Virgin Mary, *all bow.*

who was conceived by the Holy Spirit,
born of the Virgin Mary,
suffered under Pontius Pilate,
was crucified, died and was buried;
he descended into hell;
on the third day he rose again from
  the dead;
he ascended into heaven,
and is seated at the right hand of God
  the Father almighty;
from there he will come to judge the
  living and the dead.

I believe in the Holy Spirit,
the holy catholic Church,
the communion of saints,
the forgiveness of sins,
the resurrection of the body,
and life everlasting. Amen.

Liturgy

The Sacraments

Sacraments of Initiation
Baptism, Confirmation, Eucharist

Sacraments of Healing
Penance and Reconciliation, Anointing of the Sick

Sacraments at the Service of Communion
Matrimony, Holy Orders

The Liturgy of the Hours

The Liturgy of the Hours is the Church's public prayer to make each day holy. This liturgy is offered at set times throughout the day and night. In Monasteries monks and nuns gather as many as ten times each day and night to pray the Liturgy of the Hours. Parishes that celebrate the Liturgy of the Hours do so less frequently, perhaps once or twice each day. The most common celebrations of the Liturgy of the Hours are Morning Prayer and Evening Prayer.

The Liturgical Year

The liturgical year is the Church's annual cycle of seasons and feasts that celebrates the Paschal Mystery. It begins on the First Sunday of Advent and ends on the feast of Christ the King.

Advent
In this liturgical season, the Church devotes four weeks for the People of God to prepare to celebrate the coming of Christ at Christmas. The color for this season is violet, as a sign of anticipation and penance. On the third Sunday vestments may be pink, as the Advent wreath candle. This is joyful anticipation of the nearness of Christmas.

Christmas
Christmas celebrates the Son of God becoming man, God visible in humankind. It celebrates Christ's first coming over 2,000 years ago, Christ's presence with us now, and the anticipation of his second coming at the end of time. This season includes the feast of the Holy Family and the feast of Epiphany. In the current liturgical calendar, the Churches of the West celebrate the birth of Christ on December 25.

Lent

The forty days of Lent are a time of fasting, prayer, and almsgiving. Lent begins with Ash Wednesday; ashes are blessed and put on the foreheads of Catholics as a reminder of their sinfulness and of penance. Fasting, abstinence, and personal reflection on Baptism during Lent help prepare Catholics for the celebration of Easter and renewal of Baptismal Promises.

The Triduum

The word *Triduum* means, "three days." Triduum starts with the celebration of the Lord's Supper on Holy Thursday, includes Good Friday and Holy Saturday, and ends with evening prayer on Easter Sunday. Because the Triduum specifically celebrates the life, death, and Resurrection of Jesus, it is the high point of the Church year.

Easter Season

Easter, the feast of the Resurrection of Christ, is the greatest feast of the Church year. The Easter Season begins on Easter Sunday and lasts until Pentecost, fifty days later. White is the major color of this season, but gold is used in vestments as well.

Ordinary Time

This season occurs twice each Church year. The first, shorter period falls between Christmas and Lent; the second period accounts for most Sundays of the Church year, starting at the end of Easter Season and ending with the Feast of Christ the King, the Sunday before Advent begins. Ordinary Time focuses on everyday Christian life, during which we learn about Jesus' life and teaching from one of the Gospels.

Holy Days of Obligation

In addition to Sundays, there are ten holy days of obligation listed by Rome: Mary the Mother of God, Epiphany, Saint Joseph, the Ascension of the Lord, The Body and Blood of Christ, Saints Peter and Paul, the Assumption of Mary, All Saints' Day, the Immaculate Conception of Mary, and Christmas. With Vatican approval, conferences of bishops are free to set their country's holy days. In the United States six are celebrated.

U.S. Holy Days of Obligation	
Holy Day	**Date**
Mary the Mother of God	January 1
The Ascension of the Lord	forty days after Easter, or the Sunday nearest the end of the forty-day period
The Assumption of Mary	August 15
All Saints' Day	November 1
The Immaculate Conception of Mary	December 8
Christmas	December 25

Moral Life

The Ten Commandments	
Commandment	**Meaning**
I am the Lord your God: you shall have no other gods before me.	Place one's faith in God alone. Worship, praise, and thank God the Creator. Believe in, trust, and love God.
You shall not make wrongful use of the name of the Lord your God.	Speak God's name, and that of Jesus and the saints, with reverence. Don't curse. Don't call on God to witness to a lie.
Remember to keep holy the Lord's Day.	Gather to worship at the Eucharist. Rest and avoid unnecessary work on Sunday.
Honor your father and your mother.	Respect and obey parents, guardians, and others who have proper authority.
You shall not murder.	Respect and protect your life and the lives of others.
You shall not commit adultery.	Be faithful and loyal to spouses, friends, and family. Respect God's gift of sexuality and practice the virtue of chastity. Learn to appreciate the gift of sexuality by practicing self-mastery.
You shall not steal.	Respect the things that belong to others. Share what you have with those in need.
You shall not bear false witness against your neighbor.	Be honest and truthful. Avoid bragging. Don't say untruthful or negative things about others.
You shall not covet your neighbor's wife.	Practice modesty in thoughts, words, dress, and actions.
You shall not covet your neighbor's goods.	Rejoice in others' good fortune. Don't be jealous of others' possessions. Don't be greedy.

The Great Commandment

"You shall love the Lord your God with all your heart, and with all your soul, and with all your strength, and with all your mind; and your neighbor as yourself."
—Luke 10.27

The New Commandment

"I give you a new commandment, that you love one another. Just as I have loved you, you also should love one another."
—John 13:34

Gifts and Fruits of the Holy Spirit

Gifts of the Holy Spirit

- wisdom
- understanding
- counsel
- fortitude
- knowledge
- piety
- fear of the Lord

Fruits of the Holy Spirit

- charity
- joy
- peace
- patience
- kindness
- goodness
- generosity
- gentleness
- faithfulness
- modesty
- self-control
- chastity

Virtues

Theological Virtues

- faith
- hope
- charity

Cardinal Virtues

- prudence
- justice
- temperance
- fortitude

Seven Capital Sins

Each of these vices opposes the virtues and leads to other sins: pride, avarice, envy, wrath, lust, gluttony, and sloth.

Works of Mercy

Corporal Works

- Feed the hungry.
- Give drink to the thirsty.
- Clothe the naked.
- Visit the sick.
- Shelter the homeless.
- Visit the imprisoned.
- Bury the dead.

Spiritual Works

- Counsel the doubtful.
- Instruct the ignorant.
- Admonish the sinner.
- Comfort the sorrowful.
- Forgive injuries.
- Bear wrongs patiently.
- Pray for the living and the dead.

Seven Themes of Modern Catholic Social Teaching

In 1996 the U.S. Catholic bishops identified seven themes underlying Catholic social teaching. These themes run through the many statements on justice made by Catholic leaders during more than a century. Through these themes, Catholic leaders hope that the Church and its members will serve as a beacon of justice in the world.

1. Life and Dignity of the Human Person

In a world warped by materialism and declining respect for human life, the Catholic Church proclaims that human life is sacred and that the dignity of the human person is the foundation of a moral vision for society. . . . We believe that every person is precious, that people are more important than things, and that the measure of every institution is whether it threatens or enhances the life and dignity of the human person.

2. Call to Family, Community, and Participation

In a global culture driven by excessive individualism, our tradition proclaims that the person is not only sacred but also social. How we organize our society—in economics and politics, in law and privacy—directly affects human dignity and the capacity of individuals to grow in community. The family is the central social institution that must be supported and strengthened, not undermined. While our society often exalts individualism, the Catholic tradition teaches that human beings grow and achieve fulfillment in community.

◄ One of the Franciscan Sisters of Perpetual Adoration holds an orphan in Cameroon, West Africa. Several FSPA traveled to West Africa as part of a collaborative effort to address health care and social issues.

3. Rights and Responsibilities

In a world where some speak mostly of "rights" and others mostly of "responsibilities," the Catholic tradition teaches that human dignity can be protected and a healthy community can be achieved only if human rights are protected and responsibilities are met.

4. Option for Poor and Vulnerable

In a world characterized by growing prosperity for some and pervasive poverty for others, Catholic teaching proclaims that a basic moral test is how our most vulnerable members are fairing.

5. The Dignity of Work and the Rights of Workers

In a marketplace where too often the quarterly bottom line takes precedence over the rights of workers, we believe that the economy must serve people, not the other way around. Work is more than a way to make a living; it is a form of continuing participation in God's creation. If the dignity of work is protected, then the basic rights of workers must be respected—the right to productive work, to decent and fair wages, to organize and join unions, to private property, and to economic initiative.

6. Solidarity

Our culture is tempted to turn inward, becoming indifferent and sometimes isolationist in the face of international responsibilities. Catholic social teaching proclaims that we are our brothers' and sisters' keepers, wherever they live. We are one family, whatever our national, racial, ethnic, economic, and ideological differences. Learning to practice the virtue of solidarity means learning that "loving our neighbor" has global dimensions in our interdependent world.

7. Care for God's Creation

On a planet conflicted over environmental issues, the Catholic Tradition insists that we show our respect for the Creator by our stewardship of creation. Care for the earth is not just an Earth Day slogan, it is a requirement of our faith.
(Sharing Catholic Social Teaching: Challenges and Directions, p.6.)

Many Catholic organizations work in the light of the themes of Catholic social teaching. Such organizations include Catholic Charities, Catholic Relief Services, the Christian Foundation for Children and Aging, the Institute for Peace and Justice, Network—A Catholic Social Justice Lobby, and the United States Conference of Catholic Bishops.

Prayers and Practices

Sign of the Cross

In the name of the Father,
and of the Son,
and of the Holy Spirit.
Amen.

In nomine Patris,
et Filii,
et Spiritus Sancti.
Amen.

The Lord's Prayer

Our Father, who art in heaven,
hallowed be thy name;
thy kingdom come,
thy will be done
on earth as it is in heaven.
Give us this day our daily bread,
and forgive us our trespasses,
as we forgive those who trespass against us;
and lead us not into temptation,
but deliver us from evil.
Amen.

Pater noster, qui es in caelis:
sanctificetur nomen tuum;
adveniat regnum tuum;
fiat voluntas tua, sicut in caelo, et in terra.
Panem nostrum quotidianum da nobis hodie;
et dimitte nobis debita nostra,
sicut et nos dimittimus debitoribus nostris;
et ne nos inducas in tentationem;
sed libera nos a malo.
Amen.

Glory to the Father

Glory to the Father,
and to the Son,
and to the Holy Spirit:
as it was in the beginning,
is now,
and will be forever.
Amen.

Gloria Patri,
et Filio,
et Spiritui Sancto.
Sicut erat in principio,
et nunc, et semper,
et in saecula saeculorum.
Amen.

Hail Mary

Hail, Mary, full of grace!
The Lord is with you;
blessed are you among women,
and blessed is the fruit of your womb, Jesus.
Holy Mary, Mother of God,
pray for us sinners,
now and at the hour of our death.
Amen.

Ave Maria, gratia plena,
Dominus tecum;
benedicta tu in mulieribus,
et benedictus fructus ventris tui, Jesus.
Sancta Maria, Mater Dei,
ora pro nobis peccatoribus,
nunc et in hora mortis nostrae.
Amen.

The Magnificat

My soul proclaims the greatness of the Lord,
   and my spirit rejoices in God my Savior
for he has looked with favor on his lowly servant.
   From this day all generations will call me blessed:
the Almighty has done great things for me,
   and holy is his Name.
He has mercy on those who fear him
   in every generation.
He has shown the strength of his arm;
   he has scattered the proud in their conceit.
He has cast down the mighty from their thrones,
   and has lifted up the lowly.
He has filled the hungry with good things,
   and the rich he has sent away empty.
He has come to the help of his servant Israel
   for he has remembered his promise of mercy,
according to the promise he made to our fathers,
   to Abraham and to his cildren for ever.

Act of Contrition (traditional)

O my God, I am heartily sorry for having offended you, and I detest all my sins, because of your just punishments, but most of all because they offend you, my God, who are all good and deserving of all my love. I firmly resolve, with the help of your grace, to sin no more and to avoid the near occasion of sin.

Act of Contrition (contemporary)

My God, I am sorry for my sins with all my heart. In choosing to do wrong and failing to do good, I have sinned against you whom I should love above all things. I firmly intend, with your help, to do penance, to sin no more, and to avoid whatever leads me to sin. Our Savior Jesus Christ suffered and died for us. In his name, my God, have mercy.

Prayer to the Holy Spirit

Come, Holy Spirit, fill the hearts of your faithful.
And kindle in them the fire of your love.
Send forth your Spirit and they shall be created.
And you shall renew the face of the earth.
Let us pray:
Lord, by the light of the Holy Spirit
you have taught the hearts of your faithful.
In the same Spirit,
help us choose what is right
and always rejoice in your consolation.
We ask this through Christ Our Lord.
Amen.

The Rosary

The Rosary is called the *Psalter of Mary* because all fifteen of its mysteries, with their 150 *Aves*, correspond to the number of the Psalms. Praying all fifteen decades at once is called the *Dominican Rosary*. The rosary is the most well-known and used form of chaplet (a devotion using beads; from a French word meaning "crown" or "wreath"). There are other chaplets, such as those in honor of Saint Bridget of Sweden and in honor of Mary, the Immaculate Conception.

1. Sign of the Cross and Apostles' Creed

2. Lord's Prayer

3. Three Hail Marys

4. Glory to the Father

5. Announce mystery; Lord's Prayer

6. Ten Hail Marys

7. Glory to the Father

Repeat last three steps, meditating on the other mysteries of the Rosary.

The Fatima invocation (recommended by Mary to the children at Fatima in 1917) is sometimes recited between decades: "O my Jesus, forgive us our sins. Save us from the fires of hell, and bring all souls to heaven, especially those who most need your mercy."

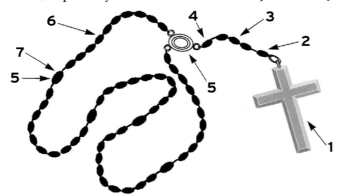

The Mysteries of the Rosary and Recommended Scriptural Meditations

Joyful Mysteries
(Mondays and Saturdays)

1. **The Annunciation** (humility)

   Isaiah 7:10–14; Luke 1:26–38

2. **The Visitation** (charity)

   Isaiah 40:1–11; Luke 1:39–45; John 1:19–23

3. **The Nativity** (poverty)

   Micah 5:1–4; Matthew 2:1–12; Luke 2:1–20; Galatians 4:4

4. **The Presentation** (obedience)

   Luke 2:22–35; Hebrews 9:6–14

5. **The Finding of Jesus in the Temple** (piety)

   Luke 2:41–52; John 12:44–50; 1 Corinthians 2:6–16

Sorrowful Mysteries
(Tuesdays and Fridays)

1. The Agony in the Garden
(repentance)

Matthew 26:36–46; Mark 14:26–42; Luke 22:39–53; John 18:1–12

2. The Scourging at the Pillar (purity)

Isaiah 50:5–9; Matthew 27:15–26; Mark 15:1–15

3. The Crowning with Thorns
(courage)

Isaiah 52:13—53:10; Matthew 16:24–28,

27:27–31; Mark 15:16–19
Luke 23:6–11; John 19:1–7

4. The Carrying of the Cross (patience)

Mark 8:31–38; Matthew 16:20–25; Luke 23:26–32; John 19:17–22; Philippians 2:6–11

5. The Crucifixion (self-renunciation)

Mark 15:33–39; Luke 23:33–46; John 19:23–37; Acts 22:22–24; Hebrews 9:11–14

Glorious Mysteries
(Sundays and Wednesdays)

1. The Resurrection (faith)

Matthew 28:1–10; Mark 16:1–18; Luke 24:1–12; John 20:1–10; Romans 6:1–14; 1 Corinthians 15:1–11

2. The Ascension (hope)

Matthew 28:16–20; Luke 24:44–53; Acts 1:1–11; Ephesians 2:4–7

3. The Descent of the Holy Spirit Upon the Apostles (love)

John 14:15–21; Acts 2:1–11; 4:23–31; 11:15–18

4. The Assumption (eternal happiness)

John 11:17–27; 1 Corinthians 15:20–28, 42–57; Revelation 21:1–6

5. The Coronation of Mary
(Marian devotion)

Matthew 5:1–12; 2 Peter 3:10; Revelation 7:1–4, 9–12; 21:1–6

Luminous Mysteries
(Thursdays)

1. Baptism in the Jordan (commitment)

Matthew 3:13–17; Mark 1:9–11; Luke 3:21–22; John 1:29–34

2. The Wedding at Cana (fidelity)

John 2:3–5, 7–10; John 13:14-15; Luke 6:27–28, 37; Luke 9:23; John 15:12

3. Proclamation of the Kingdom of God
(conversion)

Mark 1:14–15; Luke 4:18–19, 21; Matthew 5:38–39, 43–44; Matthew 6:19–21; Matthew 7:12; Matthew 10:8

4. The Transfiguration (promise)

Matthew 5:14, 16; Matthew 17:1–2, 5, 7–8; Luke 9:30–33; John 1:4–5, 18; 2 Corinthians 3:18

5. Institution of the Eucharist (grace)

John 13:1; Matthew 26:18; Luke 22:15–16, 19–20; Matthew 5:14, 19–20; 1 Corinthians 11:26; John 17:20–21; 1 Corinthians 12:13, 26–27

Stations of the Cross

The Stations of the Cross commemorate the stops along the *Via Dolorosa* (Latin: way of sorrow), Jesus' journey of about a mile from Pilate's court, the praetorium, to Calvary and the tomb. Legend has it that Mary often retraced the sorrowful way her son made on Good Friday.

1. Jesus is condemned to death on the cross.

"For God so loved the world that he gave his only Son, so that everyone who believes in him may not perish but may have eternal life" *(John 3:16)*.

2. Jesus bears his cross.

"If any want to become my followers, let them deny themselves and take up their cross daily and follow me" *(Luke 9:23)*.

3. Jesus falls the first time.

"All we like sheep have gone astray; we have all turned to our own way, and the Lord has laid on him the iniquity of us all" *(Isaiah 53:6)*.

4. Jesus meets his sorrowful mother.

"Is it nothing to you, all you who pass by? Look and see if there is any sorrow like my sorrow . . ." *(Lamentations 1: 12)*.

5. Simon of Cyrene helps Jesus carry his cross.

"Truly I tell you, just as you did it to one of the least of these who are members of my family, you did it to me" *(Matthew 25:40)*.

6. Veronica wipes the face of Jesus.

"Whoever has seen me has seen the Father" *(John 14:9)*.

7. Jesus falls the second time.

"Come to me, all you that are weary and are carrying heavy burdens, and I will give you rest" *(Matthew 11:28)*.

8. Jesus meets the women of Jerusalem.

"Daughters of Jerusalem, do not weep for me, but weep for yourselves and for your children" *(Luke 23:28)*.

9. Jesus falls the third time.

"For all who exalt themselves will be humbled, and those who humble themselves will be exalted" *(Luke 14:11)*.

10. Jesus is stripped of his garments.

". . . none of you can become my disciple if you do not give up all your possessions" *(Luke 14:33)*.

11. Jesus is nailed to the cross.

"For I have come down from heaven, not to do my own will, but the will of him who sent me" *(John 6:38)*.

12. Jesus dies on the cross.

"And being found in human form, he humbled himself and became obedient to the point of death—even death on a cross" *(Philippians 2:7–8)*.

13. Jesus is taken down from the cross.

"Was it not necessary that the Messiah should suffer these things and then enter into his glory?" *(Luke 24:26)*.

14. Jesus is placed in the tomb.

". . . unless a grain of wheat falls into the earth and dies, it remains just a single grain; but if it dies, it bears much fruit" *(John 12:24)*.

GLOSSARY

A–C

abbot—A superior in a religious order of monks who has the hierarchical status of a bishop. (*147*)

ancestors in faith—Men and women of the Old and New Testaments, who, although not ancestors of biological lineage, are those who came before us in the family of the Church. (*20*)

annulment (declaration of nullity)—A declaration by the Church, after investigation of a marriage, that it was never a valid sacramental marriage, though it was a legal civil marriage. (*182*)

apostolic succession—The unbroken line of Church leadership beginning with the Apostles and continuing to the bishops in the Church today. (*150*)

artificial birth control—Any means of preventing conception that interferes artificially with the natural action of sperm and egg during sexual intercourse. (*208*)

baptismal grace—The grace given at Baptism. (*76*)

beatitude—Complete blessedness or perfect happiness often associated with being with God. (*227*)

bishop—Highest degree of Holy Orders. Man ordained to be a successor to the Apostles and to be pastor of a diocese. (*136*)

cantor—Liturgical minister who leads the congregation in the singing of the Responsorial Psalm. (*57*)

celebrant—Presider who leads the celebration of liturgy. (*57*)

celibate life—The way of life for those who remain unmarried to serve the kingdom and dedicate themselves to God and his people. It is required for a person who vows chastity. (*102*)

character—Permanent mark imprinted on the soul by Baptism, Confirmation, and Holy Orders. (*77*)

charisms—Spiritual gifts. (*107*)

chastity—The virtue by which sexuality is integrated within a person. It comes under the cardinal virtue of temperance. (*89*)

civil divorce—State-sanctioned dissolution of a civil marriage contract. (*181*)

cloister—An enclosed place where contemplative religious live in seclusion. (*112*)

college of bishops—The society of all those who are bishops. (*137*)

commissioned—Officially sent forth to carry out an assignment. (*27*)

communion of saints—All of the faithful Church members on earth, those being purified in purgatory, and the blessed already in heaven. (*56*)

contemplative—Focused on prayer, Christian perfection, and union with Christ. (*112*)

conversion—Realization that one has done wrong, accompanied by true sorrow for doing it and a firm intention not to do it again. (*80*)

covenant—A solemn promise, or agreement, made between two parties. (*16*)

covet—To want something, or even to lust for something, that belongs to someone else. (*91*)

deacon—First or lowest level of the sacrament of Holy Orders. An ordained man who serves the Church in roles of service and in some liturgical roles. (*57, 136*)

discernment—The process of discovering what one should do, by careful study, thought, seeking of counsel, and prayer. (*14*)

disciples—Followers who are given a share in their leader's mission. (*25*)

domestic Church—The Christian family. (*61, 196*)

episcopacy—The order of bishop. (*137*)

evangelical counsels—Jesus' teachings in the New Testament that focus on growing in perfection in the Christian life more closely and removing what is incompatible with charity. The evangelical counsels of poverty, chastity, and obedience are required for those vowing to live a consecrated life. (*102*)

evangelize—To bring the Good News of Jesus Christ to others. (*27*)

evangelization—The effort of bringing the Gospel, or "Good News" of the message and person of Christ, to the whole world. This is to be done by proclamation and living testimony as Christ commanded. (*239*)

faith—A supernatural gift freely given by God that enables us to accept the truth of what God has revealed. (*42*)

faithful remnant—Exiles and former exiles who remained faithful to God. (*23*)

family—" . . . an intimate community of persons bound together by blood, marriage, or adoption for the whole of life" (*Family Perspective*, p. 19). (*192*)

free will—Human gift that allows us to make choices about how we behave. (*43*)

habit—Clothing or insignia worn by a consecrated religious to signify they are a member of a religious community. (*111*)

intellect—Human gift by which we are conscious of ourselves, God, and the world. (*42*)

lector—Liturgical minister who reads the first and second readings at Mass. (*57*)

Liturgy of the Hours—A series of daily prayers based on the Psalms, which are prayed by priests, deacons, members of religious orders, and many lay people at set times throughout each day as a way to mark time as holy and recall God's saving work in Creation; also called the Divine Office. (*52*)

Marriage—A covenant between a man and a woman, directed to the spouses' well-being and the procreation and upbringing of children (See *Catechism*, Glossary). In this Sacrament, a baptized man and a baptized woman marry and become witnesses of Christ's love for his bride, the Church. (*170*)

mission—An official assignment or task one is sent to accomplish. (*12*)

modesty—The virtue that protects the intimate center of a person. It means refusing to unveil what should remain hidden. (*91*)

monk—A contemplative male religious. (*112*)

Mystical Body of Christ—Terms used to describe the Church as a communion of many members who all have Christ as their head. (*44*)

novice—A beginning member of a religious community who has not yet taken vows. (*117*)

nun—A contemplative female religious. (*112*)

obedience—Evangelical counsel by which a person vows to obey the laws of God and the Church, the rules of his or her religious community, and the directives of his or her religious superiors. (*102*)

ordination—A sacramental ritual that brings a man into one of the Holy Orders. (*136*)

P–R

Paschal Mystery—Christ's work of redemption through his Passion, death, Resurrection, and Ascension. (*55*)

pastor—A shepherd. (*152*)

permanent deacon—Man ordained as deacon for life. He may be married or single before ordination but may not marry after that. (*141*)

perpetual adoration—The practice of keeping the Blessed Sacrament exposed on an altar for adoration at all times. It requires that members of a community take turns keeping vigil there. (*114*)

pontiff—Literally, a "bridge-maker," the title given to bishops who are to be a bridge between God and his people. (*151*)

postulant—A person who is a candidate seeking to become a member of a religious community. (*117*)

poverty—Evangelical counsel by which a person vows to own no personal possessions and to share all belongings in common with others in the community. (*102*)

precepts of the Church—Rules that connect our moral life and our liturgical life. (*49*)

presbyter—A wise elder, the second degree of Holy Orders, a priest. (*136*)

prophet—One who speaks messages from God to others. (*19*)

prototype—A first example or model on which all subsequent models can be based. (*17*)

religious formation—The step-by-step process of becoming a consecrated religious. (*117*)

S–Z

sacraments—Effective signs of God's grace instituted by Christ and given to the Church so that we can share in divine life through the Holy Spirit's action. (*52*)

Sacraments at the Service of Communion—Holy Orders and Matrimony. (*135*)

Sacraments of Healing—Reconciliation and Anointing of the Sick. (*134*)

Sacraments of Initiation—Baptism, Confirmation, and Eucharist. (*134*)

sacristan—Person who helps maintain and set up the objects needed for liturgy. (*57*)

Sanctoral Cycle—The cycle of feast days honoring Mary and the saints. (*56*)

scapular—Oblong of cloth worn over the shoulders as a sign of the "yoke" Christ invites us to carry and to follow him. Often smaller cloth scapulars take the place of the long oblong cloths. (*111*)

transitional deacon—Man ordained as a deacon on his way toward ordination as a priest. (*141*)

virtue—A habit and firm disposition of doing good. (*201*)

vocation—A holy calling from God to love and serve him and others; it is part of who God created us to be. This vocation can be lived out through the various states of life: as a lay person (married or single), an ordained minister (bishop, priest, or deacon), or as someone in the consecrated life (most often as a religious sister, brother, or priest). Members of each state of life live out their vocation through the work they do, whether it be in the Church herself or in the secular world. (*11*)

vows—Binding promises made to God. (*102*)

INDEX

P–S

Notes

Chapter 2

1. St. Thomas Aquinas, STH III, 65, 1

Chapter 3

1. John Paul II, *Chistifideles Laici* (1989), no. 16
2. *GS* 43 § 4

Chapter 4

1. *LG* 43.
2. John Paul II, *RMiss* 21.
3. St. John Damascene, *De fide orth.* 3,24: PG, 1089C

Chapter 5

1. Cf. *LG* 41; *AA* 16.
2. Cf. *Mk* 10:45; *Lk* 22:2; St. Polycarp, *Ad Phil.* 5,2: SCh 10, 182.
3. *LG* 11 § 2.
4. LK 24:26. *Presbyterorum Ordinis*, 41.
5. *Christus Dominus*, 5. Cf. Paul VI's *motv propio, Apostolica Sollicitudo*, Sept. 15, 1965.

Chapter 6

1. St. Thomas Aquinas, STH III, 65,1
2. Cf. Mt. 19:1
3. Cf. CIC can. 1057 § 1.
4. *On the Family*, 35

Chapter 7

1. CDF, *Donum vitae* intro., 2.

Chapter 8

1. *2 Pet* 1:4; cf. *Jn* 17:3.
2. Cf. *Rom* 8:18.
3. Cf. EN, no. 17